THE ART OF
THE FAKER

THE ART OF THE FAKER

Three Thousand Years of

DECEPTION

BY FRANK ARNAU

TRANSLATED FROM THE GERMAN
BY J. MAXWELL BROWNJOHN

ILLUSTRATED

Boston   Toronto

LITTLE, BROWN AND COMPANY

According to the enlarged edition of his *oeuvre* catalogue, Corot painted over 2000 pictures. Of these, more than 5000 are in the United States.

Acknowledgments

The publishers are indebted to the following for permission to reproduce copyright material: Figs. 1 and 2, Courtauld Institute, London; 5a, Phaidon Press, London; 8 and 13, British Museum, London; 10 a and b, 11, 14, 15 and 19, the author; 16, Dr. Hans Cürlis, Berlin; 20 and 21 a and b, Dr. Chr. Wolters, Doerner Institute, Munich; 33 and 34, The Trustees of the Lady Lever Collection, Port Sunlight, Cheshire; 35 and 36 a and b, Gemeente Musea van Amsterdam; 38 a and b, M. Micol, Paris; 40 and 46, Kunstarchiv Dr. Arntz; 41 a and b, and 42, ACL Brussels; 44 a and b, Kurt Wehlte; 45, Fred Ihrt.

Foreword

FORGERY has occurred since time immemorial in the fields of art, fine craftsmanship, commerce — even of industry. Any attempt to give an account of its ingredients must, therefore, be subjected to rigorous and careful limitation. There is room here to examine only the more important problems raised by the subject and to describe significant case histories. We shall, however, make a thorough examination of the technique of forgers of every category and of the modern scientific methods employed in differentiating between the authentic and the spurious.

Forgeries of works of art naturally dominate the foreground, but suitable space has been devoted to imitations of many other objects.

In the description of historic forgeries I have adopted a system of sifting and comparison which gives the most probable and best documented accounts precedence over mere anecdotes, however fascinating. It is left to the reader to decide upon one or another of the numerous versions. In this book, preference has been given to those accounts which have the best authentication. In the same way, my description of the working methods of the old masters, their imitators and falsifiers, is based on the best conclusions of the exact sciences.

FRANK ARNAU

Frankfurt-am-Main

Foreword

Contents

PART THREE
The Forger's Interests

Illustrations

PART ONE

The Forger's Province

1

❦❦❦❦❦❦❦❦

The Frontier between Genuine and Fake

IT is extraordinarily difficult for us to employ objective criteria in the realm of art because we are dealing with subjective manifestations. Creative work is a personal thing, and so is criticism. For an art historian, the distinguishing of a work of art from an imitation takes place in the field of opinion and thus assumes an interpretative form.

Objective findings presuppose trustworthy methods of research. Chemical analysis and physical tests yield measurable values, and these two forms of investigation combine to produce the best results obtainable within the limits imposed on all such projects by human inadequacy.

It is not merely a question of distinguishing "genuine" from "spurious" but of identifying reliably and unequivocally the many intermediate categories, for the gradations between original and fake are many and subtle. Creative work was frequently produced with the co-operation of assistants or pupils. Similarly, studio work often reveals the hand of the master. Some artists copy their own works for the sake of repetition. Imitations appear, together with part-originals and originals superimposed on other originals. Before it is even worthy of the name, "forgery" has occurred. The lines of demarcation become blurred, making the quest for a clear definition impossible.

One remedy might be to say that forgery begins when there is an intent to deceive and that a fake is a work which is represented as something other than it is. This, however, would place it principally in the sphere of criminal law, for the circumstances of a forgery are very difficult to pin down under civil law.

A fake can undoubtedly be a work of art. To take an extreme case, what about an original Leonardo da Vinci which has been adorned with another man's signature? It is unquestionably a forgery, even though this naturally has no material effect upon the work itself.

Similarly, a genuine work of art by an artist who is undervalued in market terms does not cease to be genuine because it has been given a more highly prized signature in order to boost its market price. It is indisputable that forgery has occurred, but in neither of the above cases has this misdemeanor exercised any material effect.

The definition of forgery and of its marginal cases applies as much to the products of fine craftsmanship and handicrafts as to paintings and sculptures. It is irrelevant to our criterion whether we are dealing with a complete forgery or a partial one, a fake or a falsification. The stylistic remodeling of a late Gothic sculpture into early Gothic is just as much forgery as an attempt to transform a painting of the sixteenth century into one of the fourteenth by masking or amplification. Indeed, even the subsequent signing of a work with the name of the artist ought probably to be regarded as a forgery, however contradictory it may seem that a genuine work can become a fake because of the post factum addition of its author's name. But does such treatment really make it a fake? Would it not be better to say that it remains what it was originally, even though it has been the subject of an illicit artifice which does nothing to affect its objective authenticity? Where does the truth lie? In an inherent sense, in both points of view.

The signing of a work with a name other than that of the artist who created it is a fraudulent act. Regarded in a purely technical sense, such a signature must constitute a material alteration of the original, a partial forgery which affects the whole of the work in question.

The indefinable nature of the boundary separating genuine from spurious can be most clearly recognized in the problems raised by the studios of famous masters. These "workshops" were attended by numerous adherents who came for instruction and practice. The master helped his pupils with their work, often specifying the subject, improving work in progress and perfecting what had been completed. What is a genuine Van Dyck? What percentage of personal intervention by Rembrandt is required to make a painting a genuine work by that master? At what percentage does its status sink to that of tyros' work? Who can distinguish with any certainty between the work of one hand and another in terms of square inches?

Is an early English silver goblet genuine if later additions have been made in the style of the original period so as to enhance its ornamentation?

When do the efforts of a restorer, the amplification or removal of defective portions, turn an original work into a falsification or even into a fake?

Is an impression taken today from an original plate, whether woodcut, steel or copperplate engraving, with the original press, ink and paper, a fake? No legal ruling of the requisite clarity has been given on this point. It may perhaps be deemed a fraudulent act, but in the abstract sense its classification in terms of criminal law is exceedingly difficult. The results of any such procedure undertaken today may be indistinguishable from those achieved long ago. The complete identity of the implements and materials used means that the modern print will be identical with one made at the date of origin. There is no perceptible difference, either chemical or physical, and no means of distinguishing a print made then from one made today. It is always possible that the latest methods of research, which employ reagents from the nuclear field, may offer a means of establishing the disparity of age. It is possible, but does that make any difference to the work as such? Yesterday the means of differentiation did not exist, so the work was genuine; today it is (perhaps) demonstrably a fake. Where is the distinction between the work as such and the work as an object of research?

Many postage stamps are worth more when uncanceled than canceled, but some stamps have a disproportionately greater value when canceled than in mint condition. For instance, Stanley Gibbons lists a 12-kreuzer Baden rural postage due which is worth £1.7. 6 mint and £185 used. If someone cancels an unused specimen with a forged stamp, the circumstances leave one in no doubt. But what if he cancels a genuine mint specimen using the original stamp and the original ink? It has certainly been "genuinely canceled" in the sense that the genuine stamp and ink have been employed, yet this cancellation is not identical with one which was applied during the stamp's term of postal validity. Is it simultaneously genuine and spurious?

What about a gold coin which has been struck, after the production of a prescribed quantity, from the original die in an alloy identical with or even superior to that of the original? Our immediate reaction is: a forgery. Yet an extremely conservative Swiss court once acquitted a man who had minted obsolete coins on the grounds that his own coins had a higher gold content than the originals. His gold coins were not originals, of course, but forgeries — what else? The fact that they exceeded the initial minting in terms of gold content in itself precluded any identity with the original coins. We are here confronted by the rare case in which a forgery is of greater material value than its original. The fact that this in itself represented definite evidence of forgery was disregarded. Three years later another Swiss court condemned a similar act as counterfeiting. Which court was right?

When is a piece of furniture "period"? What proportion of its weight, its exterior or interior surfaces, its substance, must be original work before the whole can qualify as an original? When does the piece stop being period? Where is the border here between genuine and fake?

What about Far Eastern porcelain? The mandarin used to order it from his porcelain manufacturer. The mandarin's son was supplied by the son of his father's manufacturer. The manufacturer's son used the same kaolin, the same pigments, the same motifs, the same shapes for his vases, and his son did likewise. Not until some three or four generations later did any change occur — and not always then. Are the identical products of three or four generations "originals" in period and style? When do craftsmanship and the products of craftsmanship cease to be genuine?

All these examples should help to indicate the stratified complex of problems to which the fundamental question of forgery gives rise.

As regards the forger himself, the decisive factor should be motive, since this forms the basis of any judgment in the human sphere. However, motive is only loosely related to the object of a forgery and makes no difference to the act either in the objective sense or in its material results.

There is a widespread belief that all forgers are prompted by greed. Statistically correct though this may be, quite different motives are often discernible, particularly in the more important cases.

Complete forgeries were often originals, contradictory though this may sound. Their high quality encouraged pseudo-antiquaries to conceal their true origin and represent them as other than they really were. Many works thus debased by malpractice to the status of forgeries possessed genuine artistic worth.

In the hands of unscrupulous dealers a number of works by modern artists in the Gothic style have become transformed into early medieval sculptures. Masterpieces in bronze, dating from our own century but done in *quattrocento* style, have come onto the market as originals of the period. That was when the original became a fake. The artist had no fraudulent intention when he produced his work.

In February 1959, Austria's leading salesroom, the venerable Dorotheum, had to withdraw a *Bishop with a Bunch of Grapes* previously offered for sale as a Gothic carving. It turned out to be the work of a twenty-nine-year-old wood carver called Joseph Rifesser, who lived — as he still does — in a Grödener Tal village in the South Tyrol. Rifesser had no inkling that his sculpture, sold to a Salzburg antiquarian for less than a hundred dollars, had become metamorphosed into a "Gothic original" on the way to Vienna. The art experts of the Dorotheum and their leader Dr. Herbst persisted in their opinion that the work was a "typical carving of the period *circa* 1380" until the personal appearance of Rifesser himself. A Rifesser *Madonna and Child,* which had already been knocked down at 12,000 marks (about $3000), also passed muster as a Gothic piece.

Many genuine artists and men of ability, smarting for lack of recognition, have produced works in the style of the old masters and had the satisfaction of seeing their creations hailed ecstatically by world-famous authorities. No critic worth his salt likes to acknowledge the artistic merit of works produced by modern artists in an archaic style, but it is interesting to read the paeans of praise which many experts have accorded the same works while they were still believed to be "period" originals.

Put yourself in the position of an artist who, after years spent in a vain struggle for success, finally achieves it at a single stroke by putting a famous signature to his own work. The homage paid to it derives largely from the magic aura surrounding a celebrated name.

The artist's reaction to this grotesque situation will depend upon his particular nature and temperament. It may give him satisfaction to reveal his authorship of the much-revered classical masterpiece and thereby cast derision upon experts and admirers alike. What a delectable moment when he puts to shame the connoisseurs who described his work as "dilettante" when it bore his own name, only to praise it to the skies when he presented it above the signature of a master! Ready and willing to enter the dock, he gladly asks for other cases to be taken into account. Authorities on aesthetics, museum directors and attested experts are all exposed.

"Expert knowledge" is thereupon enlisted to demonstrate the absurdity of something which was earlier proved with "infallibility."

But the artist, whose original intention was merely to bring off a successful hoax, may possibly exploit his now confirmed ability in another way. There should be no dearth of opportunities to turn his *expertise* as a forger into ready cash.

World-famous paintings frequently have to be removed from the walls of no less world-famous galleries. Pedestals in many museums bear no more than the traces where once stood "masterly" sculptures which have had to be removed from their place of honor and con-

signed to the cellars. In the British Museum, for example, an "Etruscan sarcophagus, *circa* 500 B.C.," proved to be a fake dating from
circa A.D. 1880.

The majority of forgers, and by no means the least gifted, practice their craft or trade — however one cares to describe it — for
purely materialistic reasons. A perfectly forged Corot is easier to sell
than a good genuine work by an unknown.

The forger of real distinction stands head and shoulders above
the commercial hacks of the international antiques racket. Intellectually and technically, he is a genuine artist — nor does he find
himself in bad company. Michelangelo was not averse to dubious
artifices. Rubens "treated" other artists' paintings and executed
copies to order. Andrea del Sarto was commissioned to paint a Raffaello Santi, now known as Raphael.

Where does the copyist's work end and the forger's begin? Why
did such indubitably great artists lend themselves to such questionable practices? Was it a symptom of their lighthearted age or attributable to the homage they owed their noble patrons? If a duke or
a cardinal sanctioned a fraud, did it cease to be one? Or was it only
financial gain which lured the masters on?

Forgery is at least five thousand years old. An Egyptian papyrus
of the pre-Christian era now preserved in the Stockholm Museum
contains detailed instructions for imitating precious stones in colored
glass. Seneca records that during Caesar's time there were several
workshops in Rome given over to the counterfeiting of colored
gems, and Rhousopoulus informs us that false pearls existed in pre-
Mycenaean times.

The concept of "forgery" or "plagiarism" is itself of comparatively
recent date. It was not regarded as a punishable offense even as late
as the Renaissance, although the counterfeiting of coins was a capital
crime in pre-Christian times.

Everything has been forged. Bookbindings, furniture, clockcases,

1. The Sienese triptych exhibited by the Courtauld Institute, London

2. X-ray photograph of the triptych. The machine-made nails are easily recognizable. The hinges are also modern. The gilding and painting have been applied
to wood which was already worm-eaten.

3 *a*.   Albrecht Dürer, *Michael Wrestling with the Dragon*: woodcut from the Apocalypse (*circa* 1498)

3 *b*.   Stephan Rottaler, *Michael Wrestling with the Dragon*: detail from the relief on the high altar at Reisbach (*circa* 1520)

4 *a*. Albrecht Dürer, *Noli me tangere:* Albertina, Vienna

4 *b*. Marcantonio Raimondi, *Noli me tangere*. The Dürer monogram is missing; on other copies this would be added, thus perfecting the forgery.

5 *a*. X-ray photograph of *The Feast of the Gods* by Giovanni Bellini. By means of a detailed X-ray examination of the work, John Walker has been able to establish with certainty a later overpainting by Titian of parts of Bellini's work. (Photograph from *Bellini and Titian at Ferrara* by John Walker, London, 1956.)

5 *b*. Nicolas Poussin, *Bacchanal*: Castel St Angelo, Rome

6. Giovanni Bellini, *The Feast of the Gods:* National Gallery, Washington

carpets, silver chalices, candlesticks, postage stamps, locks, sculptures, porcelain, engravings, etchings, weapons, costumes, miniatures, lace, music, manuscripts, documents, seals, snuffboxes, paperweights, rings, paper money, share certificates, coins, customs stamps, fiscal stamps — anything, in short, which will tempt a collector and is marketable at a price exceeding the cost of production.

2

❧❧❧❧❧❧❧❧

The Lure of Forgery

APART from psychological motives, the principal attraction of forgery is financial gain. The lion's share of the proceeds almost always goes to the dealer or agent, for the professional forger normally has just as little contact with the private purchaser as the thief or burglar who gets rid of hot goods through a fence who pockets the major share of the loot.

Very few important forgers have ever come into personal contact with collectors. Most of them placed and still place their wares on the market through dealers. In this connection a clear distinction must be drawn between the deluded dealer who acts in good faith (normally he does not even receive the fake direct from the forger himself) and the pseudo-dealer who is knowingly a party to the fraud. Orders are placed for spurious articles by specialist "antiquarians." Quite often the man who carries them out is unaware of the truth, and fraudulent motives cannot invariably be attributed to him.

Sometimes a dealer who operates in fakes splits up the work by getting a picture imitated by a good copyist and then giving it to a specialist to work up into an "original."

For a drawing of unknown authorship worth five, ten, or perhaps, in exceptional cases, thirty dollars, a dealer may get ten or a hundred times that sum, once it is equipped with a suitably well-known signature. If he succeeds in foisting a good but nameless drawing onto one of the old masters the profits from such a forgery may attain astronomical proportions. In this instance there is a minimal expenditure of effort on the part of the signature forger. In cases where a whole work has to be produced from scratch, the imperative requirements are consummate artistic ability allied with an unerring sense of style, sound craftsmanship and technical command.

If a forgery passes undetected the forger receives a fee which repays his outlay of effort a hundredfold, even though the dealer or agent has retained the bulk of the proceeds for himself.

The basis of the antique trade's existence is, in the broadest sense, man's passion for collecting. Price structure is determined on the one hand by fashionable trends and on the other by supply and demand. Collectors are motivated by an aesthetic sense, by an acquisitive urge, by a desire to accumulate capital and by countless other factors, not least among which are vanity, ambition, snobbery and the wish to display and enhance their personal standing by the possession of a valuable collection.

Pliny the Younger bought a Corinthian statue because it "arrests the eye of the artist and delights the layman." Goethe was so struck by the sight of Schongauer's engraving *The Dormition of the Virgin,* which he saw at Einsiedeln, that he "could never again be free of a desire to possess the same and to be able always to repeat the sight, no matter how much time elapsed."

Obsession, an unbridled acquisitive urge and the unconquerable desire to be able to call a particular *objet d'art* his own have led one man to make astronomical bids at sales and another, perhaps, to embark on a life of crime. It is a question of individual temperament.

Collecting is probably as old as the human race. It may have developed from the instinct for self-preservation which prompted the cave dweller to hoard provisions in good times so that he should have some left in bad.

Even in early times Eastern despots collected works of art, which were closely associated from the very first with religious worship and national tradition. The Egyptians and Babylonians developed a strong aesthetic sense. As early as the fifth century B.C., the Greeks were drawing up inventories in which they listed precious objects stored in the agonal temples and the treasure houses attached to them. It was these early collections of works of art, the property of the community, which first attracted a wealthy upper class to the idea of adorning their own houses with art treasures.

Rulers commissioned magnificent works of art, partly in their own honor and partly in worship of the gods. Their palaces were bedecked with paintings and sculptures. Artemisia erected a gigantic tomb for her husband Mausolus at Halicarnassus. Alexander the Great had himself sculpted in stone by Lysippus and painted by Apelles.

Mithridates Eupator accumulated a thousand gold and silver vessels and added them to his existing collection of two thousand goblets of polished onyx. Around 180 B.C. Eumenes II built the famous altar at Pergamum. He collected "art treasures of some antiquity" and his brother Attalus II "old paintings" — evidence that even at this period antiques were being hoarded and "famous old murals, which were not purchasable, copied."

From the financial aspect, scarcely any limitations were imposed on the activities of the creative artist in those far-off days. Phidias, for example, received no less than forty-four talents of gold alone for his statue of Athene Parthenos, formerly on the Acropolis at Athens but now no longer in existence. Since a talent comprised sixty minae, each weighing nearly a pound, Phidias had at his disposal about a ton of gold. The gold was alloyed with pure silver in the ratio of 1:0.153. Thus the value of the gold allocated to the artist for his Athene was roughly $1.1 million in today's terms. If we reflect that the cost of living in Phidias's day was only a fraction of what it is now we must assess the value of this early sculpture at a figure beside which our modern art prices pale into insignificance.

Since gold was always alloyed according to government specification and was open to inspection when used in statues, it was an easy matter to find out whether the sculptor Phidias had enriched himself by an admixture of cheaper metals. After this suspicion had been proved unfounded, mistrustful persons framed a charge of theft against him on the grounds that the sculptural ornamentation weighed less than the precious metal placed at his disposal. No one would have dreamt of destroying the sculpture in order to refute the allegation, but the sculptor summoned his detractors before the statue and removed its golden cloak so that it could be weighed. The result tallied. Astutely foreseeing the shape of things to come, Phidias had so constructed his work that the heavy golden cape could be easily removed from the stone figure which it covered.

For ornamenting his royal palace with paintings Archelaus of Macedonia paid Zeuxis a fee worth over $110,000 in modern terms. Seventy years before the birth of Christ, his passion for collecting turned the Roman praetor Caius Verres into a thief and desecrator: he carried off the Zeus of Syracuse and stole art treasures from the Athenians' temples, not to mention the statue of the Chian Apollo.

Caesar devoted eighty talents to the purchase of two works by the painter Timomachus dating from the time of the Diadochi, and Polyclitus's statue *A Boy Binding His Hair* fetched as much as a hundred talents. Their present-day value can be readily calculated from the sum set out above.

Under the Julians and the Claudians Rome's increasing love of ostentation was accompanied by a growing mania for collecting. The oligarchs immortalized themselves in the works of highly paid painters and sculptors. Indeed, demand was so brisk that, in order to keep up with their commitments, stonemasons mass-produced rows of figures complete except for heads, which could be modeled from the life and added later. The Romans' artistic sense declared itself in the noble coin profiles which they elaborated, ornamented and minted with ever-increasing finesse. The appearance of coins was followed almost simultaneously by that of counterfeits: the official type, so to speak, which was effected by decreasing the precious metal content, and the unofficial type produced by counterfeiters who used casts instead of stamping.

Sought-after products in the sphere of arts and crafts were also forged. The Apulians started to imitate Etruscan vases, which were in great demand. These articles, of which many examples have survived, were soon recognized as imitations because the forgers, in their ignorance of the Etruscan alphabet, had copied the inscriptions on the original vases so distortedly as to render them illegible.

With the collapse of their wealthy classes the art of the Hellenes and Romans also declined. The first half of the first century after Christ saw a renaissance of craftsmanship, but not until five hundred years later did the church of St. Sophia at Constantinople become a glittering repository of sacred ornaments, and treasure chambers gradually reappear. With Charlemagne, the accumulation of non-contemporary art treasures — antiques — began once more. The growing demand for Roman showpieces raised their value, and forgers immediately exploited the situation by flooding the market with imitations.

Even in pre-Carolingian times the trade in relics from the Near East had assumed the proportions of an industry. It was not long before forgers entered this profitable field, too. In most cases they contented themselves with simple deception, forcing up the market price of works of art by "treating" them slightly and surrounding them with some mythical tale regarding their origin. It was not enough for a chalice to exhibit good workmanship; more important was that it should be wrapped in a cloak of legend. The cup must have been used either by Jesus Christ at the wedding in Cana or by Pontius Pilate at some banquet — whichever story filled the bill.

Between the tenth and twelfth centuries there came a lull in the collection of works of art. The rulers of the house of Valois were the first to turn from the purely quantitative accumulation of gold and silver to the assembly of genuine collections. John the Good was one of the first great bibliophiles, and in 1367 his son Charles V (the Wise) founded the Louvre library. John's other sons, Louis, Duke of Anjou, Jean de Berry and Philip of Burgundy, were regarded as *the* artistic patrons of Paris, Angers, Bourges and Dijon. Thus the Church's position as protectress of the arts was gradually challenged by secular power, and what was originally and principally the religious value of works of art became associated with their formal and material value.

The Church, however, still retained her undisputed supremacy as a collector. At the same time she involuntarily and unwittingly fostered the growth of forgery, even if for religions and non-materialistic reasons. In her efforts not only to preserve works of art acquired from heathen cultures but to make them serve the Christian faith, she did not shrink from destroying their artistic unity. As late as the fifteenth century we meet a remodeled classical carving in which a contest between Athene and Poseidon has been metamorphosed into a portrayal of the Fall. An additional inscription in Hebrew gives the work its required interpretation.

Since everything done in the service of the Faith was justified —
a precursor of the maxim that the end justifies the means — this
falsification of works of art in the interest of the Church was not
confined to isolated cases. The foundations of the ecclesiastical art
collections were laid by Popes Julius II, Leo X and Paul II.

On a lower plane, primitive forgers exploited not only the new
craze for collecting but also the hoarding of gold coinage. In 1443, as
we are told in the *Jüngeres Achtbuch* of the town of Speyer, dating
from the same year, members of the *Stirnstosserbande* took obsolete
foreign coins and overlaid them with gold or silver "skimmings." If
these "improved" coins failed to tempt a purchaser he was informed that they were the pieces of silver which Judas received for
his betrayal of Our Lord. Country folk proved to be particularly
interested in this type of relic.

The *quattrocento* ushered in the age of the great patrons. The
aristocracy drew lavishly upon their inexhaustible store of wealth.
Cosimo de' Medici laid the foundations of a collection which by
1492, when his grandson Lorenzo died, probably represented the
world's largest accumulation of major art treasures. Even the incomplete inventory of the Medici collection which has survived
in a copy dating from 1512 lists works of such quality, variety and
number as to surpass our powers of imagination. The family palace,
villas and gardens were really more like museums or treasure chambers. Paintings, Byzantine mosaics, altars, tapestries, the finest furniture, the most glorious early sculptures in stone, ivory, wood or
metal; crystal and glass, manuscripts and pictures, coins, jewels of
all kinds, chains, rings, nielli, gems, nobly carved cameos and engraved intaglios, works by Florentine goldsmiths and silversmiths
— all these were represented.

The extraordinary predilection for Roman and Hellenistic works
of art quickly exhausted the remaining supplies of authentic pieces
in Rome and Athens. Unsatisfied demand was taken care of by the

forger. Michelangelo himself transformed a brand-new Cupid into an archaic one, his client being no less a person than Lorenzo de' Medici.

During the fifteenth and sixteenth centuries the collection of works of art began on the other side of the Alps. Archduchess Margaret, Hapsburg vicereine of the Netherlands from 1507 to 1530, assembled art treasures at Mechlin, Duke Ferdinand filled Schloss Ambras with them, Emperor Rudolf II collected them at Prague. The Bavarian dukes Albrecht V and Wilhelm V followed their example. Members of the plutocracy like Fugger and Hainhofer laid the foundations of important art collections at Augsburg, while the Imhoffs did the same at Nuremberg.

In the Netherlands it was principally the wealthy burghers who paid homage to art collection. Ambitious merchants such as Jakob Engbrechtz, Rauwaert, Marten Kretzer and Hermann Becker acquired notable galleries. Magnificent collections were also owned by the leading artists of their day, Rembrandt and Rubens. They were not only painters but dealers too, which may help to explain the obscurity shrouding the origin of many works. Their own, their pupils' and their studios' work were frequently amalgamated to satisfy the demands, and sometimes the impatience, of their clientele.

With the expansion of the collector's hobby, prices rose steeply. Concomitantly, forgers of every category developed their techniques. A market came into existence and the law of supply and demand immediately made itself felt.

The work of art, hitherto mainly the product of commissioned endeavor, now entered the realm of commercialism. (The artist, no less than the craftsman, originally worked in execution of instructions which were almost always framed in exact terms. The Church, like the despots of long ago, allotted strictly prescribed tasks. Even during the transitional period which ushered in the

great collectors the artist seldom worked on his own initiative, for
the idea of art for art's sake had not yet arisen. Since a work of
art was a predetermined, permanent piece of property, it could not,
except in the most abnormal circumstances, become an article of
merchandise. In the few cases where this did happen, works were
usually bartered. Two owners exchanged one for another, and
there was scarcely ever any question of buying and selling as such.)

Because an article in great demand is by definition rare, prices
soared rapidly. One of the earliest quotations for an incomparable
work of art of this period concerns the purchase of Leonardo da
Vinci's *Mona Lisa* by Francis I of France (1515-1547), who acquired the painting for the sum of four thousand scudi. This corresponds to nearly twelve tons of pure silver, equivalent in modern
terms to about $400,000.

Besides Leonardo da Vinci, Francis I also invited to his court
Andrea del Sarto and Benvenuto Cellini, whom he went so far as
to naturalize. Del Sarto was never a man to shrink from copyist's
work of a fraudulent nature, and Cellini boasted of his skill as a
coin forger — though he later declared, somewhat ingenuously, that
he had never needed to exploit it.

Artists were warmly welcomed at the various courts and their
work was highly rewarded. When, at the behest of the Great Elector, Fromantiou visited London in 1682 to attend what was probably the first art sale in history, he was amazed at the price for
which the collection of Peter Lely (1618-1680), the court painter
who was born at Soest and died in London, was sold at auction;
the modern equivalent would be about $350,000.

In 1692 Adam Andreas von Liechtenstein purchased for his collection a copy of the painting *The Triumph of Death* by Pieter
Breughel the Younger, the original of which is in Madrid. The
price was a thousand gulden — roughly $17,000 in modern money.

In Paris on August 14, 1719, the painter Antoine Watteau received 260 livres (about $4200) from the Duke of Orleans for "a small picture, *Garden with Eight Figures.*"

The first large auction house devoted exclusively to art sales was founded by James Christie in Pall Mall in the year 1766. The prices recorded were amazingly low: a portrait by Holbein changed hands for £4.18.0, a Titian fetched only two gold guineas, and Teniers' *Smoker* was knocked down at a mere fourteen shillings. This undervaluation of fine works of art appears the more inexplicable when we learn that single figures of Sèvres porcelain were bringing the modern equivalent of $280.

At an auction held at Christie's in the year 1778, prices were already showing signs of buoyancy. Van Dyck's *Portrait of Charles I* climbed to 215 guineas, Rembrandt's *Adoration of the Kings* to 390, Murillo's *Good Shepherd* to 590. (The guinea of 1778 had a purchasing power of about $66.)

In Germany and Austria, competition between wealthy collectors brought about a sharp rise in prices in almost every field of art. In 1775 Frederick the Great acquired Correggio's *Leda and the Swan* for 21,060 gold lire. The history of this picture exemplifies the fate of many other works of art. Painted in 1530, it was acquired for Emperor Rudolf II in Spain in 1603. In 1648 it was removed to Stockholm, whence, via Queen Christina of Sweden, it passed into the possession of various aristocratic families in Rome. The picture was repeatedly altered and restored. The over-pious Louis of Orleans, for instance, dismembered it and destroyed Leda's head on moral grounds. It was later reconstructed and restored by the court painter Charles Coypel, from whom Frederick the Great acquired it in 1775. In 1830 it found its way into the Kaiser Friedrich Museum in Berlin, where Leda and the attendant on her right received new heads. Although a good third of the painting has been restored or amplified in the course of its career, it cannot really be termed a fake, but might better be described as a partial falsification.

Frederick's collection of snuffboxes, which according to Nikolai comprised three hundred "costly *tabatières*" (Tiébault puts it as high as five hundred), was valued at almost two million thalers. This is hardly surprising if one considers that Frederick paid the goldsmith brothers Jordan 8500 thalers for a single enameled snuffbox, 14,000 for another, and 15,000 for yet another.

Following the example of Frederick the Great, many aristocrats by birth or purse transformed their houses into veritable art galleries and museums. Chief among them were Prince Eugene of Savoy, the Liechtensteins, Schwarzenburg, Harrach, Schönborn and Czernin. In about 1830 Frimmel counted "fifty-six picture-galleries in Austria alone."

More and more private collectors — large, medium and small — demanded their share of the limited market in antiques. Business boomed and the number of art dealers increased. In 1755 J. A. G. Weigel instituted art sales at Leipzig, and the business was later taken over by C. G. Börner. Duke Karl August of Weimar and his minister Johann Wolfgang von Goethe were among the clientele of the original establishment. In 1770 Artaria founded his gallery in Vienna.

The early nineteenth century introduced the age of the museum. Major private collections were turned into galleries or museums. In 1803, while all Europe was bemoaning the innumerable art treasures which the Little Corsican had expropriated during his successful campaigns and assembled at the Louvre, Paris saw the opening of the Musée Napoléon. London's National Gallery was completed in 1838, and in 1857 there came into being the world's first collection of arts and crafts, the Victoria and Albert Museum.

Because of the strength of the pound and the louis d'or, London and Paris developed into the main centers of the antique trade. The treasures of the Colonna estate did not go to Rome, Florence or Milan for auction, but to London. Similarly, the Renaissance paintings from the Barberini Palace were sold in 1805 at Christie's.

The ensuing decades were marked by inconsistent fluctuations in the price of *objets d'art.* Works by men who later were highly esteemed artists scarcely found a buyer. Classical pieces found their way into the permanent keeping of national and municipal museums, and the upward trend of bids in this field grew by leaps and bounds. The £11 million spent by England between 1880 and 1890 on government purchases of works of art corresponds to about £83 million in today's terms.

In 1889 the painting *Pieter van de Broeke* by Frans Hals fetched the modern equivalent of £7500, while in 1899 *A Nobleman in Black* by the same artist fetched £6000. Fashionable influences, too, occasionally gave rise to extreme short-term fluctuations in price. It seems scarcely conceivable to us today that in 1895, in the as yet very modest art dealer's shop of Ambroise Vollard at 41 Rue Lafitte in Paris, pictures by Renoir hung on the walls for a long time because they could not find a buyer at any price. The Musée du Luxembourg refused to accept even as a gift Gauguin's *Madonna and Child,* which the artist offered on his return from Tahiti. Similarly, the authorities declined to purchase Renoir's *Madame Morisot and Her Daughters* for a hundred gold francs. When, shortly afterwards, Director Chéramy was advised to acquire a Cézanne, he exclaimed in horror: "Cézanne? You'll be saying van Gogh next!"

Claude Monet's *White Turkey* fetched 96 francs at Paris in 1895; twenty years later the same figure had sprouted three zeros. In 1898 a still life by Cézanne (which the great connoisseur Huysmans described as "crooked fruit in tipsy bowls") remained unsold at a price of 600 francs. The proceeds had been intended to help Gauguin, then destitute in Tahiti, to return to Paris. It was not until its valuable carved frame was thrown in that an unenthusiastic prospective buyer took the plunge. In the space of little more than two decades the same Cézanne had multiplied in value five hundred times. The price commanded by a version of Utrillo's *Amiens Cathedral* soared from 120 francs in the year 1906 to 50,000 in 1919. After much hesitation, Ambroise Vollard acquired a Modigliani for 300 francs; during the 1930s one of the Italian's nudes fetched 350,000. The purchaser was a compatriot by the name of Benito Mussolini.

As paintings rose in price, so did old works of art of other genres. A small early reliquary soared from 5000 to 121,000 gold marks. The curator of Berlin's Museum of Arts and Crafts, Otto von Falke, made appropriations of 33,000 gold marks for a pewter tankard and 26,000 for a decorative platter, both from Breslau. The two auctions of Adalbert Freiherr von Lanna's collection of arts and crafts held in Berlin in 1911 brought a total of some 1,420,000 gold marks. The two 1910 sales of von Lanna's collection of graphic arts held in Stuttgart had already fetched 1,320,000 gold marks, and the two Berlin auctions of 1909 and 1911 produced more than 1,350,000.

Small medals went for 16,000 and 17,000 gold marks, while a medallion with the portrait of Wolfgang Gamensfelder brought 28,000, an Italian goblet of rock crystal 71,000, a Sienese plate and a Syrian glass goblet 41,000 each.

The growth of prices for great pictures of the latter half and close of the nineteenth century is illustrated by the valuations of Corot's works. In 1873 his *Nymphs and Fauns* was sold at 23,000 gold francs, in 1892 his *Entering the Wood* 101,000, in 1899 *La Toilette* 185,000, and in 1912 *Solitude* 350,000.

In 1910 Leipzig's Städtisches Museum acquired Leibl's *The Spin-*

ner for 75,000 gold marks, Böcklin's *Castle* for 28,000, Schreyer's
Wallachian Horses for 15,000, Schuch's *Kitchen Still Life* for 40,000
and Lovis Corinth's *Lamentation for the Dead* for 31,000. These
prices should be considered in the light of modern equivalents. The
gold mark of those days was worth about one dollar.

The enormous amount of capital accruing at about the turn of
the century to individual members of the new rich (not necessarily
nouveaux riches) threatened to sweep away price barriers. In 1912 a
pastel by Quentin de la Tour fetched 600,000 gold francs at
Doucet's in Paris, and Houdon's *Bust of a Child* 450,000. Degas's
Dancers at the Barre, which the original purchaser acquired for
500 gold francs, later changed hands at 435,000. Corot's *Italian
Landscape,* which scraped home at 400 francs when auctioned at the
first Corot sale in 1911, had risen in value to 180,000 gold francs
forty years later.

J. Pierpont Morgan put more than 60 million gold dollars into
his collections between 1893 and 1913. This figure includes expenditure on his incomparable Renaissance library. However, the present
value of the Morgan collection is estimated at only $600 million. He
made many bad bargains.

The collections of Andrew Mellon, Mrs. Potter Palmer, Mrs.
Peggy Guggenheim, Mrs. Isabella Stewart Gardner, Henry Clay
Frick and many other art lovers of almost limitless means all rank
behind the Morgan treasures in monetary value, but they represent
dollar sums running into at least eight and sometimes nine figures.

Raphael's *Madonna del Duca d'Alba* was required by Secretary of the Treasury Andrew Mellon in 1930-1931 from the Soviet
government under strict seal of secrecy. For this painting, which
hung in the Hermitage at Leningrad, he paid $1,166,400. Today it
may be admired in Washington's National Gallery, which Mellon
endowed.

In 1911 the middle-ranking American collector P. A. B. Widener
bought Rembrandt's magnificent picture *The Mill* from the estate
of the Marquess of Lansdowne. The price was officially given as
$500,000, but there are experts who put the actual figure much
higher.

It is hardly surprising that such prices encouraged forgers not
only to step up production but, in particular, to perfect their technique.

Growing interest in good ceramics, fine goldsmith's and silversmith's work, choice furniture, glass, ivory carvings and other antiques breathed life into other branches of the art market. This increase in demand led, almost of necessity, to the flooding of the
market with forgeries of these objects, too. Medieval majolicas from
Florence and Faenza were already fetching five-figure sums in gold
marks half a century ago. Two Salzburg tiles offered at the second
von Lanna sale at Berlin in March 1911 went for more than 18,000
gold marks. Expert forgers, their assistants, agents and dealers find
small *objets d'art* of this type extremely rewarding subjects for imitation. The same goes for valuable glass. As early as 1882 the proceeds of the Hamilton sale, which consisted largely of Venetian
glass, totaled more than eight million gold marks. Richly decorated
goblets fetched as much as 41,000, 52,000 and 71,000 gold marks
apiece.

Since the second World War, really fantastic sums have been paid
for furniture by the great *maîtres ébénistes*. In 1882 a Louis Qua-
torze *secrétaire* built by Riesener for Marie Antoinette without difficulty attained a figure of 92,400 gold marks. Fifty years later it was
quoted at one million marks (about $220,000). Pieces by Le Brun
and David Röntgen have commanded similar sums.

Aspiring nations like Venezuela, Mexico, Brazil, Peru and Ar-
gentina, to name but a few, have enlarged the circle of wealthy collectors quite considerably. Private, subsidized and public galleries

are anxious at all costs, financial included, to give their cultural progress visible expression.

Until 1950 Brazil, for example, owned no collection of international standing. In order to remedy this regrettable deficiency, the country's press, radio and television mogul, Assis Chateaubriand Bandeira de Mello, utilized the full force of those media to raise vast sums of money. Within the space of a few years the Brazilians had their Sao Paulo Museum, whose art treasures must now be worth more than $7 million — not counting the massive influx of fakes which inevitably attends large-scale buying at such a headlong pace. A selection of important classical and modern paintings from this *ad hoc* collection (the dubious works were naturally left behind in Sao Paulo) aroused great interest when exhibited in Europe and the United States, particularly since the creation of such a large and comprehensive art collection in such a short space of time represented a remarkable achievement.

In step with the growing pace of life during the same period, spurts in the market price of works of art in the last four or five decades have been far more pronounced, intense, buoyant and arbitrary than ever before. The grim, almost morbid passion for collecting on the part of potential buyers fastened itself, in contrast with the preceding century, upon works by living artists for which — despite the controversy still surrounding some of them — extraordinarily high prices have been paid.

Paris has once more become what it was in the days of the great Impressionists, the world's chief artistic center, even if this is due partly to the use of up-to-date and often reprehensible publicity methods. Artists do not achieve fame by virtue of their work: works are made famous by means of clever advertising gimmicks designed to represent their creators as geniuses. Dealers and dealers' rings purposely make their own contribution to this trend. As soon as a certain snobbish and wealthy circle reckons that the artists pushed in this way have arrived, the boom in prices begins.

Exactly the reverse prevails in the sphere of old art. Genuine works of art by deceased masters of painting and sculpture are exempt from this hectic commercialism, as are all other types of high-class antique.

Lovers of fine pieces only rarely get a chance to acquire them either at sales or when, as occasionally happens, they are offered privately. Major works which do reach the salesroom disappear into galleries, never to re-emerge. Museums do not put their superfluous items up for sale but use them for exchange purposes. New discoveries of old works of art very seldom occur in our day, and most finds should be regarded with extreme caution. While the market grows ever smaller, demand not only refuses to diminish but is continually increasing. This in itself must determine the future development of prices.

Special circumstances such as the first and second World Wars have exercised a short-term effect on the rising trend in prices. A glut of articles from areas ravaged by war and upheaval sometimes depresses prices. But even large collections which change hands as the result of a *coup d'état* very soon find a market, and prices resume their upward course.

Changes in fashion, too, can result in a slump. This almost never affects major works of war, but is confined to mediocre works or those which were never firmly established in the first place and reflect short-lived trends in style. Biedermeier, for instance, was a typical vogue. Works of this period, especially furniture and pictures, fetched high prices at various times. Then, as tastes changed, they plummeted downward, later to regain and maintain fairly consistently the more modest level to which they are entitled by merit. The same happened to the Makart and Jugendstil periods, except that they lost favor more quickly. Nevertheless, Jugendstil works have begun to fetch extraordinarily high prices again in recent years, being regarded as a forerunner of abstract art.

Paintings, sculptures and other antiques from periods deserted by popular esteem lie forlorn and friendless in dealers' warehouses, eventually to find their way into bric-à-brac shops. Collectors are not always influenced merely by dislike of their style alone, but simply doubt their artistic value.

Movements in price can sometimes result from the waning interest of individual large collectors. Suppose, for instance, that a hypothetical amateur of nineteenth-century paperweights decides to dispose of his collection. In a narrow field of this kind the discrepancy between a small demand and a large and sudden supply will have a perceptible effect on prices. Similarly, the dispersal of a collection of antique walking-stick handles will seriously affect the price level in this specialized field because the number of collectors is so small.

A factor which makes for great uncertainty in the province of modern art is that no one has even an approximate idea of how many works are being hoarded either by recognized artists themselves or by their confidential dealers. The output of the various studios is unknown.

There is little doubt that, on the death of a well-known contemporary painter, those most closely concerned will do all in their power to prevent the saturation of the market and a resulting slump in prices — whether with success remains to be seen. It is common knowledge that Madame Picasso's divorce from her husband gravely disturbed a number of people because her collection of works by the artist was large enough, especially in a slack period, to undermine the price structure for Picassos. The danger was, in fact, averted.

Meanwhile modern artists, apart from the great Impressionists, are also subject to the rising trend in prices. In London in October 1958 a Cézanne fetched over £200,000. It is said that a group of interested parties offered the well-nigh astronomical sum of £700,000 for Picasso's *Guernica,* at present on loan in the United States, without arousing any enthusiasm. Oskar Kokoschka has been paid fees of 50,000 and 100,000 marks for commissioned works. Marc Chagall asked the city of Frankfurt-am-Main for a fee of 200,000 marks ($47,000) for a painting on an agreed theme. Artists of this class now seem to be commanding such honoraria as a matter of course.

At a sale held by New York's Parke-Bernet Galleries in November 1958, a still life of flowers by Henri Matisse brought over $60,000. Until 1937 it had hung in the Städel Gallery at Frankfurt-am-Main, where it had been confiscated as "degenerate art."

At the Kirkeby sale on December 1, 1958, the New York art dealer Victor Hammer paid $28,500 for a canvas sketchily painted by Renoir with the remnants of the paint on his palette. The canvas bore a number of unrelated scenes. Hammer cut it into eight pieces which, when each had been given a frame, became eight small Renoir sketches in their own right.

The eight fragments of canvas were sold as sketches by Renoir. Total proceeds: $38,500.

Rising prices, an ever-diminishing supply of authentic works of art and antiques and an ever-expanding circle of potential customers (it is now almost *de rigueur* to go in for antiques or collect modern art) all combine to enhance the attractions of forgery. The main outcome, apart from the Paris workshops which specialize in imitations of the great Impressionists, Expressionists and greatly sought-after painters and sculptors of abstract art, has been the establishment of forgers' studios in Rome which have at their command first-class artists, technical aids of every description and an international network of successful middlemen.

One of the forger's favorite fields is that of modern graphic art, for an original can without undue difficulty be photographically transferred to a plate from which reproductions can be made on any hand press, platen or flat-bed. Regardless of whether the original print is hand-colored or black and white, imitation in the same technique is not too complicated. The number of faked modern prints runs into thousands. It goes without saying that they bear the names of the best-known and most highly prized artists.

Far less favored as subjects for forgery are works in stone, wood, ivory, metal, semiprecious stones or other materials, for exponents in the class of Dossena or Bastianini are few and far between, and the countless fakes in circulation are hardly ever of a quality to hoodwink the connoisseur. Of course, this applies only to modern forgers, not those who were more or less contemporaneous with the early masters.

Also lacking in appeal for the European forger are works from the Far East. They were largely produced on a factory scale and were never intended to be regarded as originals. Attempts by small and unscrupulous dealers to give these mass-produced articles an appearance of genuine antiquity by means of crude subterfuges can deceive only the layman. Every year that passes sees an increase in the already massive exports of porcelain of archaic pattern and ivory figures made of fossilized mammoth bone with which Japan, in particular, is flooding the world. The reverse is true of forgeries produced with unsurpassed craftsmanship and unerring sense of style in the Near and Far East, but they will be discussed at greater length elsewhere.

Antique jewelry and silver make profitable subjects for forgery, in view of the prices paid for them. Beakers, cups, plaquettes, bowls, statuettes, screw-top bottles and other articles in precious metal, whether cast, beaten, chiseled, engraved, chased or stamped, are all in great demand. Early German and English plate is much sought after. Since articles of this sort can be subjected to very rigorous methods of examination, serious connoisseurs will be deceived only by goldsmiths of superlative skill, like Ruchomovski, who in 1890 produced the so-called *Tiara of Saitaphernes* (reigned *circa* 200 B.C.). Even this first-class fake met a speedy end. Shortly after the Louvre had paid 200,000 gold francs for it in 1896 on the strength of "absolutely positive authentication," further expert opinion demonstrated that it was no more than an imitation of very fine workmanship.

Antique jewelry is so highly valued throughout the world that forgers turn gladly to the production of gorgeous pieces in the style of the rococo, baroque, Gothic and other much earlier periods. Some specialists turn out Etruscan, Hellenistic, Roman and Byzantine jewelry, and the fact that they know how to alloy their gold in the original proportions and are fortunate enough to possess abundant references for their work means that their fakes have a good chance of passing muster.

Good reproductions of Romanesque and early Gothic jewelry are manufactured on a large scale both in Italy and Germany. Though the settings are mechanically produced the pieces are finished by hand, and even the cheapest pendants, crosses, figures of St. George and similar articles, most of them crudely enameled, can be pleasing to the eye — not that they will deceive the expert, of course.

During the passage of the years the extensive ceramics field has won a wide circle of collectors and enthusiasts. Their credulity or, more properly, carelessness, renders it easier for forgers to dispose of their wares, most buyers being satisfied with the outward sign of authenticity: a manufacturer's mark. This has led to the forging of earthenware and, more especially, porcelain on a vast scale.

To the forger, the perfect imitation of old furniture means arduous work for a comparatively small return. Because high-class products by famous cabinetmakers of earlier periods can be tested literally down to the last joint, the forging of a whole piece of furniture is difficult and time-consuming, if not quite impossible.

True connoisseurs of classical cabinetwork, an extremely restricted circle, are thus ruled out as potential customers, so the forger confines himself mainly to the "revaluation" of furniture of questionable origin and age. The relative size of this branch of forgery is attributable to a clientele which is becoming, in general, less and less critical of quality. What the average purchaser looks for in antique furniture, particularly in France, where *maître ébéniste* has become a symbol of perfect craftsmanship, is the branded impression of the maker's signature. The forger exploits this proclivity by adding some trade-mark or other. Hence the not infrequent phenomenon of a nineteenth-century chest or cupboard which has been adorned with the device of a cabinetmaker who died a hundred years earlier.

In France — and elsewhere — there is a flourishing trade in forgeries of genuine antique furniture produced by the amalgamation of sound individual components which, when restored, are reborn in the shape of a new antique.

Many large workshops manufacture reproduction period furniture without any fraudulent intent, but by means of various ingenious techniques the forger can pass them off as genuine.

As a point of interest, it may be mentioned that in November 1958 at Christie's a small table was knocked down to an unnamed French purchaser for £35,000. This little piece was an authentic work by Maître Jean François Oeben, who worked for Louis XV. It contained the usual secret drawer, but this was empty. No hopes of hidden treasure had prompted such a fantastic bid: merely the unknown woman's determination to possess that particular piece. Prices like these lend wings both to the imagination and to the furniture forger, though such ambitious fakes are a risky proposition.

The counterfeiting of coins would provide forgers with a large turnover at little risk and less effort were the range of potential customers not so remarkably limited. Strange as it may seem, the difficulty of finding suitable storage for coins discourages many amateurs from entering this field. A numismatist's collection demands plenty of space and expensive cabinets which are difficult to transport and impossible to install everywhere. Quite the reverse is true of a stamp collection, for a few ounces of printed paper can be worth as much as a hundredweight of coins. The home of the coin forger is Italy. Early Roman mintings fetch high prices, but Italian counterfeiters also supply the markets of the whole world with Greek and other coins.

Another extraordinarily productive field is that of the postage stamp forger, who specializes not only in the forgery of stamps but, to a far greater extent, in the forgery of postmarks. Cancellation forgeries have considerably decreased since the advent of the spectroscope and other facilities for scientific research, but it would seem that processes have already been devised which can escape even the most modern scientific tests. Forged cancellations can no longer be detected by spectral analysis because counterfeiters have succeeded in blending their inks to match the original so that both impressions give an identical image under the spectroscope. Very strong magnification may occasionally pinpoint minute discrepancies between a faked postmark and an original, but differentiation is difficult and sometimes almost impossible in cases where a genuine old hand stamp has been fraudulently used in conjunction with inks mixed according to an original formula.

A small tributary of the main stream of forgery is plied by the fraudulent dealer in stringed instruments. The manufacture of "authentic" violins by great master craftsmen of the past is usually effected by a "rechristening" process. Contemporary violin makers have found ways and means of giving new instruments the same power and beauty of tone as that of classical specimens. The secret lies not only in their construction, which is based upon ancient designs, but in the composition of the lacquers and varnishes which play so important a part in determining tonal quality. These new instruments are sold as such and cannot be described as forgeries. Real violin forgers concentrate primarily on the restoration of old instruments, often by the amalgamation of separate components. In most cases, however, the element of deception consists in the fraudulent substitution of makers' labels. In this way, a Cappa can speedily be promoted into a Stradivarius.

Violin forgeries are more often the work of dishonest dealers than of craftsmen. Since the relabeling into a "genuine" Stradivarius or Ballestrieri or Guarneri of an Italian violin from the close of the eighteenth or beginning of the nineteenth century can turn $300 into $30,000 or $60,000, the market for stringed instruments offers immense scope to unscrupulous individuals. Their task is rendered easier because hardly any other field of art is so dominated by expert uncertainty or so characterized by sincerity and faith.

Despite varying prospects of success and a not always favorable relationship between outlay and returns, the forging of works of art and antiques still offers such remarkable profit margins that imitators continue to exist. Forgers who act from other than mercenary motives are unaffected by such considerations.

In examining the essential nature of forgery we should not forget that for many centuries the work of art — as a product of technical skill and the creative urge — was innocent of any striving after originality and executed solely for its own sake. The artist deferred to his work. It was not until the Renaissance (discounting tentative symptoms during the Gothic period) that the artistic personality started to gain ground and a desire for originality displaced the time-honored principle whereby an artist modeled himself on some great forerunner, only deviating in so far as he had to express the outward signs of a changing environment.

It is significant that the sermons of a universally esteemed master like Johannes Tauler, Dominican monk and mystic, contain the following advice (they were composed about 1330): "A diligent painter, wishing to paint himself an agreeable picture, first looks right carefully at another well-painted [picture] and then draws all the points and strokes thereof on his board, constructing his picture in accordance therewith as truly as he can." Admittedly, Tauler does use the qualification "himself," but there is a noticeable disregard of the creative "I."

A work which is a forgery by our standards but an original by those of the Middle Ages must therefore be evaluated in terms quite other than our own.

Leonardo da Vinci was probably the first to blaze the new trail as a critic as well as an observer. His treatise on painting establishes with remarkable lucidity that an original can have no copy of equal value and no limitless number of offspring, as in the case of printed work. Painting reserves its honors for the initiator alone, for only thus does it retain its value and originality. Its unique nature raises it above the sciences, which are universally disseminated. Leonardo refused copyists' work and scorned all imitations: *"Stultum imitatorum pecus."*

This attitude of mind paved the way for equality between the artist and his work and, a still more advanced stage, the promotion of the creative individual above the fruits of his creative activity. Nevertheless, the attitude of mind which not only sanctioned imitation but even admired it survived, in time at least, beyond Leonardo's day. The great likelihood that unscrupulous artists continued to devote themselves to the imitation of a model, even though the notion was already superseded and by then amounted to forgery in the modern sense, does not help us to formulate a definition of one of these early copyists' works. They should always be assessed on their artistic merits alone.

The elevation of a master above his work, the competition, the jostling for premier positions, the struggle for recognition, fame and fortune, all gave rise to phenomena which went far beyond permissible artistic rivalry and resulted in intrigues of the most discreditable nature. Great artists debased themselves into courtiers in the service of their own reputation. Correggio laid aside one of Raphael's works with the remark: *"Anche io sono pittore"* (I too am a painter). Matthias Ensinger adorned one of his works with the challenging inscription: *"Machs na!"* (Now then!).

Whereas a hypersensitive artist like Pieter van Laer took his own life because Wouwerman had imitated his works, sturdier artists countered with revolt rather than resignation. In the mid-seventeenth century the French painter Pierre Mignard, whose main work was the painted cupola of the Val de Grâce in Paris, produced a *Penitent Magdalen,* perfectly imitating the technique and style of Guido Reni, who had died some years earlier. He then aged it suitably and sold it to a Parisian collector. At the risk of losing his reputation and the fee which he had already received, he got a trustworthy go-between to arouse the purchaser's doubts as to the picture's authenticity. The collector, seriously disturbed, asked the artist himself and the art expert Charles Le Brun for their opinion. After prolonged study, the latter issued a declaration that the *Penitent Magdalen* was unquestionably a work by Guido Reni.

Mignard then sought out the owner of the picture and admitted to the forgery, but his confession was not taken seriously. The purchaser assumed that he was regretting the transaction because he had subsequently received a higher offer. Mignard, convinced of his ability to imitate Guido Reni perfectly, had carefully provided for such an eventuality. When the purchaser refused his offer to

buy the fake back at the same price which had been paid for it as
an ostensible Guido Reni, the painter produced a small bottle of
turpentine, moistened a cloth and wiped off the painted figure's
hair. What came to light, beneath it, was a cardinal's hat and
Mignard's signature.

It is not known whether the collector got rid of the picture. No
contemporary version of the story now exists, and it has survived
only in an account by Christoph Martin Wieland. It may not be erroneous to assume that Le Brun had actually recognized the forgery but preferred to ascribe the picture, whose quality could
hardly be disputed, to the dead Guido Reni rather than credit a
living artist with the virtuosity displayed by such a work of art. For
Charles Le Brun was a boundlessly jealous man, and did not
shrink from secretly treating pictures by the Swiss artist Josef
Werner at Louis XIV's court with a cloudy and corrosive varnish
which diminished the merits of their appearance. The king thereupon abandoned Werner, who had hitherto been his favorite artist.

To admire forgery as a work of art, to marvel at it and respect
it, was in tune with the spirit of the Renaissance, a period which
ascribed equal status and virtue to suicide and heroism, religion
and profanation, extreme asceticism and unbridled hedonism.

Pietro Summonte reports, in a prosaic manner explicable only in
terms of contemporary thought, that a Flemish dealer one day lent
a successful portrait of Charles, Duke of Burgundy, to the painter
Colantonio, who said he wanted to examine it more closely. The
inquisitive artist copied the painting which had been entrusted to
him with such exactitude that the copy was indistinguishable from
the original. He then returned the copy in place of the original. The
man from Flanders did not notice the deception until Colantonio's
pride and vanity prompted him to confess the hoax. One of Colantonio's pupils was Antonello da Messina. In his early period he too
tried to imitate the technique displayed by the Flemish pictures

which he saw at the Neapolitan court. Antonello, Colantonio and other South Italian painters won a great name for themselves as successful imitators.

Twenty-two years after Terenzio da Urbino's death in 1620, his biographer Baglione wrote of him that he was one of those painters who made a practice of passing off his own freshly painted works as old masterpieces. He used to soil the pictures and mount them, whenever possible, in decrepit frames. Again, he would paint over originals which had been badly or inadequately finished. "He knew how to mix paints so that his work eventually looked as though it were really old and of some value." Having finished his paintings he used to darken them with smoke, lending them a patina with variegated layers of varnish and making the frames look as though they were at least a hundred years old with the aid of shabby gilding. When a nobly carved and splendidly gilded old frame came into Terenzio's possession he used it for a *Madonna with Figures* which he had copied from an old engraving. The fake was so successful that it was admired as a genuine original.

This triumph encouraged the forger to foist his painting onto the venerable Cardinal Montalto, the benefactor in whose service he was employed, as a genuine Raphael. Not until the cardinal showed his Madonna to several experts did the forgery come to light. Terenzio lost his painting and his job, but suffered no further penalty. The concept of art forgery was as yet unknown in the legal sense.

Michelangelo, too, grew up in this atmosphere of artistic jiggery-pokery. When, as was the custom, his teacher Domenico Ghirlandajo gave him a head by another artist to copy, young Michelangelo performed the task so perfectly that the copy was indistinguishable from the original. The owner still thought himself the proud possessor of an original, but all he got back was the copy.

Michelangelo treasured the original carefully, but could not keep the secret to himself. He proudly informed the rest of the studio that he had succeeded in reproducing a drawing so perfectly that his copy had been mistaken for the original.

When one of Ghirlandajo's pupils secretly informed the owner of this fact the man immediately hurried to the painting school and demanded his original drawing back. Michelangelo denied the story, and when the two sheets were laid side by side, no one ventured to pick out the copy from the original. Michelangelo had prudently smoked and aged his copy so that there was no apparent difference in age. Only he could distinguish the two, which he eventually did. Condivi, a contemporary of Michelangelo, wrote that this occurrence "brought great fame" to the young student.

Had the purchaser known what an enormous price would subsequently be commanded by a copy from the hand of Michelangelo, he might not have been so insistent about the return of another artist's original. It is not known which drawings were involved in this fraudulent escapade, but one cannot help wondering where the original and the copy are today, if they still exist. One is tempted to assume that either of them, should one or other have survived, would be revered as an original Michelangelo. If the genuine drawing could not be distinguished from the copy in those days, it seems highly improbable that we could distinguish them today!

The boundaries between permissible and impermissible imitation, stylistic plagiarism, copy, replica and forgery remained nebulous. We are told by Vasari, the Italian painter, sculptor and writer on art, that Federigo, Duke of Mantua and a scion of the house of Gonzaga, once admired Raphael's portrait of Pope Leo X in the Medici Palace at Florence. In so doing he paid homage not only to the painter but also to the master of the house, Ottaviano de' Medici, since apart from His Holiness the magnificent painting also portrayed Giulio de' Medici and Luigi de' Rossi. Federigo admired the picture in such explicit terms that, obedient to the exaggerated laws of contemporary hospitality, Ottaviano presented it to his noble guest as a gift. It was agreed that the painting should be packed with the utmost care and dispatched to Mantua.

Scarcely had the duke departed than Ottaviano de' Medici devised a way of keeping his splendid Raphael after all. Summoning Andrea del Sarto, whose *Baptism of Christ*, a fresco in the Chiostro dello Scalzo at Florence, was held to be worthy of Raphael or Leonardo da Vinci, he commissioned him to copy the Pope's portrait. The venture was so successful that the original and copy were virtually indistinguishable.

The Duke of Mantua received the generous gift with a joy which was marred only when his close friend the painter Giulio Romano informed him of the deception. However, Romano declared, "I do not value this picture any less than if it had come from Raphael's own hand; on the contrary, I value it far more highly, for it is past nature that one distinguished man should so fully succeed in imitating and catching the style of another." And the duke allotted the copy a place of honor in his collection.

Vasari's account of these events is correct in outline, but the details do not tally with verifiable dates. To give a concrete example of how far a description of historical events can diverge from the original occurrence, here is some documentary evidence:

Federigo Gonzaga was still a marquis in 1524. He did not accede to the dukedom until 1530.

He did not visit the Florentine Medici in 1524.

It was Pietro Aretino, not he, who mooted that the picture should change hands.

The copy of the Raphael original was commissioned not by Ottaviano de' Medici but by Pope Clement VII, formerly Giulio de' Medici.

Raphael's version of the picture now hangs in Florence, Andrea del Sarto's in Naples. Fierce controversy was still raging in Italy in

the middle of the last century as to which of the two pictures was
the genuine and which the imitation. The Neapolitans claimed the
honor of possessing an original Raphael and relegated the Florentines' picture to second place. However, research into the origin and
careers of both pictures proved beyond doubt that the Florentines'
Pope Leo X was the work of Raphael. Moreover, subsequent examination of brushwork and other distinguishing features showed the
painting in Naples to be the work of Andrea del Sarto.

It is not always possible, as in this case, to pick out the kernel of
truth in the often numerous versions of one and the same occurrence. The pen quails at dismissing a copy from the hand of
Andrea del Sarto as a forgery. Yet this accomplished imitator's
motives for his course of action were just as unwarrantable as those
of the man who commissioned him. Ottaviano de' Medici defrauded a fellow nobleman, and Andrea del Sarto received payment for a forgery.

The painter and art expert Joachim von Sandrat records in his
Teutsche Academie der edlen Bau-, Bild- und Malereykünste, published in 1675, what might almost be termed a "pious" example of
art forgery:

Sundry Frenchmen acting on the King's instructions secretly nego-
tiated with the monks of an Italian monastery for one of Paolo Veronese's
finest pictures, on account of its rarity, the monks having previously had
a good copy made of it, intending to exchange this for the original and
despatch it to the King in return for a considerable amount of money.
However, the Venetian Republic was informed of this in time; the monastery raided quite unexpectedly during the packing (of the picture), the
monks caught red-handed at their task and severely punished therefor.
So that nothing of the kind should again be undertaken and in order to
keep a reminder of their discreditable act before the monks' eyes, they
were obliged to content themselves with the aforesaid copy, while the
original was transported to the Palace of San Marco and there installed.

7 *a*. Giotto, *Vision of Bishop Guido*: Santa Croce, Florence, before recent restoration

7 *b*. Present condition, with 19th-century overpainting removed

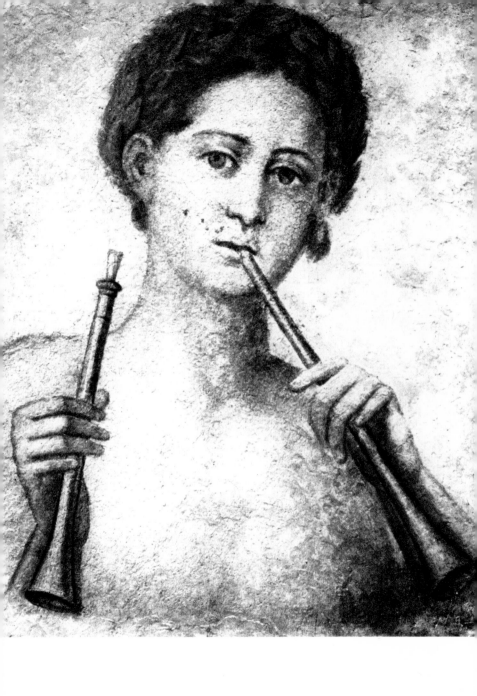

8. *The Flute-Player*, 19th-century forgery in the style of a Roman mural: British Museum, London

9. *Venus*, attributed by Marangoni to Michelangelo: Pitti Palace, Florence

10 *a*. Giovanni Bastianini, *Lucrezia Donati*: marble bust in the style of the 14th century, Victoria and Albert Museum, London. Crown Copyright.

10 *b*. Giovanni Bastianini, *Savonarola*: terracotta, Victoria and Albert Museum, London. Crown Copyright.

11. Giovanni Bastianini, *Marsilio Ficino*: terracotta, Victoria and Albert Museum, London, inspired by a sculpture by Andrea di Piero Ferrucci in Florence Cathedral. Crown Copyright.

AVE: MARIA: GRATIA: PLENA: DO

12.   Pseudo-Masaccio, *The Madonna of Humility:* National Gallery, Washington

The Lombard sculptor Guglielmo della Porta (d. 1577 at Rome) supplied "antique" marble busts to order. He even sold Pope Julius III a round dozen busts of Roman Caesars, but was forced to take them back when his more scrupulous colleagues denounced him. They were eventually sold to a Spanish dealer. Not even these fakes were condemned on ethical or moral grounds, however. The painter and stonemason P. Giacomo Alari even chose the pseudonym "Antico," so little stigma attached to the forging of works of art.

Isabella d'Este, Marchioness of Mantua, wrote to Duke Francesco Gonzaga telling him that two bronze figures which she had purchased from Maestro Raphael as antique works of art were in fact forgeries. Her steward Carlo Ghisio had apparently tried to get back the purchase price in return for the two figures, but Maestro Raphael rejected the request. When the Marchioness cited the expert opinions of sculptors such as Lorenzo and of the antiquary G. P. Columba, Raphael denied these experts any right or competence to judge the figures. He may thus be regarded as the precursor of those dealers who, throughout the centuries to our own day, have repudiated all adverse opinions — though not always with Raphael's success.

A small but extremely interesting group of art forgers is recruited from the ranks of duped collectors. Members of this species, all the more dangerous because they are unsuspected, can still be encountered in our own day. They turn to forgery from a wish to repair an injury done to themselves by re-inflicting it on others. The more deeply hurt by forgers their genuine or fancied connoisseurship of the arts has been, the easier it is for them to defend their own fraud, normally planned and executed with the utmost finesse, as an act of compensatory justice. And because many of these collector-forgers are equipped with a very sound knowledge of style and are sufficiently familiar with restoration work and — from long years of experience — trade practice, their close contact with anti-quarians and collectors makes it comparatively easy for them to dispose of good imitations and first-rate forgeries.

It is an undoubted fact that the truly great names in painting were constantly producing imitations. In his maturer years, Rubens copied works which had appeared up to two hundred years earlier. The best-known of these pictures is the portrait of Paracelsus at Brussels. In his *Christ Scourging the Money-changers,* Rembrandt copied the figure of Christ from a woodcut by Dürer, who lived a century earlier. For his part, Dürer employed as models figures by the Italian artists Mantegna and Jacopo de' Barbari.

Raphael painted the *Holy Marriage* (*Wedding of the Madonna; Wedding of the Virgin*) after a picture of the same name by Peru-gino, christened Pietro Vannucci. Born in 1445, Perugino worked in Florence and Rome but principally at Perugia, in whose honor he adopted his pseudonym. He was Raphael's teacher, and died in 1523. The *Holy Marriage* might be termed a Raphaelesque Perugino.

By the early eighteenth century a series of paintings by Nicolaes Maes, Ferdinand Bol, Govaert Flinck, Aert de Gelder, Gerard van Eeckhout and other masters had been transformed into works by Rembrandt, and a whole generation of painstaking Rembrandt scholars devoted their lives to the nice task of differentiating be-tween original productions and stylistic imitations. The identifica-tion of their origin was not rendered any easier by the fact that many works attributed to Rembrandt actually did come from his own hand, for the master did not reveal the same greatness in all his works as he did in 1656 in the *Portrait of Six,* which moved the painter and author Eugène Fromentin to exclaim: "What other painter could paint a portrait like this?" We cannot, therefore, discount the possibility that weaker pictures by Rembrandt are today attributed to other artists.

Error and fraud work in close liaison. The portrait of Cima da Conegliano in the Museo Poldi-Pezzoli in Milan very probably represents the original basis of a questionable Dürer from the year 1508 which reposes in the Graphische Sammlung at Munich. The monogram on the drawing gives rise to the well-founded suspicion that it is an imitation. The Earl of Cranbrook owns a variant of the alleged Dürer drawing at Munich in the form of a pen drawing which was published as an original by the Dürer Society in 1908. The art historian Lippmann did not include the Munich version in his *Corpus der Dürer-Zeichnungen*. It *could* be a drawing by Dürer which someone later equipped with a monogram to enhance its value. On the other hand, both picture and monogram may be a complete forgery.

PART TWO

The Forger's Methods

3

❦❦❦❦❦❦❦❦❦

Paintings

TO simulate an early picture, the forger can adopt any one of four different procedures. He may use:

(1) A genuine old work painted on wood, canvas or metal from which he has removed the original subject in whole or part. Viewed objectively, this results in an entirely or partially new picture on an old foundation.

(2) Material which is old but does not match the ostensible age of the forgery. This must first be made to look "in period" by means of various processes.

(3) Old materials which originally served quite different purposes. The rear wall of an old cupboard, for instance, can be turned into a panel picture. Old fabric can be mounted on a frame, or old copper roof-sheeting used, after careful rubbing down, as the foundation of a painting.

(4) More or less new material, artificially aged.

Whatever the subject of his deception, a forger's first endeavor must be to procure the correct material. The ground of his picture must be simulated according to the artist or school to which the fake is to be attributed. Priming and paints must correspond as nearly as possible to earlier blends of which the formulas are known, for the price fetched by a forgery fluctuates in proportion to the care and effort expended on these fundamental prerequisites.

Once the problem of materials has been overcome, the artist's work begins: original conception, stylistic imitation, or reconstitution of separate elements from several original works.

One particularly interesting form of forgery is the pastiche or *pasticcio,* which consists in abstracting various details from different pictures by the same artist and reconstituting them as a new picture in its own right. Pastiches are often very difficult to recognize as fakes from a stylistic aspect, especially if the forger is well acquainted with the idiosyncrasies of his subject (usually a near contemporary) and knows exactly what details to select for his new picture. Numerous pastiches were fabricated from the works of David Teniers the Younger and Jan Steen during their lifetime. Examination of materials is particularly important in cases such as these.

A forger's technique must thus embrace both preparation of materials and executive ability.

If, during the examination of his work, a substance were found which did not come into use until a hundred years after the picture's alleged date of origin, the forger's hoax would be established beyond a shadow of doubt. Stylistic discrepancies can be equally revealing, as when a piece of Renaissance decor turns up in a purportedly Gothic painting.

It is true that recipes and formulas have survived even from the early Byzantine period, but many techniques and implements and countless preparations of paint, lacquer, resin and oil remained closely guarded secrets. Such old recipes as have been inherited are thus of only moderate importance. It seems fairly clear, too, that old painting manuals sometimes contained purposely misleading statements. There was obviously an aversion to committing the fruits of long years of hard-won experience to the pages of a text-book.

The cardinal principle was that of the studio, of personal tuition and improvement under the guidance of a master.

What makes circumstances even harder for the forger is not only that early treatises containing painting instructions are very rare but that libraries and archives make them available only to bona fide students. The forger has to be satisfied with later editions which frequently distort the terms and specifications of the original. Errors in translation still further trouble the already clouded waters of original formulas and recipes.

Apart from original treatises and reprints, more recent textbooks give very exhaustive descriptions of the early painting techniques and materials used in the various classical periods. Max Doerner's technical work *The Materials of the Artist and Their Use in Painting* (translated by Eugen Neuhaus, Harcourt Brace, 1949) has served as my guide for the present section. Our knowledge of medieval artists' materials has grown considerably under the impact of modern science. Undisputed originals by leading masters, their pupils, studios and contemporaries have been examined under microscope and spectroscope with reference to foundation, priming, paint and varnish, and identifying characteristics have now been accurately determined.

Even the forger of superior technical education can hardly be expected to have at his disposal the results of all this research, and his insufficient knowledge of materials frequently proves fatal. Nevertheless, there are plenty of sources from which he can cull a great deal of valuable information.

When producing an imitation which is to pass as a Byzantine or *trecento* panel the forger will find detailed expositions in Cennini's account of Giotto's working methods. Byzantine art originated in the sixth century and did not make its exit until the middle of the fifteenth. The pictorial work of its earlier periods are the most valuable and accordingly the most interesting to the forger, though they are the hardest to imitate in material and style.

The wooden panel itself presents a particularly difficult problem to the would-be imitator of works from so distant an era. While wood of the Gothic period can still be procured, older pieces can be found only in the rarest instances. Even when wood can be obtained, as it sometimes can, from early Gothic buildings, there is no guarantee that it will have come from the earliest stage in their construction, wood being the building material most susceptible to the ravages of time and most frequently replaced as the centuries go by. Differences in age are hard to determine in terms of decades, but much easier in terms of centuries.

Metal sheets from these periods are almost impossible to obtain, and artificial aging is comparatively easy to detect in the case of metal.

The ground or foundation of early panel pictures was composed of layers of soap and oil. Oily varnishes darkened them so much that they sometimes give an impression of charring. Varnishes were rubbed in with the ball of the thumb, producing a result which no machine could hope to emulate. However, the use of oils of greatly varying quality shortened the life of pictorial works produced by this laborious technique.

The manufacturing of the ground presents great problems, for the inadequacies of such primitive working methods scarcely permit of consistent imitation.

Artists of the time compounded their paints of glue, lye and wax, but also used egg tempera. When constructing a picture they adhered to strictly prescribed composite tones for flesh portions, greenish in the shadows contrasted by red. The brittleness of the paints carried with it a risk that cracks would mar the surface of the picture when it was dry. To prevent cracking, it was given protective coats of dark-toned varnishes, probably containing asphaltum. The flattish texture of panel pictures was a structural inheritance from mural fresco painting and displayed ornamentation in gold leaf or, more rarely, baser alloys.

It is an uncommonly difficult and tedious task to copy the technique of Byzantine panel paintings (icons) and Italian panel pictures of the *duecento* and early *trecento*. Moreover, it presupposes an ability to maintain the iconostasis style consistently, despite its resistance to imitation and adherence to extremely rigid laws.

Probably the oldest book of paint recipes is the eighth-century *Lucca Manuscript*. This deals with the manufacture of vegetable pigments, gildings and staining oils, and also describes the *pictura translucida,* which was underlaid with tinfoil.

Another early treatise is that of Heraclius (also eighth century), who advises egg-white-and-alum colors for miniatures and illuminated lettering and gives information on oil colors.

The *Mappae Claviculae,* a manuscript which probably originated on the Venetian mainland during the thirteenth century, contains suggestions on how to prepare wax colors and bind them with glue.

The *Hermeneia* by Dionysus has gained a name for itself as "the painting manual from Mount Athos." This standard work, from which generations of painters have derived profit and instruction, discusses the structural laws of Byzantine painting and its strict code of basic rules. The handbook's date of origin is shrouded in uncertainty, but it probably dates from about 1350. As a foundation for pictures of the early Byzantine period, Dionysus suggests a gypsum and glue ground treated with soap and oil. Detailed recipes are given for gilded work, the building up of flesh tones, and decoration. These formulas refer principally to the painting of masonry. For priming canvas, the treatise suggests a mixture of glue, soap, honey and gypsum applied with egg. The author leaves to the painter the question of what proportions to use when compounding the mixture. For varnishes he recommends spirits of wine. Other formulas concern gloss colors, which can be obtained from glue and lye-impregnated wax mixed in equal proportions.

Contemporary accounts provide further valuable information. Duccio di Buoninsegna, the first great painter of the Sienese school, favored a dark green *imprimitura* to be applied over the white plaster or gesso ground, corresponding to the *proplasmos* suggested by Dionysus. The whole picture was coated with "carnation" (i.e. heightened with a blend of white lead, ocher and vermilion). Since shading was gradated toward the edges, the *proplasmos* tended to show through, creating an impression almost of tridimensionality. The red of cheeks and lips received a dark overtone. Eyebrows, pupils and deep folds, applied with *caput mortuum,* formed the uppermost layer, while draperies were always painted before flesh.

Gloss colors derived their luster from rubbing. Like egg yolk, they also served as a binding agent under the designation *cera colla.* In contradistinction to this technique with its Greek or Cretan name, early Russian icons exhibit an egg-yolk technique strongly heightened with white and displaying predominantly green, red and ocher tones.

In the course of time, the rigid laws of Byzantine painting (the *maniera bizantina*) gave way to the naturalistic tendencies first of Cimabue (d. *circa* 1302) and Giotto (*circa* 1266-1337). The most comprehensive description of the latter's technique is given by Cennino Cennini in his *Trattato della Pittura,* a treatise on painting which appeared in 1390. It is really a craftsman's textbook.

Here for the first time the student is instructed, when preparing a wooden panel for future use, to "keep it entirely free from grease."

Cennini supplies detailed information on the various preparatory stages. The panel was given repeated applications of glue-size and then covered with canvas. Onto the firm surface thus obtained was laid a gesso and glue ground composed of numerous thin layers. Finally, after much laborious scraping, the brilliant white panel was ready to receive paint.

Should a forger skimp the procedure, given here in abridged form, his efforts will not be worth while. Any substitution of a simpler technique for this extremely tedious method will only facilitate detection.

The method, as described by Cennini, of steeping a canvas in hot glue, then coating it with starch, sugar and gypsum, and finally applying an oil priming, has not withstood the test of time. Nevertheless, his suggestions on the priming of the interior panel are still, amazingly enough, rightly regarded as excellent. Nor have his instructions on high-class hand gilding ever been bettered.

For tempera painting, egg yolk was used. Mixed with the juice of young fig sprouts and water, this was rubbed into the surface to be painted. The thick, milky juice liquefied the egg yolk and increased its durability. Cennini, who warned against adding too much egg yolk, further recommended his readers to use the eggs of town-bred hens because "their yolk is lighter and more serviceable." The rule was to stir up pigments and egg yolk in equal proportions and then rub them between the hands in water. This gave the mixture more body than any mechanical process has yet succeeded in producing.

When executing a composition, the artist dealt first with architecture, then draperies and finally flesh. This invested his strongest colors with the utmost possible luminosity because they reposed directly on the white ground. The initial drawing, customarily outlined lightly in green, was toned with Veronese green earth, the pale areas being flatly modeled with two coats of white. The mixed green tone of the drawing (*verdaccio*) was achieved by blending black, white and ocher. Then came the strengthening of eyes, nose, mouth and folds with outline paint. Shading effects were obtained by a heavier application of Veronese green earth.

Flesh displayed three definite tonal values: (1) the light red terminal tone, which was obtained with *cinabrese* or light red sinope, similar to the cinnabar of Asia Minor, mixed with white; (2) the deepest tone, which was obtained from *cinabrese* with a very sparing addition of white; and (3) the medium tone, produced by mixing sinope and white in equal proportions.

The painter carried out heightening in the light tone. Transitional portions were executed in the medium tone, while the deepest tone was intensified by the green underpainting, which showed through and reacted on the reddish-white. The darkest tone was chromatically the strongest because it had to compete with the amplifying green undertone. The red showed up least strongly in the light portions where the green undertone was most diluted with white.

In the flesh portions, the first task was to apply the strong red of cheeks and lips. The darkest flesh tone, obtained from white and red, was not more than about half as strong as the full red of the lips. Intermediate tones were applied in numerous superimposed layers. Final effects were achieved by the strengthening of highlights with almost pure white and deep shadows with red-black or pure black. Draperies were likewise executed in three gradated tones.

Even the forger who is endowed with a wide knowledge of materials and great artistic ability will encounter, within the narrow sphere of a single color, an insoluble problem: since the close of the Middle Ages, natural ocher or *cinabrese* (sinope) has vanished from painting. No potential substitute produces the same results under spectral analysis. Hence, even the absence of this pigment in pictures which purport to belong to the heyday of the *cina-brese* technique must, in itself, point strongly in the direction of forgery.

To paint according to the ancient canons of tempera painting demands much greater effort than the modern technique of oil painting.

Formerly, the risk of dissolving the underlying strata of paint necessitated that a brush be loaded with the utmost care, although it had to hold enough fluid color to permit of quickly covering the undercoat with the minimum of pressure and without injuring it. A color could be strengthened only by cross-hatching it repeatedly with the tip of the brush. And because tempera painting, like any water-color technique, requires a light ground to bring it fully to life, modeled depths presented difficult problems.

After the application of parchment glue as an intermediate varnish, the panel picture had to dry thoroughly before being varnished with *vernice liquida,* normally obtained from linseed oil and sandarac. The designation sandarac has survived in modern usage as gum sandarac, but it is, in its present guise, unsuitable for tempera painting. The name was obviously applied to some other substance in those days.

The preservative substance used was a resin obtained from the crushed bark of *Callitris quadrivalvis,* a North African tree.

Also employed in the preparation of varnish, Cennini informs us, was linseed oil which had been evaporated in the sun to half its original volume.

These lacquer-like glazings with their reddish tones were what endowed tempera pictures with warmth. To achieve an even texture, the varnishes were gently worked into the picture's surface by hand. Coloration gave them the character of a glaze.

Later on, the use of oil paints came in, especially for draperies, while flesh portions continued to be painted in tempera. Giotto is said to have painted in pure oils, but Cennini does not mention this.

The extraordinary knowledge of pigments, the preparatory work, the craftsmanship and, of course, the laborious and endless task of painting itself all combined to give tempera pictures of this period a durability unsurpassed by any other technique and equaled by only a few. This also applied to mural paintings. The plaster consisted of two parts sand and one part lime, and was left to settle for several days after mixing. It was then carefully distributed over the dampened wall. After it had thoroughly dried out, the painter drew in the outlines of the projected picture with ocher and ruddle. If he was satisfied with the shape of his design, he recorded it in the form of a sketch, applied a new coat of plaster and, after the carefully smoothed surface was once more entirely dry, transferred the outlines to it. Only then did he proceed with painting proper.

One variant worthy of mention is *secco* painting, in which diluted egg yolk was applied with a sponge. This technique was also used for gilding, which was superimposed on an undertone of Veronese green earth.

The school of painting which Cennini describes in such detail not only operated in Italy but spread to southern France, Spain and the area of Cologne, where its materials and technique, Byzantine in origin, can be encountered in the works of Meister Wilhelm (Cologne, flourished 1358-1380).

The unusual characteristics of this early Italian technique were still attracting painters in quite recent times. Variations of the methods described by Cennini can be found not only in Marées but in Böcklin and many others.

Working materials used by the old masters can be imitated only partially by the forger of today. He can, for instance, attempt to replace the inner sheet of fabric, but only with cloth of much more recent origin. And canvas of more modern date is almost always subject to yellowish-brown discoloration by sodium hydrate. Early unbleached fabrics are also distinguishable from those of later manufacture both in thread and weave. The former display no dressing and are innocent of the starch pastes, mineral additives and chemicals which today foster an appearance of better quality. To employ fabric of an alien period, whether as an actual base or as an intermediate textile sheet serving to bind other layers, the forger must first boil it and bleach it in the sun. If he does not boil it sufficiently, lingering traces will be disclosed by chemical analysis. But the more thoroughly he does so the more easily detectable his intervention becomes.

Assuming that the forger has succeeded in procuring old material for coating with gesso and glue, he is now forced to blend starch, sugar and gypsum of modern manufacture, since these substances, unlike glue, can no longer be prepared as they were by the old masters.

After priming and scraping his board, the forger is faced with the difficult task of drying out the now conglomerated surface coating in a structurally correct manner. Violent heat or baking will produce fissures. The only alternative is to use alien binding and siccative agents which are easily detectable. Internal heating with infrared rays achieves no better result.

The more genuine an impression he strives for, the greater the problems a forger has to overcome. In time, his resistance to the temptation of short cuts will weaken. He will make life easier for himself and the detection of his forgery easier for the expert.

In Germany, tempera technique was joined by oil painting at a fairly early date, but the coupling of tempera and oils brought neither genuine vitality nor harmonic grace. Most of the efforts to devise a new technique miscarried. Baldovinetti's recipe, egg yolk and *vernice liquida* blended under heat, was a failure because the boiling of pigment produced a sort of omelet! Every attempt foundered on the fact that the preparation of emulsions, not in itself a particularly difficult matter, was as yet unknown.

The *Diversarum artium schedula,* a work probably written about 1120 by the monk Theophilus of Paderborn, contains recipes ranging from those based on Byzantine sources to those which figured in the Italian painting manuals of his own day. A forger can find all kinds of valuable information in Theophilus, from the priming of wooden panels with glue, gypsum or pipe clay and casein glue, to the preparation of canvases and the technique of painting on sheets of tinfoil. The monk also gives details of the principal formulas needed for tempera painting and instructions in the use of cherry gum as a painting material and beaten white of egg for light colors and large painted surfaces, though this was more customarily employed in miniatures. He describes fully the ways of achieving deep shadows by applying a preliminary undercoat of green and of heightening lights by toning flesh in redwhite. It may be mentioned that a letter from Lenbach to Böcklin dated January 14, 1867, contained a tempera recipe involving cherry-resin. Many of Böcklin's pictures reveal that he must have taken note of Lenbach's suggestions. He boiled up cherry gum with equal parts of tragacanth and isinglass. Then, before the mixture had cooled, he added spirits of wine to prevent it from decomposing. The paint remained soluble in water and presented little resistance to wear.

In his treatise on tempera, Theophilus speaks about the application of intermediate varnishes and mentions glazing mixtures compounded of oils, resins and colored varnishes. Despite the detailed nature of his account, Theophilus, like his contemporaries, knew little about the raw materials he was recommending. Oil was just oil, and so olive oil, though hard to dry, was put on a par with quick-drying linseed oil. Because olive oil remained soft, the same property was unjustly ascribed to linseed oil. The main principle was to dry a painting in the sun. Where this was impossible, oil was to be avoided. Since oils, whose properties were as yet insufficiently known, normally required a long period of drying, oil painting was not recommended. Unlike tempera painting, it allowed the application of a second coat of paint only after considerable time had elapsed.

With varnishes, it was still the rule that they should be rubbed in before and after, with the ball of the hand.

Although the practical uses of oil painting had been known in Germany and Flanders since before 1400, its true date of birth there as an artist's medium was signalized in the works of the brothers van Eyck, for it was they who reformed the time-honored methods and molded them into the technique of the ensuing centuries. The van Eycks were not by any means the inventors of oil painting, but they must be credited with having blazed the trail down which modern oil painting passed on its way to supremacy. Hubert van Eyck was born at Maaseyck in 1370 and died at Ghent on September 18, 1426. The inscription on the altar in Ghent, one of the most magnificent works produced at the turn of the fourteenth century, reads: " . . . *maior quo nemo repertus"* — "than whom none was found greater."

The discovery of the principles governing the correct use of oil paints may be attributed to an accident. Following the treatises of Cennini and Theophilus, Hubert van Eyck had laid out a freshly varnished picture to dry in bright sunlight. When he examined his work afterwards he saw to his chagrin that the board was covered with a network of cracks. This prompted him to conduct a series of tests to find a varnish which would dry in a relatively short time without the sun's aid. He eventually devised a blend of linseed oil and nut oil which proved particularly well suited to his purposes. In the course of time he produced other mixtures which, after heating, produced paints of full brilliance and a hard gloss that made pictures look as if they had been coated with varnish.

Van Eyck was, of course, familiar with the tempera undercoat which, either in monochrome or with slight additions of color, facilitated glazing with resinous oil paint and simultaneously increased luminosity without dissolving the oil paints on application.

By manufacturing an emulsion which obviated the cracking to which egg-yolk painting materials were subject, however, van Eyck exchanged the realm of discovery for that of true invention. It was the emulsifying of tempera which made possible Hubert van Eyck's structural technique, the layer-wise superimposition of tempera and oil paints. And even though this, too, had been practiced in a crude form almost two centuries earlier, it only now gained practical significance.

The working methods characteristic of paintings of this epoch present the forger with almost insuperable difficulties. To imitate them, he must employ substitute techniques which are fairly easy to detect. The ochrous oily or resinous *imprimitura* with its thin overall coat of glaze is almost impossible to simulate. The presence of contemporary varnishes and Venetian turpentine can always be established in original works to a certain degree. In section, a fake never exhibits the same authentic stratified effect, and technical shortcomings make it easy for the art historian to form definite conclusions.

The Remscheid painter Walter Ruhrmann tried to obtain van Eyck's "varnishless gloss" by using G. S. W. Clayton's "water-in-oil emulsion," to which he added $1\frac{1}{2}$ to 2 parts of concentrated sand- or balsam-impregnated oil emulsified with one part of 10 per cent strength gum solution. He did, in fact, achieve what appeared to be an almost identical effect. However, surplus oil left behind by the evaporation of the water gave the painted surface a honeycomb texture which, while it enhanced its gloss, clearly differentiated it from the original paints.

Hubert van Eyck's technique was also the basis of a patent taken out by the painter Richard Lindmar in Berlin in 1926. This related to an oily emulsion which, according to its inventor, was the sole equivalent of genuine old van Eyck paints. In fact, Lindmar used the following substances, which occur in early treatises and in van Eyck's techniques: diluted hide glue, fatty oils, boiled or rendered oil, resin varnishes, egg, casein, cherry gum, gum arabic and other additives.

Lindmar's patent colors were never marketed. They did not stand up to comparative spectral analysis. The "van Eyck type" colors manufactured from old recipes by the Parisian painters Maroger and Thièle are also quite distinguishable prismatically from van Eyck's original paints.

Max Doerner, in his admirably concise treatment *The Materials of the Artist and Their Use in Painting,* believes that it is possible to match the technique and perfection of the Flemish masters without employing original formulas. He divides the procedure into seven stages:

(1) Preparing a solid white gesso ground.

(2) Tracing and strengthening the outline sketch with ink or tempera black.

(3) Laying on an *imprimitura* compounded of red or yellow ocher oil color and varnish. Any remnants of glazing color must be wiped away with a rag. The *imprimitura* is thin and has hardly any gloss, leaving the ink drawing perfectly visible. A priming of casein or egg tempera coated with mastic varnish (or dammar) is most advantageous because it will not be dissolved by glazing.

(4) Brushing into this surface, if wet, or onto it, if dry, heightening in tempera white, applied most strongly on flesh portions, though with light brush strokes, and more broadly on draperies.

White heightening is best applied in layers. The primary, thin, flattish tone, which is distributed throughout, must afterwards be strengthened in the light portions. In shaded areas, the ocher tone shows through. Light portions, too, must be flatly heightened, though not the brightest highlights, and the same applies to the deeper shaded portions.

(5) When sufficient heightening has been applied, a resin-oil glaze thinned with varnish or balsam and blended with condensed oil must be thinly distributed.

(6) Where plasticity is still lacking, further heightening is applied to the wet surface with tempera white. Black or Naples yellow may also be used, though light brush strokes are advisable with the former.

(7) Now comes a further glazing as in (5), in the course of which a thin half-coat of resin oil paint may also be used. Glazes, too, should be gradually toned from light portions to dark. The process of deepening where necessary will readily bring out intermediate tones. The flat white-heightened modeling must also now be intensified.

Even though the forger may be capable, always assuming his stylistic competence, of producing an imitation on these lines which will deceive the unwary observer, he still has no chance of resisting meticulous examination.

Not even the most conscientious forger can copy the extraordinarily complicated technique of the great medieval masters. We must remember that artists sometimes made mistakes when mixing their paints. An imitator will have a compulsive aversion to committing the same errors, and in this respect errors themselves form an indication of authenticity. Raehlmann points out that Dürer sometimes used a copper blue under the impression that it was genuine ultramarine. The same thing probably occurred with other German, Italian and Flemish masters. This and similar details facilitate the recognition of originals.

The meticulous and painstaking accuracy practiced by the leading painters of those days becomes evident from Dürer's letters to his friend Jakob Heller, in which he writes of "four-, five- or six-fold undercoating and four-, five- and six-fold undercoating, overcoating and finishing." That done, he goes on, he then "went over the picture twice more, so that it should last longer." Far from prolonging the life of a picture, multiple applications of modern paints would tend to shorten it.

Almost insurmountable obstacles are placed in the imitator's path by the individual techniques employed in their work by Hans Baldung, Hans Holbein and their contemporaries. A manuscript from the Marciana Library speaks, for instance, of the blending of one part of coarsely ground oil paint with half a part of similar tempera paint, the whole to be kneaded in water with a like quantity of egg yolk. No artificial process can accurately reproduce the alteration in these substances which has taken place over the centuries.

After analyzing the probable manner in which Greco's *Disrobing of Christ* came into being, Doerner identifies more than thirty separate procedures which must have taken place before the final *alla prima* painting could be laid into the glaze with the utmost possible effect.

Titian's *St. Sebastian,* in the Vatican, displays marked wrinkles but very little yellowing. This points to the use of hempseed oil, although the only painting materials familiarly attributed to him and his school are mastic varnish, essential varnish and nut oil. Contemporary recipes refer to particularly pungent substances, which would suggest turpentine, linseed oil, egg-size, gum and milk. Judging by the complaints of Titian's heirs about large bills for alum, which was probably used for dressing grounds and preparing lacquer paints and madder lake, we may conclude that the artist was also familiar with this substance.

Even the greatest artists worked without any exact knowledge of how their materials would stand up to the years. Tintoretto's pictures darkened very considerably because he apparently painted on a red ground without sufficient preparation. Strangely enough, Goethe was aware of this circumstance, as we can read in his *Italian Journey*. Volpato thinks that several of Veronese's paintings deteriorated because their canvas was too thickly coated with plaster.

Velasquez invented a paint-mixing technique of his own.

The techniques of Rubens and Van Dyck are most exhaustively described in notes by Mayerne, the doctor who was a friend of both artists. In them we first find mention of pounded charcoal used in conjunction with white lead.

Rubens's work is far more complicated than that of Titian. His structural methods would require several pages of detailed description on their own. Seemingly trivial minutiae acquire significance under close analysis. Whereas it had been assumed that Rubens used Naples yellow, an antimonic acid compound of lead, tests undertaken by Dr. Richard Jacobi, head of the Doerner Institute's department of chemico-physics, indicated that Rubens's yellow was a lead-tin compound which could be reconstituted by burning three parts minium with one part ashes of tin. What was probably a unique opportunity of investigating the structural technique and layer composition of an artist of Rubens's class was provided for the Doerner Institute by an irresponsible crank who threw acid over one of his pictures and severely damaged it. Parts of the priming were eaten away to the base of the picture itself.

Just as the great old masters developed methods which were not only personal to them and inimitable from the technical and chemical aspect but also subject to considerable modification, so the succeeding centuries brought in their train a continuous change in individual approach to material, craftsmanship and style. Far though it is from Tiepolo to Leibl and from Leibl to the moderns, material and brushwork, wood and canvas, paint and varnish have preserved just as marked an individuality. Even in recent times, when great exponents were using — as they still are — mass-produced paints and equipment, they do so with a distinct individuality which, quite apart from stylistic idiosyncrasies, can be identified from the technical and material standpoint.

That was where contemporary painters who devoted themselves to forgery were considerably better off than the forgers of today. They had no comprehensive formulas, it is true, but since original works by the creative artists of the past are forever evincing new deviations in technique the detection of contemporary or near-contemporary imitations can seldom be effected by chemico-physical research. And here the judgment of experienced art historians not only comes into its own but sometimes assumes paramount importance. Whereas the modern forger of an old painting has been betrayed by the very wood with which he has framed it, the forger of earlier times runs no such risk.

Spectroscopic examination will produce results of dubious value if the picture in question is a skillful overpainting of five or more centuries ago. Moreover, a modern forger can render spectroscopic examination difficult and sometimes impossible by adding metallic salts to his overcoat of paint. X-ray pictures, too, can be "scrambled" and made illegible by prior treatment of the painted substructure with metal-impregnated substances. Admittedly, the presence of mineral salts provides almost conclusive evidence of fraudulent intervention, but it is not always easy to distinguish on X-ray screen or film between natural and artificially induced oxidization. Furthermore, such methods of detection are ineffective if an entire forgery is several centuries old.

The number of unsigned pictures, especially those of the classical periods, many times exceeds the number of works which bear a name or mark. Early forgers could thus, always assuming they had the ability, plausibly ascribe a nameless painting to a particular artist by adding his signature, their task rendered easier by the fact that varnish could be removed for this purpose and subsequently replaced without damaging the paint.

The contemporary forger was familiar with the artist's technical methods. Moreover, he had at his disposal at least some of the materials required for a convincing reproduction of the picture's foundation. If he could not procure panels of poplar wood or chestnut, walnut or pine which were exactly similar to those made available exclusively to members of the profession, there were ways and means of obtaining almost identical pieces. Their reverse side could be treated in the same manner and with the same type of ax as was used by the master or his pupils.

The modern forger lacks contemporary tools. Even the telltale marks of a plane will give him away. If he wants to work in the manner of the classical Dutch school, he will not be able to obtain the same solid oak which was cut in a slightly conical fashion and then smoothed with the large plane of the time. Again, original panels display cleanly executed beveling on the reverse edges.

The paintings of the French masters of the sixteenth and seventeenth centuries were also painted mainly on oak and less commonly on canvas. At the start of the seventeenth century mahogany appeared, and it was introduced into Holland at almost the same time. Lime, copper beech, fir, spruce, beech and nut were all used as foundations at various times and places. The real expert can often draw important conclusions from the way in which the tree has been dismembered. In Holland, the boards supplied to their members by the Guilds of St. Luke disclose extremely uniform methods of sawing and are easily identifiable, particularly by the cutting marks on the reverse. In the seventeenth century logs were cut vertically by a water-driven frame saw.

Painting bases were cut from the two inmost planks, since the outer planks tended to warp while drying, but even the former were hung up to dry for years before use. Many of them still display the identifying marks of guilds or fraternities, and it goes without saying that forgers imitated these, too. To protect the boards from subsequent warping, they were often reinforced at the back by a sort of trellis-work of jointed beading.

Disregarding the materials themselves, of course, a picture must be repeatedly analyzed on the critical plane. The difficulties involved are particularly well illustrated by the classical period of the fifteenth- and sixteenth-century masters.

The expert will by no means always be dealing with pictures which are of individual origin and authorship and give the impression of being a compact whole. Many outstanding works are the product of collaboration between a master and his pupils and testify less to the creative art of an individual than to the homogeneity of a studio. Of incomparably greater importance to the history and criticism of art, however, are works attributed to several artists rather than one, since they afford a considerable opportunity for chronological dissection of the various "contributions." This circumstance favors the imitator in that his modifications and overpaintings may be regarded as symptoms of collaboration.

In the narrow province dominated by the greatest painters of all time we encounter a new but classic instance of the imponderability of art. This is the elaboration or, if one will, refashioning of an autonomous work, as illustrated by Titian's treatment of Giovanni Bellini's painting *Feast of the Gods*.

The case has been elucidated by John Walker, whose exhaustive and unimpeachable analysis of the subject can be found in an excellently presented volume (*Bellini and Titian at Ferrara,* Doubleday, 1957).

By means of multistratal X-ray photographs, Walker established that Titian had fundamentally altered Bellini's picture and entirely painted over some of the principal figures. We can only guess at the reasons which prompted Titian to alter the static form, figures and content of the *Feast of the Gods.* The only factor of importance is that the most modern methods of research have now identified this original work by Bellini as really belonging to Titian. If there had been no means of establishing Titian's intervention, the same procedure would only have evinced that another painting underlay a hitherto undisputed Bellini. The discovery of two originals in the *Feast of the Gods* does not diminish the painting's intrinsic or extrinsic value. Indeed, the participation of two such high-ranking artists as Titian and Bellini invests it with additional rarity. Yet what a different complexion the overpainting would assume had its author been a forger! He would have destroyed a masterpiece. The art historian Eduard Hütting writes that Titian's modifications correspond "in rough terms, to the stylistic transition from the *quattrocento* to the *cinquecento.*"

It may be mentioned, incidentally, that some masterly early copies of the Bellini-Titian *Feast of the Gods* do exist, as, for instance, in the Castel Sant' Angelo at Rome, in the former Italico-Brasso Collection at Venice, and in the State Painting Gallery at Dresden.

A feeling of uncertainty assails both the collector and the conscientious expert whenever, on the one hand, hitherto unknown works of superlative quality turn up, and, on the other, when hitherto undisputed paintings and sculptures enter the twilight of controversy and doubt.

It is commonly assumed that the representative creations of the great masters have been conclusively established as originals on historical and empirical grounds. This is untrue.

An allusion to thematic similarity may become more intelligible if we remember that authorship and imitation become fused on the highest artistic plane, especially in cases where romantic by-considerations dull the critical gaze.

Few paintings have ever achieved such popularity as Leonardo's *Mona Lisa — La Gioconda.* The picture's inscrutable expression of unfathomable emotion became associated with its mysterious disappearance from the Louvre, and its return did nothing to dispel that aura of mystery — at least in the mind of a sensation-loving public. The circumstances surrounding this work by Leonardo have been obfuscated by those who, with little justification, dispute the authenticity of the painting which now hangs in its old place and voice the opinion that the original is even now the treasured possession of some fanatical collector.

The painting and its career have provided poets, composers and newspaper reporters with an inexhaustible source of material. The *"Gioconda* smile" has gained a firm hold on the popular imagination, if only because of its inscrutability.

On the track of this smile, we discover a repetition of it wreathed about the lovely lips of Leonardo's *Leda,* the magnificent painting which Ludovico Spiridon acquired in Paris and incorporated in his gallery at Rome. *Leda's* smile, rather more sensual than that of the *Gioconda,* is also invested with a certain mystery because reputable connoisseurs have questioned Leonardo's authorship, despite strong historical support for those who champion its authenticity.

Leonardo wrote of the *Leda* in his *Treatise on Painting:* "And it then came to pass that I executed a painting . . . for a lover. He wished to see the features of his goddess mirrored so that he might kiss them without arousing suspicion. Yet conscience vanquished his voluptuous sighs, for he constrained himself and put her out of the house."

Leonardo's client was Giuliano de' Medici, and the subject of the *Leda* painting was one of the most beautiful women in Florence. After the prince's marriage to Duchess Philisberta of Savoy he took leave of both his mistresses, the living and the painted, and gave the picture back to Leonardo.

What happened to it? The *Leda and the Swan* in the Gallery Borghese in Rome is designated as a copy. It is structurally and statistically related to Leonardo's *Leda,* but the background is more hilly and emphatic in treatment. The naked woman displays a *Mona Lisa*-like smile with the same carnal and sensual quality as that of Leonardo's *Leda.*

A portrait of Joanna of Aragon painted by one of Leonardo's pupils exhibits similar characteristics.

Domenico Puligo's contemporary *Leda* in the Brussels Museum is based on a composition by Leonardo which was preserved among his drawings in the library of Windsor Castle.

A further *Leda* painting founded on Leonardo's composition was identified by Tancred Borenius as the work of Vincenz Sellaer, a Frans Floris pupil who was influenced by Leonardo and was the author of a *Caritas* which now hangs in the Prado at Madrid. Joos van Cleve the Younger also painted a *Leda* which found its way into the Johnson Gallery in Philadelphia.

As for the *Leda* painting in the Spiridon Collection at Rome, attributed to Leonardo da Vinci but the subject of considerable controversy, it may either be an original work by that master, *or* a work begun by him but carried out by another's hand, *or* a magnificent picture by an altogether different person.

It is said that when Queen Christina of Sweden had the picture in her possession she also had sufficient proof of its origin to dispel any doubts about its authenticity. Nevertheless, its status as a genuine creation of Leonardo's is as often disputed as affirmed, and the thematic relationship of all the *Leda* pictures dating from this period, which embraced only a few decades, renders authentication difficult. Even the most careful sifting of exhibits undertaken in connection with the Milan Art Exhibition of 1936 — to which all the great collectors of Italy contributed their treasures — failed to shed light on the authorship of the *Leda* painting.

What argues against Leonardo's authorship is the abnormally scrupulous execution of detail, in brushwork far more meticulous than that which he usually devoted to subordinate features. Composition and tonality, on the other hand, especially in the sensually luminous flesh portions, are of a perfection which no lesser man could have achieved. In the realm of painting, of course, Leonardo was matched by the other great exponents of his age. But what raised him above every other master was the universality with which his genius declared itself, as fundamental in the field of philosophy as it was in that of mathematics and mechanics, art and invention. Leonardo is unique in this complexity. No such absolute evaluation can be applied to his painting. There was no painter like him, but there were painters who rivaled him.

If it is impossible to achieve clarity in this case, how can we hope to clear up the countless cases in which no *Treatise on Painting* exists, no deeds of ownership or sketching material?

Careless of their status and reputation, the great masters happily stooped to imitate. Two versions of Leonardo da Vinci's portrait *La Belle Ferronière* exist. No final and conclusive elucidation of which is the original and which the copy has yet been undertaken with the care appropriate to a work of such standing, though the question has been raised in the courts (see page 352).

The Munich Pinakothek once owned a *Madonna and Child* by Perugino whose original is in Frankfurt. The Munich painting was not the result of plagiarism by one of that early master's contemporaries but an unquestionable forgery which did not even belong to the same century as the original work.

The Dresden *Madonna* was long regarded as a work by Holbein, and it was only after competition from the genuine Holbein *Madonna* at Darmstadt had resulted in litigation that it was identified as a late copy.

One example may serve to illustrate the nebulous nature not only of the boundaries between genuine and false but also of the manner in which those boundaries are delineated. When first discovered, Rembrandt's painting *St. Bartholomew* was held to be an original. The New York Metropolitan Museum later classified it as "attributed to Rembrandt" and eventually returned it to the estate of the man who had bequeathed it to the museum. In 1958 the genuine *St. Bartholomew* by Rembrandt's own hand turned up in a private collection.

An excellently reasoned opinion by the Rembrandt scholar Jakob Rosenberg distinguished between the original and what he conjectured to be a contemporary copy. (Since St. Bartholomew symbolically holds a knife in his hand, the picture was long thought to be a *Portrait of Rembrandt's Cook*.) Jakob Rosenberg regarded the original work as one of the most characteristic expressions of the master's transition from youthful portraits to his later group portraits.

Expert handling of X-ray equipment will clearly reveal the cruder attempts at deception. Radiographic scrutiny of a picture

13. *Julius Caesar*: 18th-century forgery, bought as authentic by the British Museum in 1818

14. *The Tiara of Saitaphernes*, work bought by the Louvre for 200,000 francs in gold, and pronounced by the experts to be a genuine masterpiece of the 3rd century B.C. It was found to be the work of the Odessa goldsmith, Israel Ruchomovski. Musée des Arts Decoratifs, Paris.

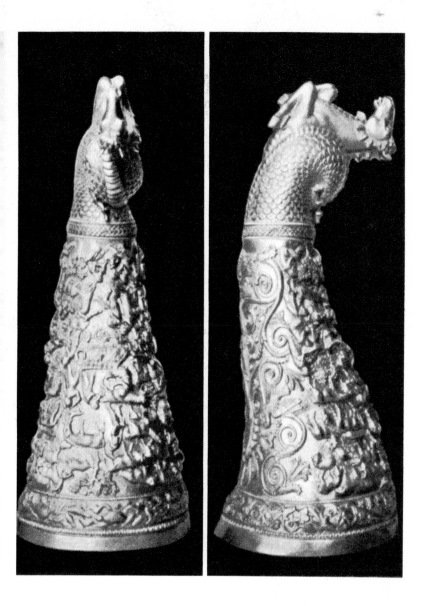

15. *The Golden Jug* (rhyton) by Ruchomovski. In this work the lack of coherence in the ornamentation is so obvious that there was no possible doubt as to the date and origin of the piece. Reitlinger Collection.

16. Four works by Alceo Dossena, which show his incredible capacity for copying any style, from Greek to Etruscan, from Sienese to that of Donatello.

long attributed to Adrian van Ostade disclosed that beneath the peasant couple visible in the "masterpiece" lay the painted image of a poultry yard which had served as the fake's foundation.

In London, the Courtauld Institute of Art exhibited a triptych which apparently belonged to the Siena school of the fifteenth century. X-ray examination disclosed that it was a skillful modern forgery.

Only in the case of pictures painted upon metal do X-rays cease to be effective. This is because metal absorbs them less easily and most of them are reflected. In such cases experts must fall back on spectroscopes and fluoroscopes or other combined optical and chemical methods of research.

One curiosity worthy of note is that a picture by Leonardo da Vinci was verified, although leading experts had earlier pronounced it to be the work of a pupil, because dactyloscopic examination revealed a fingerprint identifiable as da Vinci's. However, the ascription of authorship in such an abnormal case should not rest merely on the presence of a chance fingerprint, for it is quite likely that a master handled his pupils' work repeatedly, leaving papillary impressions which were easily retained by the sensitive surface. It is illogical to assume that a painting comes from the hand whose fingerprints it bears, although the discovery of identical fingerprints at several different points on a picture would seem to increase the likelihood of such an inference. Early masters very often followed up brushwork by smoothing the paint with their fingers, so the repeated appearance of dactyloscopic evidence may well be causally related to authorship.

In Rubens's workshop, which might better be described as a factory, there was a complete blurring of the lines of demarcation between "masterpiece" — work by the master — master-pupil collaboration and pupils' work. Burckhardt grades the pictures associated with Rubens's name into six categories:

(1) Pictures entirely by the artist's own hand.

(2) Works which the artist sketched for his assistants, supervised and later touched up.

(3) Works in which a formal division of labor took place.

(4) Workshop pictures, painted in the spirit of Rubens by his assistants, in which his personal share was small.

(5) School copies without the artist's personal participation.

(6) Copies executed by painters of other schools, sometimes to order.

Part-originals, minimal originals, masterly contemporary copies and contemporary imitations in impeccable style are intermingled in such countless gradations that they offer the modern forger many different chances.

Contemporary forgery, too, was made easier by the engravings and woodcuts of great masters. Weijermann asserts that "thousands of pictures were painted from Rubens' engravings." Jan Pieters won international fame for his mass-produced fakes of the Antwerp artists. Originally assistant to Sir Godfrey Kneller in London, he started by painting backgrounds, draperies and clothing for him. When he later became an art dealer and found that he could not buy up enough originals on his journeys to Holland to satisfy his London clientele, he remedied the deficiency by forgery. For less exacting customers he contented himself by painting over engravings which, when stiffened with board, he marketed as sketches by Rubens and other artists. He also faked Italian pictures, being careful to paint them on Italian canvas with indigenous pigments.

During the seventeenth and eighteenth centuries forgers seized upon all the important Dutch and Italian masters. The Dutch art dealer Gerrit Ulenborch, originally an untalented painter's assistant, gathered about him in his capacity as an antiquarian a circle of young and gifted artists whom he set to forging the works of whichever master best suited their particular style and technique. In the year 1671, Ulenborch sold the Elector of Brandenburg thirteen "Italian masterpieces." Unfortunately for him, the prince submitted the pictures to the painter Hendrick van Fromentiou, formerly one of Ulenborch's "suppliers," for certification. Litigation ensued. Fifty art experts appeared before the magistrate of Amsterdam, of which half pronounced the controversial pictures to be originals and the other half fakes — a comedy of errors to which we have more than once been treated in modern times.

The verifiability of material, technical execution and painting aids on the one hand, and, on the other, expert opinions based on comparison with undisputed originals set highly unwelcome limitations upon the activities of the picture forger.

If he uses an old painted ground for his picture he runs the risk of detection by X-rays, for the abnormal undulations of the outer surface will usually arouse the suspicions of a genuine connoisseur. An additional risk springs from the varying reactions to each other of different types of paint applied at different points in time. The new layer of paint superimposed on the old either "creeps," after its marriage to the original substratum, and inevitably creates a displacement of the interior structure, or, if it reposes on the underlying paint as though on priming, lacks stability. Any forger wishing to eliminate this factor of uncertainty is left with only two choices: he must either remove the original painting, whatever its value, with pumice stone, glass-paper, emery or very fine steel wool, or wash it off completely. If he decides on the former course, mechanical treatment of the base will leave recognizable traces, especially on the edges of the picture; if he chooses the latter, vestiges of oil paint will remain despite all his efforts. Should he decide to use a strong detergent, unmistakable traces will again be left, whether on wood or canvas. Moreover, the laws governing the capillary attraction of pigmental solutions will cause the formation of strata of differing heights which will not escape detection under a powerful magnifying glass.

One trick favored by the well-schooled forger is *marouflage*. This technique involves the gluing of a genuine old base of wood or canvas to the non-contemporary base of the forgery. The glues employed are abnormally resistant and stand up well even to the strongest solvents. The telltale crack which would reveal where the fake had been laminated to the old base is entirely masked by paint. All that the prospective buyer sees is the reverse of an entirely unobjectionable old canvas or wooden board completely in harmony with the "period" painting on its face.

Fundamentally, this is a reversal of the *rentoilage* process in which a genuine old painting is married to a new canvas. In this case, by contrast, a new fake is married to an old canvas.

Obvious repairs to old pictures, particularly those painted on canvas, are always worthy of attention. They are suspicious because genuine renovations, as in the case of invisible mending, are always carried out so that they do not disturb the eye. The forger, on the other hand, snips a little piece out of his opus, pulls the exposed threads apart and splices them with an alternative cloth which he carefully cements, primes and paints. He then draws the prospective purchaser's attention to this "flaw," pointing out that old works of art usually exhibit unimportant defects which in no way detract from their value.

Since *craquelure* lends a painting an appearance of age and authenticity, a forger achieves it with the aid of two different quick-drying varnishes. The slower-drying varnish which forms the first or underlayer causes the top layer of quicker-drying varnish to crack in many places. Dirt is then rubbed into the resulting fissures with a pad of cotton wool. If these specious tokens of antiquity are excavated with a pin and their contents submitted to expert examination, they will prove to include minute particles of material of very recent date. The hasty forger achieves his *craquelure* merely by scoring pictures with a pin — a simple method whose detection is equally simple.

A relatively undemanding form of forgery is the signing of a weak picture with the name or device of a celebrated master. In rare instances the nameless picture possesses qualities which lead even the connoisseur to regard it as a work by the master whose name the forger is abusing, and it can happen that not even an art historian will doubt the signature's authenticity. This makes it all the more essential to scrutinize a signature with the utmost care, especially as this presents no undue difficulty. Even famous masters occasionally produced pictures of doubtful merit, a fact which forgers have exploited to considerable advantage.

This narrow field offers the forger several different procedures.

(1) He can paint out an existing signature and replace it with a more valuable one.

(2) He can erase the original signature, cement and prime the damaged patch and insert a counterfeit signature.

(3) He can transform an existing signature into foliage, decoration or folds of drapery, according to its position. The new signature is then inserted in an entirely different part of the picture and fixed with a varnish of appropriate texture.

Each of these procedures harbors its own particular risk of detection, whether by superficial or X-ray examination. One possible means of evading discovery lies in first drawing the outline of signature or symbol on the picture's surface with a pin, then excavating the paint with a graving tool, and finally embedding the counterfeit in the depression thus obtained. In this case there is no perceptible irregularity in surface texture. An organic part of the picture, the signature lies in its own bed of paint without becoming fused with the surrounding mass. Even the most conscientious of examiners will be misled, provided the forger has been clever enough to dissolve the varnish over a sufficiently large area and replace it with one which is identical to that originally employed. This technique anchors the counterfeit signature so firmly to the body of the paint that it will withstand moderate cleaning.

Forgers are often prone to place signatures or symbols in positions which conflict with an artist's normal style. F. W. Rohrich, for instance, probably the most prolific nineteenth-century forger of Cranachs, adorned many of his thirty versions of *Patrician and Her Son* by placing the master's signature on the hat-brim of the lady depicted. No one has yet explained why Rohrich not only selected this curious position for his own imitations but prescribed it for those of his pupils.

In passing, it may be mentioned that falsifications of signatures also exist. A Cuylenborch, for example, has been turned into a far more valuable Poelenborgh. Works by the little-known Munich painter Eibl have been "modified" into pictures by Leibl in the hope of promoting them from the fifteen-dollar class to the $15,000. (In this instance the forger's efforts were defeated by the inadequacy of Eibl's work.)

In order to achieve an aura of antiquity, countless other little tricks are used, such as artificially induced paint blisters, artificial mildew and the infliction of bacteriological damage on unimportant parts of a painting.

The reverse side of an old fake often bears a multitude of counterfeit stamps of authentication, certificates, museum seals or seals of leading collections, on the principle that one forgery lends support to another.

It is not difficult for the forger to obtain information about the composition of old paints and inks used for writing and stamping. For imitation early medieval inks, vegetable sap can serve as the vehicle and soot as the coloring agent. Iron gallotannate inks did not come into use until the close of the Middle Ages.

If the forger is obliged to remove an old inscription chemically or mechanically before inserting his own, this preliminary treatment will be very easily detectable. If, on the other hand, he is dealing with a picture whose reverse side is bare of inscriptions, his work may withstand the most exhaustive scrutiny, always assuming that he has executed it in contemporary style and with contemporary writing materials, i.e. quill and ink.

The examination of a picture should be entrusted only to an experienced specialist, since the solubility of paints when treated with alcohol, turpentine and other agents varies so widely that irremediable harm may sometimes be done.

Everything that applies, from the technical and stylistic aspect, to forgeries of works from earlier periods is logically applicable to fakes of later date. The closer pictorial works are to our own period the greater attention should be paid to detail, for modern subjects naturally present the forger with smaller material and technical difficulties. The trial of strength between forger and expert is now conducted more in the artistic, stylistic and technical sphere.

Fundamentally, therefore, the criterion applied to forgeries of modern pictorial works is one of artistic merit. Paints, materials and implements such as those used by Spitzweg, Corot, Defregger, Leibl, Manet, Uhde, Monet, Liebermann or artists still closer to our time are equally available to the forger, who can either buy them commercially or procure them with relatively little trouble. So it is the art historian who plays a leading role where works of more recent times are concerned — not that this rules out the careful use of chemico-physical methods in doubtful cases. No secret should be made of the fact that experts are continually succumbing to error, and the collector should be warned by the cases, reported in detail elsewhere in this book, where expert opinion has gone very seriously astray. Moreover, the fact that even scientific research in this field can lead to sharp differences of opinion helps to illustrate the extraordinary difficulty of separating wheat from chaff.

Marcantonio Raimondi (*circa* 1480-1534), whose amazing versatility as a draftsman enabled him to work in the spirit of Raphael and, no less proficiently, to forge Dürer's woodcut series, *Life of the Virgin,* has found fellow practitioners in our own day who manage to imitate the creations of others with alarmingly deceptive accuracy.

In the province of modern and very recent painting special regard must be paid to the origins of a picture, especially as the history of its ownership over the last fifty years or so can usually be ascertained with less difficulty and more prospect of continuity than in the case of a work of art with a career centuries old.

Where the forgery of a living artist's work is concerned, consultation of the painter himself provides an almost infallible method of control. But, whether affirmative or negative, his answer should, astonishingly enough, be treated with a certain amount of reserve. Cases have been known in which painters who had modified their style fundamentally over the years were so reluctant to acknowledge many of their earlier works that they flatly disowned pictures painted by them in their youth. Other artists, of the more fluent and prolific type, often find it impossible to affirm or deny their authorship with absolute certainty, principally in the case of sketches but also in that of smaller and less important works.

Mention must here be made of a species of forgery which springs from kindness or good nature. A large number of artists of earlier times would occasionally sign their pupils' works.

It is known that, to fit them for a readier and more profitable market, Corot put his own signature to many works by needy and unsuccessful colleagues who painted or drew in his style.

Forgeries of the moderns can sometimes be recognized by radiographic examination of the substrata with reference to brushwork. Even if the imitator tries to employ the same technique, his inability to maintain consistently a style of brushwork alien both to hand and instinct will soon become apparent. Additional means of identification are supplied by the chemical and physical examination of paint, since it is known what paints were favored by many modern artists. A further distinguishing feature worthy of note is the change in manufacturing processes undergone by certain specific paints in the course of chemical and technical development. The knowledge that a certain painter used a certain paint of a certain make at a certain time is thus of only relative importance to the forger, for the same factory now supplies under the same name paints considerably different in chemical composition from those of ten or thirty years ago. And, since paint manufacturers usually keep their processes a closely guarded secret, it is almost out of the question for a forger to transform the spectral values of today's paint into those of years ago. The same applies to siccatives, varnishes and, above all, to priming technique. Segantini painted his Alpine landscapes on a special red primer which is still detectable even in completed pictures and scarcely permits of imitation by the forger.

It is common to speak of *the* forger, but it would frequently be more proper — at least in the case of pictorial fakes — to say *forgers*.

The ability to execute every type of motif and theme perfectly is a heaven-sent gift. Even among the greatest creative painters there were few who displayed consistent mastery of every aspect of their art, from figure work to background and from ornamentation to landscape. One artist will always make the hands his favorite mode of expression, another the eyes or folds of drapery.

In the plastic arts, too, the tasks of carving, enchasing and gilding were frequently shared between three men.

Similarly, the high-class fake often proves under closer examination to be a co-operative venture. If the thematic composition of a picture exceeds the forger's technical or stylistic competence, he will get a specialist to rough it out for him.

In 1928, several very talented painters were collaborating in a Viennese studio which restored old works with a high degree of perfection. The studio also undertook the renovation of fragments, and in the course of time there left the premises "old masterpieces" of which nothing was genuine save their foundation.

The work of the Viennese studio was always characterized by the consistently high quality of its every feature. Figure work, decoration and thematic treatment combined to produce pictures which were homogeneous whatever their motif, whether interior or landscape. Each one had been painted by a specialist.

One of the forger's happy hunting grounds is the field of classical drawing, especially Italian. Unfinished sketches of figures and roughly outlined ideas for larger compositions, both plastic and pictorial, occupy a leading place among the interests of collectors and arouse equal enthusiasm — almost of necessity — among forgers.

The forgery of medieval drawings is to some extent aided by the fact that an expert's requirements with regard to stylistic purity are far more easily satisfied in this field than in that of painting. Countless examples of such early sketches exist. Also very profitable and not unduly hard to simulate are two-dimensional working sketches of the theme, figure work and construction of an original sculpture, done on suitably aged paper in a homemade chalk identical to the one originally used. The same applies to the falsification of genuine old sketches. Unfinished drawings are amplified and unsigned sheets adorned with a cipher, initials or signature which will bring them into a substantially higher price range.

Where the paper and crayon used are in period, it is remarkably difficult to spot a forgery. In such cases a physical examination of materials will only evince that everything is, in the empirical sense, genuine — a finding which is in conflict with the true facts.

Here, therefore, the last word must rest with the art critic. Where crude imitations, amplifications and signatures are concerned, of course, his contribution to the establishment of the truth is comparatively easy; but the more perfect the work, the harder it is for stylistic criticism to demonstrate that forgery has occurred.

Paintings and sculptures provide the exact scientist and the art historian with countless "tangible" points of reference. Drawings, on the other hand, exhibit a minimum of identifying characteristics, and the more reliable of these can only be ascertained by the investigation of drawing materials and paper under laboratory conditions.

The pencils of early painters actually contained lead alloyed with a base of tin. Our own pencils, by contrast, are entirely devoid of lead, being made of dense, compressed graphite.

Cennini refers to the composition of the early pencil in his treatise on painting. Its extremely soft alloy consisted of one part beaten tin and two parts lead. Since the first plumbago mines (at Barrowdale in England) did not come into operation until the mid-sixteenth century and their products were not immediately marketed in Europe, drawings which reveal the presence of graphite can scarcely have originated before 1560-1570.

The forger may try to exclude the risk that graphite will be discovered by melting down lead and tin in accordance with the old formula. However, the task of finding either metal in a condition corresponding to the impure and crudely processed lead and tin of the Middle Ages will probably prove beyond him. Thanks to rapid developments in smelting technique, metals have been increasing in purity ever since the middle of the last century. It can thus be established what type of lead and tin are present in the forger's alloy.

The fineness of a pencil point, too, can provide a valuable source of information, for really sharp points and fourteen grades of hardness did not come in until the introduction of the new material.

The earliest drawing papers were manufactured in northern Italy during the thirteenth century. From Lombardy they spread to the southern regions of Germany, and the end of the fourteenth century saw the establishment of the first paper mills at Ravensburg and Nuremberg. All these papers bore a watermark designed to give information about their origin or quality.

For drawings of later times, the recent past and the present, chemical and physical examination must always be amplified in doubtful cases by the stylistic verification of an art historian. Prints by Toulouse-Lautrec, sketches by Rodin, pencil drawings by Menzel and many other artists who were working just before or after the turn of the century bring substantial prices only exceeded by the sums paid for pictures by Paul Klee and other abstract painters of equal status. Paul Klee's works can be identified by referring to the excellent records of the Klee Foundation in the Bern Museum and to Klee's own oeuvre catalogue — which is more than can be said for the works of most other modern artists.

It seems incredible but is nonetheless true that countless fake Picasso drawings, not to mention those attributed to many other living artists, happily go the rounds of the international art market today. Moreover, the former's inaccessibility makes personal identification by him exceedingly difficult to secure.

Because the circle of water-color enthusiasts is a relatively small one and the prices paid for this type of work are low compared with those fetched by oil paintings and sculptures, the water color plays a subordinate role in the forger's craft.

Water-color painting of high quality demands an imitator of equal finesse. This is why signature forgeries are far more common than complete fakes in the case of certain highly valued water colorists. When the Austrian painter Rudolf von Alt temporarily came into vogue, for instance, skilled forgers got hold of every available water color which was in any way reminiscent of his style and added his signature, an easy matter in view of its simplicity. The water colorist's technique in itself makes the detection of a forgery by chemical or physical means incomparably harder than in the case of oil paints, primarily because the manufacture of water colors has been subject to far fewer modifications than that of the more complex oil and tempera paints, and, secondly, because a signature added in water color became almost imperceptibly wedded to the underlying paints, since these are dissolved, at least superficially, by the water in the forger's brush.

It goes without saying that every picture has its frame. Picture and frame are so closely related, in fact, that it seems idle to inquire why two such entirely different things have come to represent such a unity in our minds.

The history of the picture frame has always come in a poor second to the investigation of specifically artistic activity, but if we trace the reasons for this amalgamation of ideas, for so long instinctively felt to be an organic whole, we arrive at some noteworthy conclusions.

The framing of pictures may possibly be attributed to two motives: (1) The desire to "enclose" a picture just as our view of the outside world is enclosed by a window, and (2) The intention that a frame should provide suitable protection for the vulnerable edges of a picture.

Early frames unmistakably accord with the wish to protect a picture. Since layers of priming were most liable to crack at the edges of a picture, that was where they had to be protected from harm. Beveled moulding similar to that which shielded windows and doors from rain and seepage introduced an architectonic element into the originally utilitarian nature of the frame, and what was once a practical feature gradually evolved into a structure of artistic design.

For various obscure reasons, far fewer genuine old frames have survived than genuine old pictures. "Period" frames are thus at a premium.

The frame maker of the fifteenth and sixteenth centuries worked rather like a sculptor. Consciously or unconsciously, he was still guided by the desire to protect a picture, and he used mixtures laced with ox hair and waterproof glues which rendered wood and mount more resistant to decay.

The forging of old frames presents almost the same problems as the forging of sculptures. A forger will try to procure old material, but the "uniform irregularity" of the ornamentation on the often extremely large face- and profile-sections of wood is almost impossible to imitate. Fake frames do not stand up to careful scrutiny, especially when stucco relief and gilding is involved. They betray the forger all the more easily because he is working without any intimate reference to a particular painting. The early frame makers and even the master frame makers of the closing years of the nineteenth century maintained a very close liaison with painters themselves. The influence of the painter on the frame maker produced a harmony of technical and artistic design which later lost ground with increasing rapidity until its sun finally set with the advent of the modern frame factory.

Picture frames frequently display wood carving reminiscent of ecclesiastical interiors, and the unity of painting, ornamentation and frame is particularly well illustrated by painted polyptychs regarded as frames in the broader sense.

The aim of the picture-frame forger is to enhance the value of a more or less genuine painting, sometimes dignifying a mediocre picture with the aid of an architectural frame in early ecclesiastical style. Similarly, a genuine but unmounted altarpiece will gain in appearance from a "period" frame. In such cases the weaker member, the spurious frame, is designed to bolster up the stronger, the genuine picture.

It is a time-honored practice to shed luster on forged pictures by means of genuine frames. Here the frame specialist is confronted by the task of marrying two objects — frame and picture — which are not normally a perfect fit. He may either have to cut down an overlarge frame or enlarge one which is too small. When examining old frames, therefore, it is always advisable to pay particular attention to joints in the wood.

Less exacting is the imitation of monochrome, usually black-toned, frames of smoothed and polished natural wood. Holland and England, in particular, were the early home of the exaggeratedly simple frame made of nut wood which consciously acknowledged the superiority of the painting itself. Since nut wood required priming only for the scanty gilding which was customary, the forger can avoid priming by using some form of filler, though only if it corresponds to the purported date of origin.

These frames, mainly of plain design, spare the forger much complicated gilding work. He need only give them faint traces of gilding which will seem, at least under superficial examination, to bear witness to the ravages wrought by the passage of centuries.

4

❧❧❧❧❧❧❧❧❧

Sculptures

ORGERS take a far smaller interest in sculpted works. The reasons for this are twofold: first, the considerably greater difficulty of imitation, and, second, the substantially smaller market. The circle of amateurs of good sculpture is restricted when compared with the vast multitude of lovers and collectors of pictures and antiques. Few in number though they are, moreover, collectors of sculpture are normally an exacting and well-informed race of men.

Whereas a demand exists for pictures and other works of art of almost every era, the demand for three-dimensional works is centered principally on earlier specimens. Sculptures from every stage of the Gothic, Renaissance and baroque periods are particularly favored. The considerable but often artificially engendered and fostered interest in sculptures by modern artists, especially the abstractionists, is of only minor significance by comparison.

Works of the highest rank are extraordinarily rare, and Romanesque originals in good condition scarcely ever reach the market.

It is the counterfeiting of sculpted works of the most sought-after periods which presents the forger with most problems. Materials alone are hard to obtain in the requisite quantity and bulk. Priming, too, poses considerably greater problems in the three- than in the two-dimensional field.

While a work in stone or metal may represent a less exacting task for the forger than a wood carving, a convincing imitation, either of weathering, in the former case, or patina or lacquer, in the latter, is extremely hard to achieve.

The fundamentals of sculptural forgery are best exemplified in the works of the Gothic epoch.

Hubert Wilm's book *The Gothic Wooden Figure* (Stuttgart, 1942) gives an excellent illustration of the skill and technique of the Gothic artists, whose originals are characterized by virile, monumental strength of design coupled with gorgeous ornamentation.

It is no exaggeration to call the enchasing of these works of art inimitable. Their glassy-smooth, ivory-colored chalk ground was painted in glowing azure, fiery vermilion, clear green, tender rose, and warm brown, and they were bathed in the luster of gossamer-fine gold leaf, delicately applied.

The unique quality of Gothic sculpture rests on an inner harmony between plastic modeling and painting. Many unpainted carvings from these centuries may strike us as disappointing, but this is because they were originally designed to be seen in glowing color. In the sober tones of wood alone they seem almost unconvincing. It is quite otherwise with works, such as choir-stalls and church cupboards, which the early masters carved without any intention of adding a brilliant finish. The carvings of Tilman Riemenschneider

are devoid of gilding and painted ornamentation: they have no need
of it, such was the artist's skill in lending splendid animation to
wood alone.

Sculpture very early became a medium in its own right, yet a
close connection with painting is discernible not only in important
examples of sculpture proper but also in three-dimensional translations of two-dimensional works. The altar in the Church of St.
Lilian at Heilbronn incorporates a carved figure of the Virgin copied
in every detail from a section of Martin Schongauer's *Crucifixion*.
There are two sculptures based on the masterly *St. Sebastian* engraving which bears the signature "E.S.," one dating from about
1480 and one from about 1490. In 1520 Stephan Rottaler modeled
a carved relief for the right-hand wing of the high altar at Reisbach
on Albrecht Dürer's woodcut *Michael Wrestling with the Dragon*.
Similar translations of two- into three-dimensional works are far
from rare.

Gothic carving is, fundamentally, a transitional stage between the
miniature technique of the goldsmith and Romanesque sculpture, with its increasing tendency toward larger forms. If ivory and
precious metals were the favored materials of artists between the
tenth and twelfth centuries, the thirteenth and fourteenth saw stone
and, following on its heels, terra cotta, alabaster, and finally
(though it had been used since early times) wood enter and dominate the scene. While this evolution was going on the plastic arts
gradually assumed full three-dimensional form, and Romanesque
abstraction adopted a more substantial shape.

In respect to motif and theme, a wide panorama of choice con-
fronts the forger who wants to produce stylistically plausible work.
However, the actual transposition of an engraving or painting into
sculptural terms presupposes suitable material and adequate technical ability.

Anyone proposing to counterfeit a Gothic wooden figure of

high quality must be a master in two respects, for the carving demands supreme craftsmanship and so does the "enchasing" of a sculpture with paint and gilding.

With sculpture as with painting, the forger's task becomes easier when he is dealing with works of art of more recent date. Although the problems raised by the imitation of baroque figures are hard of solution where materials, composition and decoration are concerned, they are markedly easier to overcome than those posed by pre-Gothic works and those of the fourteenth and fifteenth centuries.

If various types of brush and the ball of the hand occupy a major place in the equipment of the forger of great early painters, tools are of even greater importance in the plastic medium, if only because of their very multiplicity. The masterly carvings of the Romanesque and Gothic periods were often produced with axes of strange and no longer familiar design which forgers were obliged to grind themselves or get made for them, even in the eighteenth and nineteenth centuries. The flat chisels and bent double-edged chisels forged at a sharp angle were all unique in shape. The majority of these implements were used by sculptors as early as the Gothic period, as can be seen in *Wood Carver in His Workshop,* a choir-stall relief from Pöhlde. Specific tools leave specific marks, and any imitator wishing to produce identical results must work with identical equipment.

We have already mentioned the difficulty of obtaining suitable wood in our discussion of panel paintings. The far more voluminous proportions peculiar to sculpture render the problem of material almost insoluble — and it was upon material that the old masters bestowed their chief attention. On March 12, 1517, Anton Tucher entered in his household accounts an item of six pounds paid to the bailiff Linhart Pemer for a lime tree and its transportation from the Sebalder Wald to the workshop of Veit Stoss (Wilm).

By July 17, 1518, Veit Stoss's *Annunciation,* a carving in lime wood, was already installed in the choir of the Lorenzkirche at Nuremberg. It would seem from this that Veit Stoss had used fairly fresh wood, but it is more likely that the *Annunciation* was carved out of old workshop stock and that the log from the Sebalder Wald had been stored for drying. Contemporary artists ordinarily used nothing but old logs which had entirely dried out, in order to minimize the cracks and consequent distortions which inevitably resulted from warping.

Numerous woodcuts and copperplate engravings supply us with information about the technique of Gothic and later sculptors. A woodcut by Hans Sebald Beham from the year 1531 portrays, apart from an illuminator and an organist, a wood carver at his bench. This bench was fitted with an adjustable end so that it could hold logs of varying length, while the logs themselves could be revolved on their axis, allowing the sculptor to bring the portion to be carved into whichever position was most convenient.

Before work commenced, holes were bored at either end of the log to enable it to be clamped to the bench by means of two pointed pegs.

On completing his work, the wood carver plugged the borehole at the head of his figure with a well-fitting peg. When this eventually fell out, it revealed the cavity where it had once reposed. The hole at the other end was frequently dispensed with. After a figure had been removed from the bench it was usually subjected to further carving at the base, so that the place where the borehole had once been was taken away with the offcuts.

Finally, any heart was removed from the back of the carving, which was usually flat, to prevent subsequent splitting. Where a work had been carved from the full circumference of a tree trunk it was hollowed out from the base for the same reason. Small works carved out of fully rounded material required only the outer wood of a trunk. Since this did not contain any heart, hollowing was unnecessary.

Wood carvers used to mask their excavation of the flat back by means of a carefully fitted board which they attached to the figure with wooden pegs. Canvas was then glued over the joints and concealed by the final enchasing, so that the finished piece looked as if it had been carved from a single trunk.

Small rolled strips of parchment bearing a handwritten note of the date of origin and the wood carver's name have often been found in the peg-holes. Many figures display initials and others inspection marks or guild insignia branded or stamped into the wood. This was probably a protective measure aimed against contemporary forgers or wood carvers who did not belong to the guild in question.

Guilds and societies formally prescribed the methods to be used by their members when handling materials. The basic rule was to work from a complete block, whether of wood or stone. The only portion of a figure which might be added as a separate component was a prominent feature such as a hand, bishop's crook, crown or halo. The rules of the guild permitted the jointing of two or more blocks only if a composition was of abnormal size. Works in stone were cemented together and anchored with iron pegs which increased their stability and strengthened unsupported details.

Technical errors were committed even by the leading artists of early, medieval and later periods. On the other hand, these were sometimes occasioned by shortage of materials. Few could bring themselves to abandon an almost completed work and start again from scratch merely because of some small defect. In such cases the normal practice was to mend and make do. If small pieces have been cemented into a wood carving or stone sculpture, therefore, it does not necessarily mean that they are later additions: they may very often be corrections made by the original artist.

Sculptures in stone and metal were much less often forged than wood carvings.

Just as the materials used by stonemasons ranged from granite to softer types of stone less resistant to the elements, so their tools varied from the coarse, flat chisel to the finer and more delicate chisels suitable for finishing-work. The expert can date a work with a fair degree of accuracy from the technical methods employed, though not without reference to stylistic considerations as well. However, to attribute a work to a particular stonemason is a much more problematical question, except in the case of forgeries of more recent date which are either obvious copies or easily recognizable imitations in the classical style.

It is very much harder to recognize later imitations or reproductions of Greek and Roman stone sculptures. In this connection we must again remember that in earlier days no stigma and even less penalty attached to the author of a masterly copy, an imitation based on a great original, or even a downright fake.

Michelangelo himself was a child of his age in this respect. As a youth he had found favor with the stonemason Bertoldo, whom Lorenzo de' Medici commissioned to produce sculptures for his private park. Determinedly, Michelangelo took up the tools himself. His first work of any importance was a copy of an early faun's mask with a damaged set of teeth. The latter detail offended his aesthetic sense, so he omitted it. On examining the finished sculpture, Lorenzo de' Medici drew the young stonemason's attention to the discrepancy between the original faun's mask and the copy with its perfect set of teeth. After comparing his imitation with the original, Michelangelo at once took his finest shaping-chisel and removed a tooth from its upper jaw so deftly that it seemed to have fallen out, root and all, from old age. Even in his youthful years, Michelangelo displayed an amazingly well developed hand, eye, and brain.

Recognizing his superior ability, Lorenzo de' Medici commissioned the artist-craftsman to ornament his park and mansion with sculptures in stone. Michelangelo fulfilled his patron's wishes, but also found time to produce free-lance sculptures like the *Sleeping Cupid*. The prince did not find this reclining figure decorative enough for his park, though he entertained no doubts about its beauty. He suggested that Michelangelo should put his *Cupid,* which was executed in the classical style, to speculative use by "so treating it that it could be sold in Rome as an antique" for a much higher price than any copy could command.

Michelangelo concurred, and the figure's date of origin was put back by fifteen hundred years. By today's standards this was sheer fraud, especially as both patron and artist were motivated by hope of financial gain. To contemporary eyes, fraud did not enter the question. Admiration was accorded to ability per se.

Having skillfully aged the *Sleeping Cupid* by burying it in sour earth, Lorenzo de' Medici sent it to the art dealer Baldassare de Milanese in Rome. The latter sold the "archaic" work of art for two hundred gold ducats, an extremely large sum for those days, to Cardinal Riario of San Giorgio. He kept 85 per cent of the proceeds for himself, however, and passed on a fee of only thirty ducats to Michelangelo.

When the art-loving cardinal learned through devious channels that his *Sleeping Cupid,* far from having slept for fifteen hundred years, had been laid to rest in Florence only a short while before, he sent a confidant to institute inquiries there. There can be little doubt that Lorenzo de' Medici got wind of this, for he hastily dissociated himself from the venture. The cardinal's envoy eventually found his way via Ghirlandajo's workshop to the stonemasons working in Lorenzo's park. When he told Michelangelo that Riario had paid two hundred gold ducats for the sculpture, the young sculptor acknowledged it as his own. Pointing out that the only chance of retrieving the two hundred ducats from Baldassare lay in Michelangelo's giving evidence, the Roman nobleman persuaded the artist to accompany him to Rome.

When Michelangelo appeared at Baldassare's establishment to demand a more equitable share of the two hundred ducats, the art dealer simply pointed to the *Sleeping Cupid,* which he had been forced to take back in return for the full amount of the purchase price.

Michelangelo did, in fact, retain the thirty ducats which had been paid him for his part in this peculiar transaction. An attempt to secure an audience with Riario failed. The cardinal could not guess that the young man who had vainly sought access to his house would one day be numbered among the greatest names in the history of art.

Michelangelo's *Sleeping Cupid* vanished into the darkness of a century dominated by the interplay of dark powers and forces. The *Sleeping Cupid* on show today in Turin is regarded as a sixteenth- or early-seventeenth-century forgery.

The historian Paolo Giovio, a contemporary of Michelangelo, records that the *Sleeping Cupid* was once more buried, this time in Rome, so that it could be dug up "accidentally." Baldassare de Milanese had seen to it that the sculpture was provided with the few slight traces of damage characteristic of almost all genuine old finds. Paolo Giovio adds in a postscript to his account that "Michelangelo's 'aged' *Sleeping Cupid* brought him great fame."

In 1560 there appeared another *Sleeping Cupid* which may well have been the original upon which Michelangelo based his imitation. However, it is impossible to establish any connection between the two, and no one can say for certain whether the greatest of all sculptors had ever encountered an archaic *Sleeping Cupid* before he produced his own and aged it.

Partly to satisfy their vanity and partly for financial gain, sculptors of every class produced large numbers of classical copies and works in archaic style. The dignitaries of the Renaissance, both secular and ecclesiastical, cherished a great liking for classical sculpture. Because damaged examples of archaic art offended their aesthetic sensibilities, they had them renovated. Even a missing ear lobe had to be replaced. Everything had to be perfect and, in the material sense, beautiful. It never entered their heads that to repair may mean to destroy and that restoration work on a large scale is to be avoided from the stylistic aspect because it militates against the essential unity of a creative work. When there were no more defective old sculptures left to renovate, forgers set about their piratical work.

The more fastidious collectors not only avoided imitations but realized that restoration could impair stylistic unity. In 1567 Count Hans Fugger wrote to David Ott: "You report, by the by, that he has patched up an old head . . . beware, for such patchwork is nought but old and new mingled together."

It had become the habit to collect as many fragments as possible and reconstitute them as seemingly intact works. As early as 1525 the Roman master builder and sculptor Lorenzetto di Lodovico was running a large workshop for the repair of damaged sculptures.

In the course of time many restorers combined their ill-paid craft with the more profitable activities of the forger. Art historians like Vasari, Baglione and Passeri were already decrying the amalgamation into a single person of artist, restorer, dealer and forger — "from the most eminent down to the hawker of bric-à-brac," as Burckhardt put it.

The exact sciences have considerably less chance of determining the age of a stone sculpture than that of a work in wood or metal.

It is true that within certain limits complicated methods of research can distinguish between a genuinely old and an artificially aged surface, but the far more comprehensive tests applicable to the paint, varnish and gilding of pictorial works must here be dispensed with almost entirely. A stone sculpture which has been left a prey to every quirk of wind and weather for one or two hundred years is so thoroughly and genuinely aged that the verdict of genuine or false must devolve upon the art historian alone — regardless of the possibility of error.

In October, 1957, during the construction of the coast road from Rome to Naples, some four hundred marble fragments were unearthed in the vicinity of a village called Sperlonga. Photographed individually and built up into a montage, they apparently formed a Laocoön group. This find kindled the flames of a controversy among art experts over the authenticity of the Vatican's Laocoön group, which had never hitherto been disputed. If the four hundred fragments were reconstructed they would produce a monumental work almost twice as large as that in the Vatican.

Who was competent to decide which was the original and which the copy? It might even be that the fragmentary Laocoön was merely a replica on another scale and that both were original works by the same artist.

After the excitement over the new find had died down, Professor Jacopi launched an attempt to reconstruct it from the separate fragments. The result entirely refuted the Laocoön theory and encouraged a belief that the group portrayed Odysseus standing at the prow of his ship surrounded by companions. It was further postulated that the scene represented Odysseus's voyage between Scylla and Charybdis.

In the course of detailed research, however, a fragment of the socle came to light. It bore the name of the Rhodian sculptor Agesander, who had collaborated with his sons Polydorus and

Athenodorus in producing the Laocoön monument in the Vatican.

In October, 1898, one of the Berlin Museum's proudest exhibits was an "original sculpture of an excellently preserved female marble head from the later stages of archaic art." Kekulé von Stradonitz devoted his expert attention to this new acquisition and, after thorough study, pronounced it to be a "modern Italian imitation of the eighteenth century." On January 18, 1899, the administrative council of the Royal Museums acknowledged at Berlin that "the marble head acquired as a Greek original is a modern work."

There are strong indications that the studio which had, via sundry middlemen, supplied the museum with its "marble head from the later stages of archaic art" also produced the four forged marble heads described by Furtwängler, of which the most celebrated, the *Hera of Girgenti,* found its way into the British Museum. A fifth and very similar sculpture was offered for sale in Paris in 1888, while a sixth for a long time adorned the Ny-Carlsberg Gallery in Copenhagen. The heroic sculpture *Athlete from the Time of Phidias and Polyclitus* from the same collection also proved, on closer examination, to be a modern forgery.

On June 1, 1958, shortly before his death, the distinguished art historian Professor Matteo Marangoni of Pisa University discovered a six-foot figure of Venus in a side-passage in the gallery of the Palazzo Pitti in Florence. After careful study he announced his conviction that it was a work by Michelangelo.

Other eminent connoisseurs beside Marangoni also confirmed Michelangelo's authorship. Dr. Procacci, a director of the Palazzo Pitti, based his assertion that the Venus was a work "fully in keeping with Michelangelo's working methods" on an analysis of the technique employed. It had not been modeled, he said, but hewn from the stone, and the marks left by the notched *gravina* chisel were the same as those on other, uncontested works by Michelangelo. Professor Mario Salmi, vice-president of Italy's highest Arts Council and former director of the Institute of Art History in Rome, agreed that the statue had been begun by Michelangelo but thought it had been completed by one of his pupils. And Professor Ulrich Middeldorf, director of the German Institute of Art History in Florence, regards the Venus as a work either by Pierino da Vinci, grandson of the great Leonardo, or by Tribolo, dating from the period between 1500 and 1550. This case illustrates the extreme, if inevitable, uncertainty which prevails in regard to authorship and date of origin in the field of stone sculpture.

Undisputed originals demonstrate the fact that archaic Greek sculptures were hewn equally from all sides, whereas Hellenistic sculptures were produced in two stages, front and rear, after which the intermediate ridges were chiseled away so that they conformed to the modeling of the rest of the surface. The same technique, which approximates to that employed in the carving of reliefs, is exhibited by the work of medieval stonemasons.

In the course of decades and centuries, stone sculptures in the Greek and Roman style as well as works of the Gothic, Renaissance and baroque periods have been repeatedly copied and imitated. Sculptures of alabaster and marble, the latter preferably veined and multicolored, ranging from first-rate and valuable imitations to cheap fakes, usually of Italian origin, have saturated the world's antique markets, which are also kept abundantly supplied with forged works in clay.

In the rare cases where stone sculptures were painted, pigments, as well as any gilding or silvering, were applied on a very thin chalk ground in conjunction with oil. Stonemasons' work being often exposed to the elements, it was decorated principally with oil-based materials which made the stone more weather-proof.

The forger will attempt to provide his stone sculpture with

tokens of authenticity. By burying it in acid-steeped earth he can go a long way toward achieving an appearance of genuine age. Should the fruits of his labor be discovered — with a little encouragement on his part — during the course of excavations, few doubts will be raised as to their value. People have not changed much since Baldassare's day.

Even leading national collections have succumbed to tricks of this kind. (And not only with sculpture — research conducted by the laboratories of the British Museum under the direction of R. P. Links indicated that an "early Roman mural," *The Flute-Player,* which was among the prized possessions of the Museum, was a modern fake.) Until the turn of the century, the National Museum at Naples fondly displayed a *Fountain Relief from Pompeii* which was regarded as a remarkably beautiful and representative work. A German art historian established that the figure work was beyond a shadow of doubt based on a drawing by Albrecht Dürer. With a heavy heart the museum authorities banished their Pompeian treasure: it had originated in a Roman forger's workshop.

A head of *Julius Caesar* acquired by the British Museum in 1818 had, after scientific examination, to be declared a carefully aged eighteenth-century fake.

Evidence of forced aging on the surface of marble sculptures can be identified by microscopic examination. The calcium carbonate crystals in marble are of a rhomboid shape characterized by pointed corners and sharp edges which become blunted by contact both with humus acids and air. The surface of a genuine old marble sculpture displays crystals which are not only blunted but sometimes entirely dissolved. If the forger leaves his work buried for too short a time these characteristics will not develop. If he attacks the surface with quick-working acids, on the other hand, this fact will be chemically detectable. Nevertheless, the value of a test may well be nullified by a true master of his trade if he has undertaken the aging of a work with sufficient care and patience and knows enough about the properties of calcium carbonate.

Fundamentally, the same principle applies to sculptures in alabaster, whose crystalline structure is that of calcium sulphate.

The element of uncertainty governing wax sculptures is best illustrated by the case of Wilhelm von Bode's bust of *Flora,* which has never been satisfactorily resolved. The distinguished expert Adolph Donath, art critic of the *Berliner Tageblatt* and author of some major works on art criticism, maintained that the sculpture was genuine, and the results of chemical analysis tended to support this view. Gustav Pauli, on the other hand, Alfred Lichtwark's successor at Hamburg's Kunsthalle, pronounced the *Flora* to be a fake. In 1927 Edmund Hildebrandt, a man of great scholarship, extolled it as "an incontestable work by Leonardo da Vinci." Weighted against this was an assertion by the English sculptor Lucas that his father fashioned the bust and that he collaborated with him in painting it and producing the original clay model.

Art critics wrote imposing treatises justifying their championship or refutation of the sculpture's authenticity. Dr. E. Raehlmann subjected the work to microchemical analysis. Minute fragments of paint were removed from an unimportant spot and placed in four test tubes containing water, alcohol, ether and a weak solution of hydrochloric acid respectively. Since enough authentic pigment has survived from the whole range of medieval art to enable us to know how contemporary substances react under the above-mentioned forms of analysis, their age, at least, can be determined almost to within a decade. In the majority of the paints Raehlmann found a medium, translucent under the microscope, which never recurred after the seventeenth century. A series of other factors reduced the area of potential doubt. For instance, traces of mycelium or mushroom spawn were present, a special characteristic of the orseille paint which was in common use between the fourteenth and six-teenth centuries. This would encourage one to assume that the bust of *Flora* could not have originated later than the mid-seven-teenth century. But, even if these scientific findings were correct, it might still be argued that the forger could somehow have em-ployed old pigments. Consequently, any attribution of authorship, whether to Leonardo da Vinci or some other contemporary sculp-tor, must rest solely on the opinion of one expert, while any denial of the same must be based on the opinion of another. Finally, what about the allegations of the younger Lucas?

As an art historian, Gustav Pauli declared that the *Flora* was reminiscent of porcelain figures of Queen Victoria. This case pro-vides a striking illustration of the difficulty of verifying wax sculp-tures. What explanation can there be for the fact that in 1910 the English art scholar E. V. Lucas referred to the *Flora* as a work by his namesake, while in the London *Times* in 1924 he pro-nounced it to be an original?

To the art world, the conflicting opinions about Wilhelm von Bode's *Flora* came as a rude shock. The controversy as to whether the bust was a work by Leonardo (or at least one of his contem-poraries) not only affected the question whether the extremely high price paid for it was justified: the name and reputation of Wilhelm von Bode was also at stake. Eminent scientists gave it as their opinion that the presence of argil in itself established the sculpture's age, since this material had ceased to be used by the sixteenth century and had entirely vanished from the market. In 1911, however, Theodor von Frimmel established in connection with research into the *Flora's* date of origin that argil was still ob-tainable long after the sixteenth century. It could certainly have been procured in London in the middle of the sixteenth century, which was when, in the view of the *Times* article, the sculpture originated. Frimmel published his thesis in 1911 in the periodical *Blätter für Gemäldekunde.*

According to Augusto Jandolo, another *Flora* (this time of marble) was acquired for fifty lire by Alfredo Barsanti, a self-taught man who had taken up art dealing, and sold to the Boston Museum of Fine Arts for 48,000 lire. In his *Catalogue of French and Roman Sculptures,* L. D. Caskey described this marble bust as one of the collection's crowning glories.

After this effortless and highly successful deal, Alfredo Barsanti purchased from a Florentine restorer a *Flora* by Verrocchio, who had taught the great Leonardo da Vinci. For this he paid two thousand lire. In Rome, where Barsanti tried to market his *Flora,* dealers and experts pronounced the sculpture to be an obvious fake.

Barsanti was familiar with the techniques used by Florentine forgers. He knew that, in order to simulate the patina which developed in the course of centuries, they applied various varnish pastes in layers. Convinced that beneath the glazed surface lay a genuine work of art, he unhesitatingly cleaned the bust. If he were wrong, there were plenty of specialists who could restore its original appearance.

Miraculously enough, cleaning merely restored the sculpture's pristine splendor.

The first man to acclaim the resurrected *Flora* was the Italian art historian Ruddioro Schiff. Later, when the bust had been acknowledged as the work of Verrocchio, it was acquired by Sir Joseph Duveen of London, though doubts about its authenticity continued to be voiced. Just as Wilhelm von Bode regarded his *Flora* as a work by Leonardo da Vinci despite the fact that other experts pronounced it to be a fake, so a question mark remained poised above Barsanti's genuine sculpture.

It was no less surprising when, in 1936, the Cerveteri sarcophagus

17. Leonardo, *Leda:* Borghese Collection, Rome. A painting of Leda which the master must have executed for Giuliano de' Medici during his stay in Rome (1513-15). The original is thought to have been lost, and only copies are extant.

18 *a*. Leonardo, *Leda:* Spiridon Collection, Rome: attributed by Venturi to the master.

18 *b*. D. Puligo, *Leda and the Swan:* Musée des Beaux-Arts, Brussels. One of the many imitations of the famous Leonardo subjects.

which had for decades been one of the treasures of the British Museum disappeared from its accustomed place. The splendid modeling exhibited by this "classical masterpiece of the fifth century B.C." had long been an object of admiration not only among experts but also among the art lovers and museum visitors who gladly accepted their judgment.

This "pre-Christian" work turned out to be a co-operative venture on the part of the Pinelli, a family of Italian stonemasons. The sarcophagus had been produced under the direction of Pietro Pinelli and published as a "find from the neighboring hill-graves of Cerveteri." It was not until the discovery of a remarkable similarity between the inscriptions on the Cerveteri sarcophagus and inscriptions on Etruscan sarcophagi in the possession of the Louvre that experts from the art world, and eventually Scotland Yard, decided to investigate the matter. The sarcophagus has reposed in a cellar in the British Museum ever since.

Sculptures in iron, bronze and other metallic alloys are, from the formal aspect, tempting propositions for the forger, but any idea that it is easy to age them is entirely erroneous. On the contrary, the convincing imitation of works of distant date poses particularly difficult problems in the case of metallic substances. Patina, not only in the sense of chemical surface transformation but also as evidence of a sculpture's long existence, is almost impossible to reproduce. The eye may be comparatively easy to deceive, but chemical and physical examination of metal permits the expert to determine age with much greater accuracy than in the case of stone. In particular, the chemical violation of metallic surfaces is simpler to detect than the artificial aging of stone.

Chemical analysis of the coating of lacquer especially characteristic of early Italian bronzes can lead to far-reaching conclusions, but the composition of the casting itself can also supply valuable information because the alloys used in a wide range of indisputably genuine metal sculptures have been carefully recorded.

Metallurgists specializing in the artistic field, such as Berthelot, von Bibra, Le Chatelier, Loeb, Morey and many others, have examined metallic sculptures from Alaska to Tierra del Fuego and from northern China to the Malayan Archipelago. They encountered sculptures and utensils dating from a time when copper was known as an alloying agent but tin was not yet in use. The alloys of the early Bronze Age suggested that the men who cast them very often failed to distinguish tin from lead. Since it was not until Roman times that cadmium from the Spanish mines began to be alloyed with bronze, the boundary between this period and that which preceded it, at least, can be drawn with certainty. If a bronze work in a much earlier style contains cadmium, it can only be a stylistic reproduction or an imitation from a later period. This affords some means of differentiation, however elastic. Metallographic tests of a more exhaustive nature can within certain limits enable a closer identification of the particular period.

Valuable conclusions may be drawn from the composition of an alloy. The various casting techniques, too, produced differing surface structures according to the cooling process employed, and further scrutiny of the metallic skin can be carried out with the aid of microphotography.

Mindful of the good prices paid for archaic and medieval casts of high quality, forgers often try their skill at recasting. Casts of numerous genuine old metal sculptures being readily available, the imitator uses their close approximation to the originals to produce more and more "period" bronzes.

Another imitative process involves the use of stone sculptures whose surface the forger cements so as to facilitate the making of a casting-bed in sand. There also exist a large number of metal sculptures modeled more or less free-hand on old paintings or copperplate engravings. These sometimes achieve a certain stylistic purity.

Genuine bronze patina is a carbonate of cuprous oxide, and its color depends on the alloy used. Analysis of the alloy, on the one hand, and the patina, on the other, can help to determine whether the cuprous oxide is genuine, i.e. born of old age, or artificially induced. It is quite fallacious to suppose that a "thick" bright green patina is necessarily a symptom of authenticity. Patina may range in color from dull to light to dark green, and from dark green, via gleaming brownish intermediate shades, to a blackish green. Where a metallic surface has been exposed to vegetable acids, patina of a light yellow shade results. Crystalline cuprous oxide can even produce an almost reddish color. The forger naturally has at his disposal all the chemicals needed in order to create an artificial patina of the type desired.

It became the practice in Italy during the fifteenth and sixteenth centuries and in the North shortly thereafter to coat bronzes with a dark-toned artificial patina which made them look old. Although forgers have succeeded in reproducing this patina it can easily be detected by gentle rubbing, for the original patina remains stable while the more recent imitation comes off. However, really excellent fake patinas do exist, and their detection is extremely difficult.

Of course, the true expert will often be able to tell whether he is dealing with a genuine old work or a fake by the thickness of the casting itself. Remarkably enough, there are few craftsmen alive today who could match the thinness of casting achieved by the author of *Boy Praying*. This sculpture, which is owned by the Kaiser Friedrich Museum in Berlin, weighs less than ninety pounds.

The metallographic instruments employed in the elucidation of forgeries are so highly sensitive that they need less than a gram of material for analysis. So small an amount can easily be removed from a casting without risk of damage. Metallographic research gave experts reason to believe, for instance, that early bronze works found in West Prussia originated in southeast Hungary. As further investigation subsequently revealed, the bronzes had actually been exported to West Prussia in exchange for amber.

Many connoisseurs assert that they can tell whether a bronze is genuine simply by feeling the surface. While there certainly are more things in heaven and earth than are dreamt of in our philosophy, it would be unwise to attach any practical value to this procedure. It is a known fact that many eminent numismatists can spot a genuine coin by its "feel." The transcendental field remains as yet unexplored, unfortunately, and there is still no satisfactory explanation, for instance, of the dowser's rod. But without flatly dismissing a supersensitive person's ability to sense things, we must agree that this phenomenon lacks the objectivity desirable in a scientific method of examination. Any such opinion must therefore be treated with the utmost caution.

Forgers also take advantage of the fact that sculptures of artistic merit are frequently damaged by inexpert cleaning. They subject the external and interior surfaces of their fakes to rough treatment and then carry out a certain amount of "restoration." Prospective buyers are informed that, since a sculpture has been damaged by careless cleaning, it is being offered at a particularly favorable price.

These remarks about bronze sculptures and the many other alloys are only partially applicable to iron castings. Consequently, there is considerably less scope for metallographic and chemico-physical testing of surface and oxidization in the latter.

There is no room here for a detailed examination of every material ever used in the plastic arts. However, in view of the high prices commanded in the art market by ivory carvings and wax colorings, here is a brief summary of the types of forgery characteristic of these two materials.

The forger of ivory carvings must possess an unerring sense of style and great technical ability. The fineness of the work and the fragility of the material carries with it a great risk of splitting the ivory. To undertake repairs may be not only time-consuming or quite impossible but also, in view of its small scale, detrimental to the stylistic unity of the work — unless, of course, the forger *intends* his figure to exhibit a flaw.

One serious problem is that of aging the ivory's exterior. The freshly carved surface must be darkened by artificial means in order to simulate the enchanting and incomparable shade characteristic of genuine, delicate old works of art carved in ivory. Apart from this, old ivory acquires a unique form of *craquelure* which is exceedingly hard to imitate.

Ivory discolors very slowly, and the process of darkening takes place in gentle gradations over a long span of time. Even in carvings of the Middle Ages and still earlier periods, this darkening consists of little more than the gradual emergence of varying tonal values. The darkening of folds of drapery or other recessed areas is more pronounced.

Both ivory and the fossilized mammoth bone often used in its stead can be artificially discolored, but almost invariably without achieving the same harmonious transition between the various tonal values. On the contrary, artificial discoloration results in a harsh contrast between the too dark and the too light.

This difference can best be illustrated by a comparison. To give meerschaum pipes their traditional warm, honey-colored shade as rapidly as possible, manufacturers sometimes "smoke" them by mechanical means before marketing them. Within a few hours the meerschaum heads have become as thoroughly impregnated with the nicotine and tars from tobacco as they would be after years of leisurely smoking. However, the forcible nature of mechanical smoking creates harsh marginal shades. No time-saving process can conjure up the same characteristics as long years of gradual impregnation. The surface of artificially discolored ivory creates an equally unnatural impression.

It is extremely difficult to authenticate Asian ivory and bone carvings unless one is dealing with crude mass-produced exports or European imitations. Genuine ivories from the Far East are often coated with a colored varnish of remarkable smoothness which indigenous forgers know how to reproduce perfectly, and special attention should be paid to works of art displaying this technique.

The buyer should be particularly on his guard against forgeries of original works which are not accessible to a wide circle and are thus familiar only to a few art lovers. Even though these fakes do, in the last analysis, lack the same inspiration as original works, their composition is so "genuine" that an art critic's assessment of their merit can hardly be regarded as conclusive without reference to and comparison with the originals.

Master forgers of early works in ivory frequently take contemporary pictorial compositions and reproduce them sculpturally on a smaller scale. Any modifications they make are intended to prevent critical analysis from revealing the fake's connection with the original work of art, and the further a forger diverges from his model the greater chance he has of concealing its derivative nature.

Imitations based on large sculptures and figures found in or on medieval buildings are also on the market. Despite their greatly reduced size they often reproduce style and form in a remarkably convincing manner.

Ivory carvings of the greatly prized Byzantine and early Gothic periods were frequently decorated with gold leaf and inlaid enamel. The imitations to which modern forgers devote their energies are easily distinguishable under close scrutiny not only from the finely beaten gold foil of the old craftsmen, its application and affixing, but also by technique and material in general. If the ornamentation is removed — always provided that this does not endanger the whole work — the form of graining to which the under-surface has been subjected or the boreholes made in it can provide surprising disclosures, especially if the latter prove to have been made with a modern dentist's drill. Medieval craftsmen worked with rather different instruments! The molten glass colored with metallic oxide and used for enamel decoration is obtained in our day from industrially produced materials which are spectroscopically distinguishable from the substances used in early enameling.

Genuine ivory has a typical, smooth surface and shows a distinctive graining on all cross-sections. Forgers often use fossilized mammoth bone as their raw material and, for smaller articles, the teeth or bones of other animals, these being considerably easier to carve. The recognition of illegitimate carving materials presents no difficulty.

It is comparatively easy to deceive the naked eye in the case of wax embossings. The dust which settles on them in the course of decades or centuries becomes so thoroughly wedded to the waxen skin that a similar appearance can be created by applying an artificial layer of dirt particles. All that need be done is to spray the whole piece evenly with a diluted solution of turpentine, using an atomizer (a scent spray will do the trick). Then, before the turpentine has dried in, dust is blown onto the still absorbent skin of the wax, lighter or darker in tone according to the age which it is required to simulate. Liquid and particles of dust become evenly bonded to the surface. The older practice of applying liquid with a brush often left brush marks which could be detected with a magnifying glass, and the pressure of a brush tended to rob the delicate waxen outlines of their clarity. A spraying procedure eliminates these defects. Of course, chemical analysis will identify not only turpentine or any liquid used as a substitute but also the "old" dust and dirt, which is by no means as easy to procure as might be supposed. Nevertheless, there is no reason why the fake should not withstand superficial examination provided that the forger has committed no stylistic blunders and has followed the technical procedures used by the old exponents of wax embossing. The simplest way of achieving an outward appearance of authenticity is to use a wax casting. This form of time-saving does, however, run the greatest risk of detection.

One fraudulent activity which may be regarded as coming within the scope of art forgery is the large-scale production, often by leading studios, of archaic Hellenistic and early Italian works of art. Forgeries are so widespread in Italy that space forbids one to list even the most important of the various genres. However, mention may be made of at least a few of the products especially favored by the Italian forging fraternities.

Foremost among them are the "pre-Christian" *objets d'art* offered with varying degrees of exaggerated secrecy to tourists visiting Pompeii. Unscrupulous dealers sell them under the counter as museum pieces of illicit origin.

It is an astonishing fact that, far from diminishing the enthusiasm of most prospective buyers, a dealer's admission that his wares are the proceeds of theft or robbery merely tends to increase it. Once again, delight at getting a bargain overrides every other consideration. To have given good money for a mass-produced and in most cases poorly faked "find" is a meet reward for anyone who buys from such motives.

There is a great demand for genuine early Roman statuettes, which bring high prices. Forgers satisfy that demand, but the only genuine thing about their wares is the volcanic rock which is available to them free of charge and in unlimited quantities in the regions surrounding Vesuvius and Etna. Even a moderately close scrutiny will disclose that these lava sculptures — principally heads, because they are much easier to manufacture than figures — often bear the traces of carborundum-tipped dentist's drills, forgers being far too busy to waste time on manual work with the delicate tools of the creative artist.

Similar sources supply innumerable catacomb lamps, small cult vessels, vases decorated with erotic motifs or nymph-and-faun sculptures in obscene poses. Fakes of this type can be detected with the fingernail, being nothing but yellowish-white castings which have been discolored, aged with the aid of dust and soot and slightly damaged in places to simulate the appearance of an archeological find.

5

❦❦❦❦❦❦❦❦

Printed Works

PRINTED works represent a wide field, ranging from incunabula to Matisse prints to reproductions of abstract art. Fundamentally, however, their manufacture is governed by only three processes.

Surprisingly enough, a grave disparity exists between the care devoted to stylistic study on the one hand and knowledge of reproductive processes on the other. Even some of the leading collectors of printed works fail to bestow enough attention on details of technical or mechanical production, regardless of the rule which applies here as everywhere — namely, that insufficient knowledge on the buyer's part is grist to the forger's mill. Moreover, since forgeries of printed works are mostly fakes based on photomechanical processes, the decision between genuine and false must devolve less upon the art critic and his stylistic assessments and proportionately more upon the expert judge of manual and mechanical techniques.

That is why, before dealing with the numerous and extremely

diverse types of printed forgeries that exist, we shall first devote space to a brief introduction to printing processes and methods of manufacture.

The printer's is among the oldest of all handicrafts. There is an erroneous belief that printing originated in medieval Europe, but the Chinese were familiar with the art, if only in the rudimentary form of deeply engraved signets, when Europeans were still clearing their forests and drinking mead from horn cups.

Although Gutenberg is regarded as the inventor of letterpress printing, people were printing "block books" from wooden plates engraved with text and illustrations and from engraved plates with movable characters long before his time. Gutenberg's most important contribution was a casting device which allowed the manufacture of type in any given quantity. This first piece of mechanization, a quite uncomplicated forerunner of our modern linotype machines, coupled with the development of the printing press, provided the "black art" with its strongest impetus.

Two printing processes have existed from the very beginning, and since the end of the eighteenth century there have been three: (1) letterpress ("raised"); (2) intaglio ("recessed"); (3) lithography ("flat"). Time has wrought no fundamental change in these processes, though great technical advances have been made.

(1) *Letterpress* printing, still the commonest of all the processes, works on the following principle. Ink is applied to raised surfaces and then transferred to the material to be printed, normally paper. For this process, the image of the characters or pictorial blocks in the "chase" must be reversed in order to appear the right way around when printed. A simple example of letterpress printing can be seen in the rubber or metal stamps used daily by commercial firms. In letterpress, characters or pictures protrude from the sur-

face. They take ink from a cylinder which passes over them at a given speed, and transfer it to the material. It is immaterial whether the ink is applied with a hand-roller or by mechanical means, nor does the principle of letterpress printing change because it is produced with a simple manually operated press or with a complex flat-bed or rotary machine.

Apart from complete lines and solids, letterpress printing can also produce half-tone effects in which dots of varying thickness correspond to areas of light and shade. The finer the "screen," the more delicate the tonal gradations possible. Fineness of screen is limited by the surface texture of the paper employed. The coarser the surface of the material to be printed, the coarser must be the half-tone screen. If a fine-screen half-tone block were used on newsprint, for example, the closely set dots would spread and run into each other on the absorbent surface, producing a black and meaningless mass. Glossy art paper, being less absorbent, will allow the correct tonal values to emerge.

(2) *Intaglio* is distinguishable from letterpress in that ink is not conveyed by the protruding surfaces of type or pictorial blocks but lies in depressions from which it is taken by the paper as it passes over them under pressure. In other words, the outlines of lettering or illustrations do not project from the printing surface but are recessed into it. The basic principle of this process is the same whether these recesses are produced by hand with a burin or chemically with acid. When pressed against the plate and its ink-filled recesses, the material to be printed removes the ink partly because of its absorptive properties and partly by vacuum effect. Intaglio printing can be done with a hand press of the most elementary type or with a multicolor rotary gravure machine. In photogravure, photographic etching of the printing surface creates minute recesses impossible to achieve with a burin or pantograph.

Consequently, the surface of the finished product is smooth, whereas the products of other types of intaglio printing exhibit pronounced ridges, as a brief glance at any engraved business card or die-stamped letterhead will reveal. Take a steel-engraved bank note and run your fingernail gently over it without exerting any pressure. It will feel as though you are touching an extraordinarily fine file. The volume of ink removed from the comparatively deep indentations made by an engraving tool in a steel die or copperplate, on the other hand, is so substantial that it remains on the surface of the paper in the form of raised veins. Furthermore, the pressure exerted is so great that the edge of the plate will leave an impression in the paper which is known to the trade as the "platemark." This forms an intentional feature of some invitations or business cards.

In the photographic process used for intaglio printing by cylinder (photogravure), text and illustrations are transmitted to a pretreated metal surface and etched into it with acids. Machining does not leave any marginal impressions.

(3) *Lithography* is commonly supposed to be a "flat" process. This is really a fallacy, for it shares some of the attributes of letterpress and should be regarded, in principle, as the "flattest" method of letterpress printing. In fact, the only protrusions on the printing surface are formed by the ink's own bulk. In lithography, ink is distributed by an image which is neither protuberant nor recessed: the raised surface of the ink itself constitutes the printing agent. The whole process is based on the relationship of oil and water, which, as everyone knows, are mutually repellent.

The original form of lithography, on stone, was invented by Alois Senefelder in 1796-1797 and patented by him at Munich in 1799. The so-called lithographic process involved the drawing of text or pictures in greasy chalk on a smoothly polished slab of slaty limestone, after which the surface was etched with a solution of gum arabic and mineral acids. Being greasy, the printing ink adhered only to the image, while the rest of the surface was kept moist and remained free of ink. Senefelder began by drawing the pictorial plate or lithograph proper and then transferred the image in reverse to a machining stone from which he took his actual prints.

Out of this process developed offset printing. Thin and flexible sheets of metal took the place of limestone slabs which were not only very expensive but could weigh several hundredweight. Even with the most up-to-date rotary offset machines, however, the same principle applies. Text and illustrations are photographically transferred, the right way around, to a metal plate. From this surface the image is passed, exactly as in the case of Senefelder's hand-transfer, to a rubber cylinder or blanket on which it appears in reverse, and from there to the printed material, once more the right way around. The intervention of the rubber cylinder eliminates the necessity for heavy pressure, though it also rules out the sharpness of image attainable by other processes.

Each of these three forms of printing has its own special idiosyncrasies. Every sheet to leave a machine betrays the method of its manufacture, and the expert can tell from the characteristics of a printed image how it was produced.

Intaglio reproductions of a woodcut are fairly smooth, the printed areas being only slightly rough to the touch. Copperplate engravings always feel distinctly rough and are characterized by projecting ridges which can be detected with the fingertips, even when they correspond to the finest grooves in the engraving. Photogravure and lithography produce a flat image but one which always has a rather viscous and greasy finish. Outlines are softly defined. Letterpress printing from type and blocks is sharply defined and produces a somewhat glassy surface. However careful the "make-ready" or preparatory work, the latter process normally leaves perceptible indentations. Too much pressure can result in raised impressions on the reverse of a sheet, which are familiarly referred to in the trade as "braille."

Naturally enough, the hand presses in Gutenberg's workshop did not have the thousandth-of-an-inch precision of some modern machines, but the complete revolution in technique which has led to such vast differences in the finished product has done nothing to alter the fundamentals of printing.

The prices paid for rare incunabula are a great temptation to the forger, but an extremely limited circle of potential buyers makes it imperative that any forgery should be of the highest quality, for no fake will pass muster unless a great deal of time and professional ability have been devoted to it. Once again, the first problem is to obtain materials. Medieval paper, normally protected by a watermark, can only be produced sheet by sheet if the original manufacturing methods are employed.

One remedy is to use unwatermarked paper and equip it with the artificial watermark appropriate to a particular period and locality. Changes in the composition of paper were not so pronounced between the fifteenth and sixteenth centuries that they permit the expert to date any one sheet to the nearest decade.

Since large numbers of genuine books of the *cinquecento,* principally of a juristic nature, are available in the market at reasonable prices, their unprinted flyleaves provide the forger with one source of original paper.

The watermark, whether in the shape of symbolic lines, coats of arms, monograms, names or letters, came into being as soon as the pulp was dipped from the vat, for the metal symbol selected was attached to the rectangular mold. Where the pulp had settled on it during dipping, the finished product was correspondingly thinner. The first handmade papers of the late thirteenth century were not as yet watermarked with letters or trade-marks, but with symbolic lines which merely identified their district of origin. It was the paper manufacturers of Ravensburg who first introduced the true watermark in the fifteenth century: a turret with three crenelations. This simultaneously represented a guarantee of quality. Rejected paper was watermarked with a horn hanging on a loop.

There are three fundamentally different types of paper: (1) handmade paper, identifiable by the lines or "laid" marks which result from the dipping procedure and from which watermarks later evolved; (2) silky Japanese and Indian papers, manufactured from bamboo fiber; (3) machine-made paper, developed in the late eighteenth and early nineteenth centuries. The earliest papers go back to Chinese manuscripts and stamped impressions of the second century B.C.

The Frick brothers and Hans Holbayn, who together founded the first paper mill in Ravensburg, are commonly regarded as the inventors of rag paper. According to another view, the first paper mill to be brought into operation was at Erbach in the Odenwald. There is no definite evidence to connect the introduction of this process into southern Germany with immigrant paper makers from Lombardy.

For the forger, the imitation of age-old paper is a near impossibility unless, of course, he cares to adopt the original procedure. This would entail — among many other things — laboriously pulverizing linen and cotton rags, soaking them in water, mixing them in a pulp vat with the correct proportions of contemporary size and bleach, pouring the pulp into a mold equipped with a sieve-like mesh of wire-cloth and, after draining the water, carefully drying the residue.

Since about the middle of the last century, handmade paper has been manufactured industrially, but it has never been possible to reproduce the irregularity of hand-dipped vat-paper. However, forgers have devised ways and means of fabricating effective substitutes for watermarks.

Old unwatermarked paper can, if generously moistened beforehand, be fraudulently converted into watermarked paper by the application of a heated stamp. The process is expensive and difficult. The whole sheet is placed in a pre-heated metal press, which must be fairly large, as incunabula often far exceeded crown octavo in size. The watermark being engraved into the metal plate, the sheet dries slowly in the deeply recessed areas where it is not brought into contact with the hot metal, and rapidly throughout the rest of its heated surface. In this way the recessed portions remain more translucent than the surface as a whole, which has been evenly dried under pressure.

The difference between a genuine watermark created by the dipping process and one which has been artificially added under pressure can be easily recognized with the aid of a microscope. But there is another, chemical method of identifying a spurious watermark added subsequently in the manner just described. If moistened with an alkaline solution of natron (a sesquicarbonate of soda), the transparent design which has resulted from slower drying will vanish within a few minutes. Natron causes the body of the paper to swell rapidly and regain its original bulk. A genuine watermark swells in like manner when treated with natron solution, but shows up with even greater clarity as soon as it is dry once more. This test must not, however, be used on hand-colored or illuminated works, since very few inks remain fast when treated with natron.

Some painstaking forgers fake their watermarks by applying them to the surface with a raised stamp, normally made of rubber and moistened with a weak solution of sulphuric and nitric acid.

The stamp should only be applied quite gently to the paper, which must be thoroughly washed as soon as it has absorbed the moistened outlines. Drying may on no account be accelerated by heat.

In areas where the sheet has come into contact with acid, the texture of the paper takes on a parchment-like appearance coupled with greater transparency.

Despite immediate washing, however, traces of acid can still be detected by chemical reaction long after the event. No time limit can be set on the efficacy with which microscopic examination will reveal the artifice, for where paper fibers have been affected by acid they melt away and display horny malformations.

Another type of watermark forgery is effected with emulsions of glycerine, vaseline or paraffin. These are easily detectable, both chemically and microscopically.

Since watermark experts have ascertained and recorded the design of every major watermark together with the duration of its use, it will not often happen that a forger who specializes in this peculiarly difficult field fakes an incunabulum of the period *before* A.D. 1500 on a sheet of paper bearing a watermark of the period *after* A.D. 1500.

Charles M. Briquet's work *Les Filigranes,* published in Geneva in 1907, listed in order of date and origin every known watermark from 1282 to the beginning of the seventeenth century. In a compilation which appeared in 1861, Hausmann published all the watermarks present in indisputably genuine Dürer prints between 1496 and 1528. Five years later Bodmann assembled examples of all the watermarks on genuine incunabula, while Heitz published all those that could be found in the libraries of Basel and Strasbourg. Available literature on watermarks will frequently permit the serious collector and expert to distinguish between genuine and fake without resorting to empirical methods of research, forged watermarks being almost without exception guilty of deviations from the original — in respect not only of lines and ornaments but also of over-all length and breadth. Whether applied by hand, rubber stamp or engraved plate, the forged device will inevitably diverge from the original in size.

Watermarks apart, the sheet itself should be tested in doubtful cases, at least with regard to its age. And here the decisive factor is the composition of the pulp.

The first clear-cut line of demarcation between hand-dipped and machine-made paper came into being in 1806 in the shape of resin size, which replaced the animal glues used hitherto. Printed matter dating from before 1806 cannot, therefore, have been produced on resin-sized paper. Resin-sized paper takes on a pronounced violet shade when moistened and pressed against commercially obtainable tetramethylparaphenyldiamin litmus paper.

The second line of demarcation came in 1840 with the introduction of wood pulp into paper manufacture. Thus a graphic work of earlier date than 1840 cannot have been printed on paper with a wood-pulp content. Wood-pulp paper turns yellow if moistened with a solution of 5 gr. aniline sulphate and 50 gr. distilled water, and red if moistened with a solution of 4 gr. hydrochloric phloroglucin, 25 c.c. alcohol and 5 c.c. pure hydrochloric acid.

Practical tests in the laboratory will readily establish a paper's pliability, strength, structure, composition and resilience in comparison with that of an indisputably genuine paper. Such tests require only a very small quantity of material, but, because a damaged sheet naturally depreciates in value, they should only be employed when, as principally happens in criminal proceedings, absolute proof of forgery is indispensable.

Modern forgeries of early printed works are extremely rare because the time and effort involved bears little relation to the rewards. When forgeries of items from the early days of letterpress printing do turn up they almost always take the form of single sheets, never complete works. A copy of the *"zweiundvierzigzeilige Bibel"* (each page comprises forty-two lines), very probably printed by Gutenberg himself in 1454-1456, changed hands some years ago at a price of about a million dollars. Details of the transaction were not communicated to the public at large. A single page from such a work would be immensely valuable, but there is little chance that even the most perfect forgery would find a buyer. Fust's and Schoeffer's *Psalterium* of 1457 and the *Catholicon* printed by Gutenberg in 1460 are other treasures which would tempt a forger from the point of view of price were there not almost insuperable difficulties in his path.

"Block books" and incunabula of the highest quality form a class of their own, in price as in other respects. Printed works which originated only a few years later do not fetch such very high prices in these days, as most auctions tend to show. (This does not, of course, apply to rare works which are sought after by wealthy collectors or public libraries either for prestige purposes or because of their historical and, very often, local interest.) Even the *Schedelsche Weltchronik,* an extremely beautiful work printed in German and Latin by Anton Koberger at Nuremberg in 1493 and illustrated with woodcuts, failed to fetch more than 5000 marks (about $1200) when it was sold in 1958.

With the growing popularity of woodcuts and copperplate engravings in their various forms, whether as single sheets or series, creative artists became increasingly dissociated from the actual presentation of commissioned works, which were often tastefully bound. And therein, perhaps, lies the especial characteristic of the work of art which exists in many originals. While it was formerly rare for an artist to repeat one of his own works, numerous printed "originals" could now derive from the same hand.

Wood carvers and copperplate engravers naturally directed their efforts toward the most promising market available, and, because portrayals of religious motifs sold best of all, most early woodcuts and engravings are devoted to Biblical themes. Later, since it was easier to work from an old drawing or painting, they exploited mythological themes as well.

A handmade printing surface furnished many hundreds of original copies, and these copies had to be marketed. As a consequence of this, there came into being the professional dealer who formed an intermediary between creative artist and potential buyer.

A copperplate engraving could, according to the fineness and depth of the engraving or etching, give between 300 and 350 very good copies, and then another 400 good copies, and finally an unspecified number of more or less serviceable copies. Prints from the same copperplate may thus vary considerably in condition.

The quality of a print exercises a decisive effect on its artistic and commercial worth. Very considerable differences in value exist between prints which display full delicacy of line and those in which the definition has lost its clarity.

Prints taken from a worn woodcut normally exhibit blots, the image being marred by cracks which have developed in the wood. Prints from a worn metal plate are characterized by loss of quality in areas where the surface has become flattened.

An especial value is attached to the test prints, often as yet unsigned, which an engraver makes to help him appraise his work and enable him to amplify or improve it. Several very different prints may thus have come from one and the same plate. Sometimes, for instance, the experimental print lacks a background because the artist could not decide what tonal values were indicated until after he had seen it.

By comparing an experimental print with prints from later stages in the engraving of a plate and, finally, with the finished product, the art historian can elicit valuable information about the artist's working methods.

A trial print of Albrecht Dürer's *Adam and Eve* shows us the background in a state of near completion. The two figures, on the other hand — except for Adam's fig leaf, the upper and lower portions of his right thigh, and his foot — are only sketched in outline. The serpent has been elaborated but the apple is still a flat disk — as is the figure of Eve. The panel which in the final "state" bears an inscription giving the name and date is merely a blank patch.

Rembrandt modified one of his major prints, *The Three Crosses,* several times. In the fifth state of *Ecce Homo,* a print of oblong format, the figures in the foreground have disappeared and the architecture has been refashioned.

In engravings, the artist's name is often followed by the words *sculpsit* or *incisit* (abbreviated to *sculps., sc.* or *inc.*), meaning "has engraved," or *fecit* (*fec.*), "has made." In engravings based on original paintings or drawings the name of the painter or draftsman is followed by *pinxit* or *delineavit* (*pinx., delin.* or *del.*) and, less commonly, *invenit* or *composuit* (*inv.* or *comp.*).

The signing of examples of graphic art came into fashion in about 1455-1460. The cipher of the so-called "master of the Berlin *Passion*" also appeared at about this period. The earliest monograms date from about 1465, as, for instance, that of the artist "E.S." A combination of the initials of Christian name and surname, the monogrammatic device was intended to throw light on a work's authorship. But, despite the growing tendency to regard a work and its creator as a single unit and publicize them as such, it was several decades before anonymity gave way to the statement of an artist's name in full.

Many artists made ornaments out of their initials or monograms, each according to his temperament, thus transforming them into a sort of trade-mark. Others, like Schongauer, combined a clue to name with a clue to origin.

The practice of imitating the personal cipher of some great and celebrated master became particularly widespread in the graphic arts, as the countless numbers of Dürer prints testify. However, this abuse should not be equated absolutely and in every case with signature forgery in the present-day sense. It may much more frequently have served ends not immediately apparent to the modern observer.

If this were not so, it would be hard to understand why so many of the imitators who copied woodcuts or copperplate engravings with remarkable accuracy went on to add ciphers or monograms in a haphazard manner which immediately marked them as forgeries. Many copyists of well-known artists adorned all their words with emblems or devices which, while similar to the originals, could never have been mistaken for them. (Quite the reverse applied to forgers of gold- or silversmiths' hallmarks, whose only concern was to lend their work an authentic appearance by imitating a punch with the maximum of accuracy.)

The designation "woodcut" cannot be applied indiscriminately to all early works, since metal plates, too, were occasionally treated in woodcut fashion. Woodcut effects can be achieved with a large measure of success by linocuts, which are much easier to deal with.

When producing woodcuts, the artist drew the reversed image of his picture — sketched either in detail or outline, according to personal preference — on a wooden block, which was filed smooth, completely flat, and always cut with the grain. The initial drawing was done either with crayon or a cutting knife or, too, by tracing a reversed image on to the block in advance. The large areas which were to remain white were then removed from the block with a gouge. That done, the artist was ready to begin the delicate task of cutting.

If the work was to include textual matter, the wooden block

could be pierced to make room for typesetting. The early masters of this craft preferred to make their blocks out of pear-tree wood and walnut. From the eighteenth century onwards, English exponents made boxwood their favorite material. The hardness of this wood necessitated the use of a graver; consequently, "wood engraving" might be a more apt description of this technique.

The nineteenth century saw the appearance of the *Tonstich,* in which black became the neutral background and white the illustrative medium. There being nothing really new under the sun, this technique did, in fact, have a sixteenth-century forerunner in the so-called chiaroscuro engraving, which was used in making the first multicolored prints. Finely carved or engraved into the wood, the lines combined to form faint mixtures of color when the separate blocks were superimposed.

It was rare for any corrections to be made in metal engravings, woodcuts or wood-engravings after the first "state." Corrections could, in any case, consist only in the enlargement of white or non-printing areas. Substantial alterations made it necessary to excise largish portions and replace them with uncarved blocks of appropriate dimensions which had to be cut with the utmost accuracy and closely fitted to the original surface.

The easiest way of telling whether a print comes from a wooden or a metal plate is to study its outlines. Metal, being far more difficult to work with, is usually characterized by less clarity of definition.

A further variant of metal engraving is the paste print, of which only about a hundred exist. The unrecessed surface was made receptive to ink by being punched. Most of these prints are single examples. Metal plates treated in this manner could only be used in conjunction with specially prepared paper. The indentations in the printing surface were imparted to a thin crust of size overlaid with gold leaf. Because of the malleability of this crust, the punched design showed up on the negative ground in the form of a diffused impression.

Engravers of earlier centuries often made a number of additional trial prints from their blocks or plates for the benefit of collectors who were happy to pay a higher price if they could acquire a rarity.

For the same reason, there has been a sharp increase in the number of "artist's proofs" since the end of the Second World War. The artist produces these for particularly demanding buyers, some before the addition of title or signature, some with signature but without title, some with title but without signature, some on special paper as a "first series" lettered from A onwards, some as a "second series" designated by roman numerals from I upwards, and some as a "third series" with Arabic numerals also from 1 upwards. "State" prints like these, which are really nothing of the sort and merely exist to satisfy extravagant whims, naturally leave the door wide open to forgery.

The only forgeries of early woodcuts which represent any danger to the serious collector are those which originated at roughly the same time as the originals.

The first forger on a really notable scale was Marcantonio Raimondi (*circa* 1480-1534). The Prague art historian Friedrich Lippmann wrote of him that he became Raphael's engraver "thanks to a rare ability to adapt himself to an alien artistic manner" which permitted him to take a sketch hastily dashed off by someone else and produce an engraving "rounded off and intimately modeled in the spirit of the original."

This forger-engraver was connected via Raphael with Albrecht Dürer, who (if we are to believe Vasari's account) gave the former a self-portrait as a mark of his esteem. This was executed in water color on a very fine-grained canvas so that it could be viewed from either side, and its highlights were achieved not with white paint but by using the bare and translucent texture of the canvas itself. Raphael likewise sent Dürer a number of his own drawings and several engravings, which were printed at Bologna.

Marcantonio had much admired Dürer's *Life of the Virgin*, and his first engravings of that work appeared while Dürer was painting his *Madonna of the Rose Garlands* in Venice. Dürer at once lodged a protest with the Signoria of Venice, the city-state's supreme authority. Since an artist's signum was recognized as "a valid token of protection," an edict was published forbidding Marcantonio to adorn his engravings with Dürer's monogram, "A.D." In accordance with contemporary law and the indifferent attitude then adopted towards mere plagiarism, no measures were or could be taken against their publication *without* Dürer's signature.

Apart from the seventeen sheets comprising the *Life of the Virgin*, Marcantonio also faked thirty-seven smaller woodcuts from Dürer's *Passion*. Art historians unanimously agree that the imitator's copperplate engraving technique reproduced the essence, character and feeling of the woodcuts with remarkable accuracy. Just how Marcantonio succeeded in eliminating, even over extensive areas, the striking dissimilarity in surface between copperplate and woodcut prints is hard to explain. The marginal impressions left by a metal plate are always sharper than those of a wooden block.

While there is little chance of proving it, the probability is that dealers were responsible for overprinting Dürer's monogram on Marcantonio's forgeries, which ceased to incorporate the "A.D." after the Council of Venice had published its decree. At all events, new sixteenth-century forgeries of Dürer prints with monograms subsequently overprinted are constantly coming to light.

The papers which Dürer himself used for his prints bore specific watermarks. The primary method of differentiating a contemporary fake from an original, therefore, is to compare their watermarks.

The forging of Dürer's work, which included both the slavish copying of his engravings and the deployment of his major figures against other backgrounds, gained such proportions that in the year 1512 the town council of Nuremberg, heedful of the artist's complaints that his "signs manual were being fraudulently overprinted," issued an official warning to forgers.

In Germany, the leading exponents of imitative engraving were Hieronymus Hopfer (*circa* 1470-1535) and Virgil Solis (1514-1562). Twelve-year-old Jan Wierix (1549-?), a youthful prodigy, produced imitations of Dürer's work which were never surpassed, either in power of expression or technical ability.

When Dürer died in 1528, there were more forged Dürer engravings in existence than genuine — not to mention a plentiful supply of copies and stylistic imitations of his paintings. His widow Agnes Dürer petitioned the magistrate of the town of Nuremberg for "protection of her privileges," and did, in fact, receive a grant towards the buying up of some forged blocks "since this was the only means of preventing the manufacture of further prints from the same."

The uncertainty which rules where early engravings are concerned is well illustrated by the case of the *Apostles*. In 1906, after an exhaustive analysis of a *Study of Heads for Dürer's "Apostles,"* the Swiss Dürer expert Heinrich Wölfflin reached the conclusion that this drawing, which had until then been regarded as unquestionably genuine and served as a model for Dürer's *painting* of the Apostles, was of dubious authenticity.

In the decades following Dürer's death, the painter Hans Hoffman (flourished 1570-1603) produced a number of imitations based on the master's work. There was, in fact, no need for him to resort to forgery, for his own originals were of a high standard. One

recognized forgery is the *Ecce Homo* from the Gallery of Count
Nostiz in Prague, which probably originated in about 1620. It bears
the date 1500 and an excellent imitation of Dürer's monogram.
This monogram, which had become a symbol of supreme quality,
was pressed into the service of every kind of technique. It has even
turned up on inferior imitations drawn in printing ink.

The spirit of the times is exemplified by an entry made in his
"secret journal" by the contemporary collector Hans Hieronymus
Imhoff, which (according to M. Tausing) runs as follows: "My late
father had Albrecht Dürer's cipher painted in at the foot of a
Madonna done in oils on wood, but no one could really have believed that A. Dürer was responsible for it."

The painter J. von Sandrart wrote in his notes: "Hans Birkmayer
painted a self-portrait in which he adorned his own name, Hans
Birkmayer, painter, 44 years old, 1517, with the regular cipher of
Albrecht Dürer."

The wide field of Dürer forgeries even embraces certain "recognized" imitators such as Jobst Harich, Paul Juvenel and Hans
Glaser. Contemporaries found their copies extremely marketable.

In the mid-seventeenth century there were no less than sixty-eight
patently forged Dürers in the collection of Archduke Leopold
Wilhelm of Austria alone, and even in the centuries that followed a
brisk trade was still done throughout Europe in forged Dürer
paintings, woodcuts and engravings. On the death in 1665 of the
Frankfurt book-dealer Christof le Blon, who had made quite a
reputation as a copperplate engraver, veritable bundles of fake
Dürer prints were found among his effects, probably the work of
le Blon himself and his brother Michel.

Artists early recognized the spiritual and material threat which
forgers represented, although it is probable, in view of their arti-
san's background, that they were motivated principally by professional and financial considerations.

When, after consultation between the guilds and the authorities, a "decree concerning marks" was published, the sign manual became more than a mere indication of creative authorship. The practice which had grown up since the latter half of the fifteenth century, whether from ambition or caution, of identifying a work by means of a house-mark, cipher or monogram, now assumed the nature of an obligation.

It was from this "obligation to sign," which sprang partly from statutory or guild law and partly from the contractual relationship existing between an artist and his clients, that there evolved the spiritual and material significance of the signature, monogram or cipher. A work signed by its author was of incomparably greater value than an anonymous work. This circumstance was exploited even by engravers of the class of Israel van Meckenem, who also succumbed to the temptations of forgery. His method was to acquire plates from the effects of deceased engravers whose technique had approximated to his own, work them up in his own style, and add his personal signature.

There are more Wierix prints in existence bearing Dürer's "A.D." monogram than there are with Wierix's own signature. Later forgers often removed this masterly imitator's signature and replaced it, sometimes on prints and sometimes on the blocks themselves, with Dürer's monogram.

An artist's monogram is sometimes accompanied by an additional cipher. This is attributable to the fact that many old masters practiced a division of labor. Holbein, for instance, drew his picture on wood, but the actual cutting was done by Lützelburger, who also worked for Hans Burgkmair. Lützelburger put his monogram to one of Holbein's *Dance of Death* prints. It is significant that Dürer, too, made use of other men's hands, at least for rough work, and many other artists followed his example.

Even when the anonymity which had hitherto been customary

finally gave way to the signature, opinions as to an individual's rights over his work fluctuated long and continuously before the notion of copyright began to take shape. By the sixteenth century, the rudiments of copyright protection for written works and a ban on pirated editions engendered a clearer legal concept of intellectual property in general. It was not until the eighteenth century, however, that it received formal definition in Johann Rudolf Thurneysen's *Dissertatio de recusione librorum furtiba,* which in 1738 described unauthorized reprinting as *"furtum usus."*

Some excellent reprints of Dürer engravings were brought out by the state printing office at Berlin. They are identifiable as facsimiles by an embossed and a flat stamp, the latter applied with document ink. Forgers have taken advantage of these official reprints. After careful steaming, they iron out the raised stamp of the state printing office, repeating the process until all signs of embossing have disappeared. The surface of the paper, once rough but now ironed smooth, is then carefully pressed between two contrary graining-blocks. The expensive rag paper used for these reprints by the state printing office is of a type which permits the ink stamps to be bleached out. Although the chemicals employed in this process (mainly a volatile solution of chlorine) damage the paper fibers, this defect can be remedied by spraying on a colorless solution of 6 per cent cellite. The paper thereupon regains its original structure and resilience.

The above procedure can be detected with the aid of microscope and spectroscope. However, if the forger ages the whole sheet by darkening it, adding spots of mold and, as is sometimes done, perforating it here and there with minute holes to simulate the incursions of woodworm, gullible customers may be so impressed by its appearance that it will never occur to them to scrutinize it more closely.

Woodcut prints by medieval, recent and contemporary masters

of the art are no longer reproduced by hand but by photographic means. The image, whether woodcut or linocut, is photographically transmitted to a zinc plate, and from there, after the outlines have been retouched by hand, to paper. The result is as unsatisfactory, when subjected to rigorous tests, as the procedure is simple.

The print to be reproduced is photographically transferred to a metal plate in the proportion of 1:1. This process will in itself produce a discrepancy of the order of a thousandth or ten-thousandth of an inch between original and copy because the outlines of the image which appears on the camera's opalescent screen will not show up with the hair's-breadth accuracy necessary for an identical print. Furthermore, areas of any size are subject to distortion by the photographic lens. If original and reproduction are accurately measured, preferably by running diagonals from opposite corners, their disparity will immediately become apparent. In the case of an early original, examination of paper and printing ink should confirm the results of such tests.

Imitations of old or modern prints can be detected with near certainty by photographing a section and magnifying it to a high degree. No great difficulty is involved in photographing a few square centimeters from a portion of the original which is particularly heavily hatched, enlarging it fifty times, and holding it up against a similar enlargement of the suspected forgery. This procedure will reveal discrepancies from the original of as little as a thousandth of a millimeter which have escaped even the most powerful magnifying glass. And neither manual nor mechanical reproduction can maintain accuracy of such an order over any wide area.

Naturally enough, the methods of research described above need only be used in doubtful cases.

Of far greater danger to the potential buyer are printing blocks fraudulently produced by "direct" transfer. This process assumes that the forger is in possession of an original print. Instead of photographing it he transfers it directly to a chemically treated zinc block, thereby obtaining an image which is fully identical with the original both in dimensions and proportions, much as a simple photostat is. The printing surface results from the etching away of such of the metal face as has not been chemically pre-treated against acid. The etching process does produce microscop-ically small variations from the outlines of original block, but it offers no chance of establishing a discrepancy by the measurement of diagonals. The only alternative is to compare contours by greatly enlarging them as previously described. It becomes apparent from our account of the way in which they are executed in the first place that the faking of copperplate engravings must founder on almost insurmountable technical difficulties. Forgers make up for this by swarming over every other province of the graphic arts. Nevertheless, intaglio plates engraved or otherwise hand-worked in copper have been faked, even though they are never likely to mislead the expert. The much finer linear complexities of copper-plate engraving are so much more demanding than those of the woodcut that mechanical reproduction always creates a crude im-pression, while any attempt to engrave the plate by hand is futile.

The commonest forgeries are made from plates which have been photographically "pre-etched." A forger uses as his pattern the most clearly defined original print available. Just as in the zinco-graphic process so, in the making of a copperplate, a print is trans-ferred in reverse to a copper sheet with a sensitized coating. But, however meticulously the procedure is carried out, chemico-me-chanical reproductions of this type are always lacking either in depth or, if etched deeply enough, delicacy of line. This is because a generous use of acid will attack the "ridges" themselves, causing the recessed lines to merge.

19. *Madonna and Child,* ivory, triptych of the 13th-century French school (left, closed; right, open). The Louvre experts were able to identify this as a 19th century forgery. The hinges appear to be contemporary, but the holes for them have been made by machine.

20. X-ray photograph of the El Greco forgery shown in Fig. 21 *a*. Beneath the figure of St Peter an 18th-century figure of St John can be seen clearly.

21 *a.* *St Peter*: an El Greco forgery, inspired by an original by the master, now in the Escorial.

21 *b.* Using X-ray photographs as a guide, the overpainting has been gradually removed, revealing the head of St John.

22. Thomas de Keyser (1596-1667), *Mother and Daughter.* 19th-century forgery. Private collection. The pastiche has been produced by using a composite of the *Portrait of a Child* by Govert Flinck (left) in the Mauritshuis, and the *Portrait of a Lady* by Ferdinand Bol (right), in the collection of Capt. Holford, London.

A copperplate produced by photo-mechanical means lacks the modeling which only an artist working by hand with a burin, pin or other instrument can achieve. Prints taken from it will give either a flat or a blotchy effect. Even when a forger uses genuine old paper, his fake looks quite different from an original print made with a hand-engraved plate.

Apart from this, photographic reproduction is almost always betrayed by luminous dots, sometimes infinitesimal, which the retoucher has tried to remove from the negative, glass plate or metal surface. Minute symptoms like these are enough to differentiate imitation from original.

Reprints from old blocks such as the aforementioned prints published by the state printing office at Berlin and other, unofficial, prints taken from genuine woodcut blocks have no connection with forgery. Enthusiastic collectors of old blocks often have prints made for themselves or their friends. Hans Albrecht, Baron von Derschau, not only collected drawings and copperplate engravings but had prints made from them, without, however, using contemporary paper or reconstituting inks from old formulas. After his death in 1824, many of his reprints turned up in an artificially aged condition.

From equally disinterested motives, William Baillie, who built up an important collection of graphic art in London during the eighteenth century, had some pulls taken from the original block of Rembrandt's *Hundred Guilder Print,* which was in his possession. There was no fraudulent intention on his part, of course. He could not foresee what misuse would be made of his prints by unscrupulous individuals after the sale of his collection at Christie's in London in 1811.

At Paris in the year 1906, Alvin Beaumont brought out reprints of some original engravings by Rembrandt which had survived in varying degrees of preservation. He identified them as facsimiles with a publisher's stamp which forgers promptly removed, thereby creating an abundant supply of "original" prints. To distinguish these reprints from the genuine article is a task for the expert, since forgers aged them and often provided them with artificial watermarks.

Countless reprints, frequently from retouched copper and steel plates, came into being during the eighteenth and nineteenth centuries. They constitute the bulk of the forgeries in this field. Prints by Marcantonio, Rossi and Lafreri, together with similar reproductions from old plates, served as facsimiles and were subsequently worked up into would-be originals,

The rising prices paid during the first third of the nineteenth century for woodcuts and metal engravings by the masters of the fifteenth and sixteenth centuries attracted copyists of every complexion, from the crudest to the most adroit. Specialized publications by Bartsch, Passavant, Retberg, Rowinsky, Middleton and others contain whole collections of copyists' works. They detail and catalogue the features which differentiate them from originals.

The prices of old graphic art vary enormously. Rarity, general condition and, in particular, width of margin may all decisively affect the sum paid for a print.

At the Holford sale in London in 1893 a "first state" print of Rembrandt's *Self-portrait with Saber* fetched £2000, a price equivalent to more than ten times that sum in modern money. The *Hundred Guilder Print* in first state was knocked down at £1750. Dürer's *Knight, Death, and the Devil* brought £700 at Fischer's in London in 1892. In a sale at Goncourt in Paris in 1897 *La Troupe Italienne* fetched 760 gold francs as against the 5320 paid for Debucourt's *L'Oiseau Ranimé*. In 1920, when Bürner of Leipzig auctioned the Paul Davidson collection of masters of the fifteenth to seventeenth centuries, more than ten million inflationary marks poured into the coffers, a sum approximating to $470,000 in present terms.

Monochrome and polychrome prints by modern artists, especially fashionable favorites from the turn of the century onwards, are far from overshadowed at sales by the graphic works of old masters. On the contrary, they often bring much higher bids. Even well-preserved woodcuts by Dürer and many of his contemporaries and followers may occasionally be picked up at an auction for thirty dollars or less.

Original blocks and plates by the major old masters either belong to museums or have become the treasured possessions of wealthy private collectors. As such, they are inaccessible. Nevertheless, genuine old woodcut blocks are always coming to light, especially those originally used for letterpress purposes. Old copperplates can still be found in secondhand dealers' shops, antique shops and the metal stores of old printing houses. Although they are much rarer today than they were fifty years ago, they are by no means to be regarded as great rarities. According to the forger's period and ability, these blocks and plates will display signs of modification and retouching. If an original bore a valueless signature, it could easily be hammered out and a more sought-after and remunerative engraver's signature engraved into the repolished surface. Unsigned plates make forgery considerably easier. In the case of woodcuts, an original signature may be sawn out together with the surrounding areas of the block and a piece of wood furnished with the new and valuable signature carefully fitted into its place.

Dr. Heinrich Leporini, much respected curator of the Albertina in Vienna, considers that the question "how far a later reprint from an original plate may not be regarded as genuine depends on the particular circumstances."

This rather generous interpretation would not seem to be legally tenable. The seal of absolute authenticity can only be awarded to original prints which were made by the artist or his assistants. Exactly what attitude to adopt toward reprints made at a later date from original plates on contemporary paper with contemporary ink is, of course, another matter.

Also to be ranged in this group of fakes and falsifications are prints made from a genuine woodcut or engraving which has been retouched in order to simulate the appearance of a first or second state and reap the higher financial rewards accruing. Re-engraving is not the only way in which a worn plate can be rendered usable by the qualified craftsman. Parts of an engraving may be hammered out and repolished or sections of the image filled with powdered chalk, talc or other readily cohesive material to prevent their taking ink and so appearing on the print. This method produces a renovated "state."

The careless manner in which early prints were often kept is responsible for the fact that many of them have sustained serious damage. Because their value depends to a large extent on the width and condition of their margins and rises in relation to their mint state, a paying branch of forgery is devoted to amplifying or extending margins and washing, bleaching and renovating paper.

Innumerable prints have been damaged by being placed in books, framed, stored or devoured by small creatures. Paper provides sustenance for the common weevil, several species of cockroach, the so-called bookworm, various kinds of mite, death-watch beetle, book scorpion, meal worm, teredo and silverfish. Many of these are attracted only by certain ingredients in the raw materials from which paper is manufactured, notably size. This predilection accounts for the destruction of strongly sized papers, bookbindings and, in particular, the interior of a book's spine.

Prints look extremely unattractive when riddled with small holes as though by shot-gun pellets. Many beetles even drive regular canals into the body of the paper. Although the repair of these damaged areas may not be downright forgery, it is, strictly speaking, fraudulent to simulate the pristine condition of a print by renovation. What must definitely be regarded as forgery is the insertion of sizable patches in order to re-create extensive areas of the original. A print's state of preservation is vital to its evaluation, both from the material and artistic aspect. On this principle, the term forgery must be applied to any form of renovation which involves the refashioning of substantial parts of a print or its amplification with components taken from other genuine but damaged sheets. (It is a favorite trick to concoct a new and "perfect" engraving by cannibalizing the ruins of several others.) Another definitely fraudulent practice is to affix missing margins.

While this type of forgery can be extraordinarily tedious, it is no less profitable. It entails accurately cementing-in the missing areas with paper taken from old sheets or pages, mainly unprinted flyleaves, which bears at least some resemblance to the print under repair. This the forger soaks and either inserts into damaged areas or adds to outside edges, whichever is appropriate. Then, before the whole surface dries, he irons-in the substituted sheet. If the texture of the paper exhibits variations after this treatment, it may be homogenized by spraying-on a solution of cellite or nitrocellulose, which not only protects it against disintegration but makes it receptive to ink.

If renovation has been undertaken on an extensive scale it is advisable to immerse the entire sheet in a solution of nitrocellulose diluted with amylacetate, thus effecting uniform penetration. This process is detectable by microscopic and chemical examination, but it will normally deceive the naked eye.

The removal of spots of mold caused by various species of fungus and other bacteria comes under the heading of restoration.

Microphotography can yield valuable information about any

suspect print, from early woodcuts to modern linocuts and from medieval ruddle drawings to graphic works by living artists. Light cast onto the sheet from different angles renders it possible to distinguish just as surely between the strokes of a lead, silver or graphite pencil as between those of a goose quill and a steel nib or between a genuine copperplate print and a zincographic reproduction.

Forgery and falsification are equally prevalent in the sphere of old maps. These excite enthusiasm among collectors not only because they are often beautifully engraved and enriched with decorative pictorial representations of great charm but also, and more importantly, because of their geographic, historical and cultural significance. Complete atlases being as valuable as they are rare, it is a profitable form of activity to replace missing sheets. If deficiencies of this kind are remedied by the addition of genuine loose sheets, the operation counts as repair. However, because genuine sheets are extremely difficult to come by, forgeries are enlisted to take their place. The large format of a map in itself makes reproduction by any printing process difficult, so the forger's only alternative is to draw it by hand. This invariably leads to detection.

Another very profitable line is the hand coloring of monochrome woodcuts, engravings and even atlases of which contemporary colored originals exist. The sheets are aged by being left to bleach in the sun.

One substantial difficulty posed by the coloring of old prints lies in the porousness of the paper. Contemporary hand coloring, whether of early woodcuts or single-plate, i.e. monochromatic, French and English copperplate engravings and lithographs, was carried out immediately after printing. The paints thus lodged in the outer surface of the paper because binding agents in the original pulp prevented them from penetrating it.

If painting is carried out on old paper, however, the water colors will infiltrate it so thoroughly that their presence will be betrayed on the back of the sheet.

One way of preventing water colors from seeping through is to coat the sheet by spraying it with one of the solutions used to bind its ingredients. Careful overpainting can be detected only by chemical and structural examination, and these tests become even more difficult if the forger, having applied his paints with due regard for contemporary formulas and technique, has subjected them to natural bleaching.

Special attention should be paid to engravings originally printed in several colors, i.e. from several different plates. Colored engravings which have faded to any great extent command a far lower price than those with still brilliant colors. This circumstance lends an added attraction to forgery by means of hand coloring and retouching.

"Oeuvre catalogues" provide both experts and dealers in the rich and varied field of graphic art with valuable points of reference. These put into dictionary form the total output of major wood carvers, copperplate engravers and etchers, paying due regard to the all-important question of historical development. They also describe the origination of individual prints in every known state.

The scientific research of which these works are a distillation makes it possible to identify any print with a probability bordering on certainty. If a print exhibits even the slightest divergence from an oeuvre analysis, this circumstance is enough to excite the gravest suspicion.

Le Peintre-Graveur, an oeuvre catalogue in French by Adam Bartsch, devotes twenty-two volumes to the graphic art of the fifteenth to eighteenth centuries, while Loys Delteil's illustrated oeuvre work comprises no less than thirty-one volumes. Bjørklund and others concentrated principally on Rembrandt. Gustav Schiefler devoted his oeuvre catalogue, constructed on similar principles, to the work of the painter Max Liebermann. Käthe Kollwitz's output was exhaustively dealt with by Klipstein. H. W. Singer's *Handbook for Copperplate Collectors* lists the oeuvre catalogues dealing with this specialized field of artistic-cum-scientific research.

To obtain reliable material based on the latest results of scientific research, it is always advisable to consult the most recent technical literature.

Sale catalogues and other prospectuses identify works of graphic art by means of abbreviations, capital letters, roman and arabic numerals, and names. All these serve to pin down the exact origin of a particular print. The letter B, for instance, stands for Bartsch's oeuvre catalogue, while the Arabic numeral following it refers to the section in which the print is described. Roman numerals stand for the state of a print, e.g. I is a first state.

Some specialized works deal with the output of individual sculptors and painters partly on the same basis as an oeuvre catalogue and partly on other lines. Others devote themselves to individual periods and genres. None of these books, however, achieves the same complete coverage in the province of graphic art as an oeuvre catalogue.

Collectors, experts and dealers attach considerable importance to the pedigree of a print, and its value is enhanced if it bears a stamp of origin from a good house. The reputable and discriminating collector includes only items of high value in his collection, and a print with such a background speaks for itself.

The Dutch art connoisseur Frits Lugt spent decades in a quest for stamps of ownership, and embodied the results of his research in *Les Marques de Collections, de Dessins et d'Estampes*. Valuable conclusions may be drawn from the facsimile reproductions and descriptions contained in this volume. Any print which displays one of these stamps should to some extent be judged from that angle, too.

Fake stamps of origin occur on genuine as well as forged prints. In the former case they serve to enhance the value of a pedigree, and in the latter they discourage closer scrutiny, a stamp being evidence of a background which should in itself vouch for the authenticity of a print.

6

❦❦❦❦❦❦❦❦❦

Objets d'Art

AT every period in its history, humanity has set store by the glowing radiance of gold and the gentle luster of silver. Whether of a religious, ornamental or utilitarian nature, gold and silver articles from all periods and regions of the inhabited world are numbered among our most precious and eloquent cultural possessions.

Gold was known even in early Pharaonic times. The Egyptian royal tombs have yielded up countless works of art, ranging from small rings to complete masks, made of the precious yellow metal. The Etruscans fashioned crowns and drinking vessels out of gold. Greek artists cast sculptural works of incomparable purity in gold and finished them off with the graver.

Gold was not employed in works of art or utensils merely for its rarity, intrinsic value and beautiful color, but also because it possessed a durability, in the widest sense of the word, unsurpassed by any other known material. It was known empirically, if not scientifically, to be acid-resistant. It was not susceptible to the effects of weathering or oxidization. The golden utensils, jewelry and religious articles which accompanied the Pharaohs into their tombs so many thousands of years ago have survived, intact and unaltered, as no other man-made objects from such far distant times have ever done.

Goethe makes Gretchen say in *Faust,* Part I, "All strives for gold and all on gold depends." And it is hardly surprising that gold has always been a favorite target of the thief, wherever and in whatever form it has been hoarded, whether in the Near or Far East or in pre-Columbian Central and South America. Because sculptural works and coins made of gold could be identified, they were ruthlessly melted down. That is the main reason, apart from migrations, natural catastrophes and wars, why early art treasures made of this time-resistant material are so extraordinarily rare. All that survive in any quantity are specimens, mainly in damaged condition, of gold coins which once circulated in large numbers.

It has never yet been established beyond doubt where gold was first discovered. The Sumerian works of art unearthed not long ago in Mesopotamia, the area bounded by the Euphrates and Tigris, would seem to date back at least to the fortieth century B.C. Yet gold may well have existed in prehistoric times. As much as five thousand years ago, Menes, the founder of the Egyptian First Dynasty, used small batons of crude gold as a standard of value. Weighing the modern equivalent of 14 grams and inscribed with hieroglyphs signifying his name, they were probably a rudimentary form of gold coin.

Gold is the most malleable of all metals. It can be drawn into fine wire 1/1000 of a millimeter in diameter and beaten or rolled into a foil 1/14,000 of a millimeter thick. In the latter condition it becomes translucent, which is probably the best illustration of just how delicate gold foil can be.

Goldsmiths were exploiting this outstanding characteristic of the precious metal in very early times, for it permitted an extraordinarily varied and effective treatment of surface. Very delicate modeling can even be done with hardwood tools or by polishing.

COINS

The forgery of works in gold and silver is probably as old as the use of those precious metals itself, and there is definite evidence that it was practiced on the earliest coins. A distinction must here be drawn between two types of forgery: (1) the semiofficial debasement of an alloy, which economized on precious metal and made a profit for the authorities, and (2) counterfeiting, in which molds made from original coins were used to cast pieces from gold-colored metal or other material which was later gilded.

The first gold coins known not only to have served as a model for all later coins, both in shape and method of manufacture, but also to have been forged at an early date were minted by Gyges of Lydia in 670 B.C.

Counterfeiting was from the very first punishable by death. There has been no substantial change in the methods, either of falsification or forgery, even in the most recent past. Whenever a ruler's coffers yawned in a threatening manner, the remedy was to fill them with ducats whose fine gold content was appreciably lower than the standard officially laid down and publicly adhered to, or silver thalers whose pure silver content had been debased. In Spain, for example, there was a period when more counterfeit and debased silver coins — notably the "duro" — were in circulation than genuine.

Originally manufactured for utilitarian and commercial reasons, coins early came to be regarded as a new and welcome medium of artistic expression. Portrayals of deities and rulers, symbols and emblems, inscriptions and, later, coats of arms with national insignia, were all reproduced in sculptural terms with ever-increasing perfection.

Coining is a far more tempting proposition than forging individual examples of the gold- and silversmith's art, for objects produced mechanically and in great quantities lend themselves more easily to imitation. Nevertheless, the outlines on molded counterfeits always show up in far vaguer relief than those of the minted originals, and are easily detectable. There also exist, though in smaller numbers, genuine cast coins, whose counterfeit versions are extremely difficult to identify as such because they were produced by exactly the same technique as the originals. Forgers also used and still use genuine dies. Provided that the material used is identical, imitations produced in this way cannot be distinguished from original coins. We are here confronted by the same sort of problem which was posed by prints taken from genuine blocks on contemporary paper with original inks. This does not, as we have already mentioned, prevent the more perceptive collector, expert and dealer from claiming that he can tell whether a coin is genuine by "feel."

In 1588 Enea Vico wrote a now almost unobtainable work dealing with the counterfeiting of ancient coins. Entitled *Discorso sopra le Medaglie de gli Antichi,* it attempted to analyze the forms and methods of forgery in this specialized field.

Coins of the ancient world which had been illicitly minted at or shortly after their date of origin were much sought after and highly prized as collectors' pieces. Forgers needed no second bidding: they prepared two-piece molds from old minted coins, fitted them together, and proceeded to cast counterfeits. Only experienced connoisseurs could tell a minted from a molded coin, especially when the forger pared off the ridges or extrusions and skillfully went over inscriptions and reliefs by hand afterwards. Remarkably convincing results could be achieved in this way, especially as the expert had to rely on the naked eye, magnifying glasses being not yet in use. Today, coins counterfeited by the casting process can be detected with comparative ease by accurate measurement. Metal contracts when molded, so that the counterfeit will differ from the original in both thickness and diameter. The more ingenious forgers evolved various methods of counteracting this phenomenon, but even when they succeeded in keeping it within narrow limits delicate measuring instruments will still distinguish unerringly between genuine and fake. Counterfeits were hawked around the dealers, who got rid of them on inexperienced collectors. Pieces of particular value were occasionally unearthed in graveyards in the presence of a numismatist or conveniently discovered in burial urns and other receptacles. Only collectors with a delicate and highly developed sense of style never allowed themselves to be duped by counterfeits of high quality. In the year 1568 a dealer offered Count Fugger, the wealthy merchant and distinguished collector of coins, a gold piece bearing the profile of Seleucus I Nicator, Macedonian ruler of Syria. The connoisseur declined the coin in a written note which ran: "I consider the Seleucus to be a casting and modern, whatever Juan sculptor may say."

The fact that people had to be, and were, very much on their guard against counterfeits of ancient coins, even in the seventeenth century, is illustrated by a letter sent to Duke Philip of Pomerania and Stettin by the Augsburg antiquarian Ph. Hainhofer in 1610: "I know nothing of antique coins, it is true, nor, for lack of time, have I devoted myself to them; but others, who imagine that they do, consider numismata to be original and authentic mainly because they have come from a reputable source and been accumulated for many years at great pains and expense."

Coins are collected for a number of very different reasons. Many ancient coins are veritable little works of art with splendidly elaborated reliefs of rulers, emblems or symbols which evoke a high degree of aesthetic pleasure. Others are collected for their value alone, and still others from a wish to see periods of past history expressed plastically in a valuable medium.

It is the most insatiable collector who most easily falls prey to the forger. The coin cabinet of one of the first major collectors, Duke Jean de Berry, contained innumerable counterfeits of Dutch and French origin.

But was he really a victim of forgery? Wilhelm von Bode thought he had found indications that the duke filled gaps in his collection by having the missing coins made for him.

Similar motives prompted Valerio Belli, a gold- and silversmith of the Renaissance, to counterfeit coins himself. Francesco Hollanda noted in his *Discourses* that Belli had shown him "fifty medals of purest gold which he had produced with his own hands after the manner of the ancients, in so wonderful a way that it caused the high opinion which I had of the ancient world to seem exaggerated."

Vasari records that the painter Marmita of Parma gave up his own craft and "devoted himself entirely to the making of medals in the ancient fashion." Marmita's son Ludovico, too, forged coins with a proficiency which Vasari described as of *"grandissima utilità."*

To satisfy the growing demand, regular counterfeiters' workshops were set up of which the foremost were at Padua. Their imperial Roman coins and medals, which became known as "Patavini," penetrated even the French and German markets.

Two master coiners of wide repute were the antiquarian Giovanni Cavino and the architect, painter, archeologist and author Pirro Ligorio (1493-1580). Cavino plied his craft so conscientiously that he used to consult the historian Alessandro Bassiano in doubtful cases.

GOLDSMITHS' AND SILVERSMITHS' WORK

With the growing craze for collecting gems (mainly in gold settings) and other small works of art from the ancient world, all of
which had in their time found imitators ranging from the slavish
dabbler to the master craftsman, coiners started to devote their skill
to this type of valuable, too, often using an early imitation as a
model. They also executed special pieces to order. It is significant
that an artist of Ghiberti's class should have openly admitted in
his *Memoirs* that he had carved "three antique figures" on a carnelian and furnished the stone with "an inscription appropriate to
the scene depicted" — *"lettere antiche titolate nel nome di Nerone,"*
to be exact. The man who employed him to do this was none other
than Cosimo de' Medici. It is probable that Cosimo was also responsible for ordering someone to engrave a carnelian in the Medici
collection with the cipher of the Hellenistic stonemason Pyrgoteles.

Apart from forgeries of sought-after contemporary *objets d'art*
or coins, the Middle Ages also brought forth, as a result of the
newly awakened admiration for Roman and Hellenic art, archaic
forgeries so convincing that they can represent a danger even to the
most experienced of modern collectors. Medals, articles of religious
significance, sacrificial lamps, rings, brooches and pieces of jewelry
— especially those adorned with precious stones — passed from the
forger's hands into even the most celebrated collections.

A high price was set on the artistic handiwork of gold- and
silversmiths, and the substantial sums disbursed by churches and
monasteries for sacred vessels, chalices, candlesticks, crucifixes and
monstrances provided these craftsmen with so strong and continuous an incentive that their violent competition gave birth to some
magnificent pieces of jewelry. The art of working with precious
metals was far more intensively developed at Nuremberg and
Cologne than in other cities. There is no very concrete explanation

for this, for master craftsmen did not by any means receive all their most important commissions from the area where they worked. Holland and other countries also had districts which specialized in goldsmith's work.

The silversmiths of Cologne had already gained an international reputation by the middle of the thirteenth century. When, in 1494, the city councilors of Frankfurt-am-Main resolved to make a presentation to a royal guest and his consort, they sent for a range of choice jewelry made by the gold- and silversmiths of Cologne with the object of selecting a suitable piece in plenary session.

Frankfurt's own goldsmiths' guild lodged a formal protest against the council's intention to give preference to Cologne-made work. However, since the councilors had already picked out two pieces of jewelry and were unwilling to reconsider their decision, the Frankfurt goldsmiths resorted to a simple but, by present standards, not very ethical expedient: two masters of the guild, Daniel Fogler and Bernhard Weidelich, were commissioned to copy the pieces.

We are prompted to ask ourselves what term should be applied to imitative works of art like these, which came into being at the same time as their originals: copy, imitation, or forgery?

The lack of respect with which the Frankfurt council treated creative work by the master craftsmen of Cologne can probably be judged only in the spirit of the period, which we have already discussed elsewhere.

While strict regulations laid down by the guilds in order to safeguard honest gold- and silversmiths might render the manufacture and sale of inferior gold- and silverware difficult, they could never exclude the possibility that forgers and falsifiers would continue to devise new ways and means of marketing their products, which they naturally adorned with fake hallmarks and emblems. When the first pieces of hallmarked silver appeared on the market there also appeared, almost simultaneously, the first imitations of these punched marks of inspection or symbols identifying a particular craftsman or workshop. Hallmarks form a special field of expert research and have been dealt with in an excellent work by Marc Rosenberg, *Der Goldschmiede Merkzeichen* (Frankfurt 1889, new edition 1956).

High-class forgeries dating from the same period as the originals are remarkably hard to identify in cases where a forger has used the same alloy as the creative goldsmith. Examination of materials may fail to settle the question, and there is also a limit to the efficacy of stylistic criticism when a forger not only copied the shape of a piece meticulously but was as imbued with the spirit of his time as the original artist himself. If he economized on materials and employed an inferior alloy, of course, empirical evidence of forgery will not be hard to obtain.

Nearly two hundred works by the Florentine goldsmith and sculptor Cellini (1500-1574) are preserved in museums and private collections. The majority are definitely not by Cellini, and the fact that most of them are furnished with documentary evidence does not put their authenticity beyond dispute. In 1850 the Berlin Kunstkammer acquired a "silver basin by Benvenuto Cellini depicting a battle of the Amazons" from a Cologne antiquarian for a thousand friedrichs d'or. With this work of art went a learned treatise which claimed that it had been made by Cellini for Ercole d'Este in the year 1559. In Volume IX of the *Organ für Christliche Kunst,* published at Cologne in 1859, attention was drawn to the similarity between this work and silverware in the possession of Don Carlos, pretender to the Spanish throne, which had been made by a Toulouse-born goldsmith working in London.

Recent or present-day fakes are seldom made of inferior material unless they are crude and primitive imitations. Men who counterfeit valuable originals do not economize on gold and silver, being only too aware that practical tests will infallibly give them away, while a critical appraisal of smith's, embosser's, stamper's, engraver's or molder's technique need not always be feared.

Apart from trivial alterations in the shape of certain tools and in the method of soldering, adjusting and setting, gold- and silversmiths' technique has undergone scarcely any basic change from the earliest times to the present day. The tools now commercially obtainable are made of different material and display certain modifications in shape, but they can easily be adapted to conform with those of earlier periods. Works in gold or silver are almost entirely free of the knotty problems which must be overcome when imitating or forging old paintings and sculptures, in respect to wood, canvas, paints and even brushes. The forger can bestow his whole attention on the problem of style. This is of supreme importance, for there must inevitably come into play, in the forging of old works of art on a very high plane, every obstacle between the actual creator and the imitator which can possibly arise from the incompatibility of spiritual experience in two different epochs.

To be absolutely precise, the term "smith" is a misnomer when applied to the worker in precious metals, for articles of gold and silver may be manufactured by cold processes as well as hot, and a piece which has been cast, punched, rolled, or stamped from dies has no connection with smith's work in the exact sense.

The designation "smith" has been transferred from the blacksmith who operates on glowing iron with a sledge hammer to the craftsman who shapes precious metal with a small hammer which is normally double-headed, smaller on one side than the other, and convex on both.

This form of technique might be more aptly and explicitly termed "chasing," because the sheets of gold and silver, which rest on a firm but resilient base, have the design chased or embossed into them. Hammer blows applied to the reverse side produce recesses or indentations which are crude at first, become finer as work progresses, and finally assume clearly defined outlines.

The further a relief is embossed into a sheet — or out of it, depending on the point of view — the thinner the metal becomes. The extremities of a face in profile, or a hand which almost reaches out of a composition, will be only fractionally as thick as the unembossed areas. It is this variation in the thickness of material which differentiates the embossed relief unmistakably from molded and, still more, from mechanically produced work, whose "walls" display very much less contrast.

Masters of the classical period used to hammer jugs with tapering necks and swelling bodies from a single sheet of metal. The *Apfelpokal,* the "apple cup" designed by Albrecht Dürer and executed by the Nuremberg silversmith Ludwig Krug at the beginning of the sixteenth century, exhibits an almost incredible mastery of technique and material. Another piece whose shape and ornamentation make it a miracle of workmanship is an early seventeenth-century silver ewer by the Utrecht master Adam van Vianen. A contemporary writer noted with amazement and admiration that it was likewise *"uyt een stuck geslagen"* (beaten out of one piece). A conventional hammer could not be used for work of this sort because the neck of a jug was too small to admit a human hand. Accordingly, the metal sheet was beaten out with a long-handled, jointed hammer of ingenious construction which the goldsmith introduced into the vessel's interior. The small hammer at the nether end of this gadget worked rather like a firing pin and was operated by a movable lever set at an angle.

The true masters of the gold- and silversmiths' art imposed the most exacting standards on themselves and their work. Others, not excluding many talented members of the profession, were not averse to short cuts. If it required too much effort or skill to beat a particular composition out of a single sheet, they constructed it from several separate components. When making a jug, for instance, they would beat the sheet into a cylindrical shape as work progressed, leaving the whole surface accessible to the hammer at every stage. Eventually they rolled up the embossed sheet until the two ends fitted exactly. Soldering was applied so that it was largely disguised by the ornamentation on the handle. Where it was still visible the outer skin was hammered into the general design or ornamental beading, giving jug or cup the appearance of a unified whole. The base of the vessel was affixed with soldered joints on the interior or exterior.

The more three-dimensional a relief and the smaller and more delicate the figure work or ornamentation, the greater the variety of tools needed to produce it. Corrections could be made only by hammering out any areas which had been too deeply embossed. The connoisseur should have no difficulty in distinguishing handiwork of this kind from a mechanically produced article or even a finely engraved casting.

Forgery using the craftsman's original technique is unremunerative. Even though fantastic prices are paid for fine examples of early gold- and silversmiths' work, the risk that the fruits of his extremely arduous endeavors may be unmasked is out of all proportion to the forger's potential gain.

As early as the second century B.C. a tendency toward simplification gave rise to the techniques of stamping and punching sheets of precious metal. Then, as now, the soft gold or silver was compressed between two dies, made of some hard material, which fitted into one another. The resulting effect was similar to that achieved by beating, in that one side of the sheet exhibited indentations while the other was raised.

In the technique of stamping, which is really identical with the primitive "striking" (as of early coins), the design was originally borne by only one surface. When the hard metal die, almost always engraved in negative or matrix form, was driven into the softer precious metal, the surface of the latter took on the shape of the former in reverse. The use of both negative and positive dies later enabled each side of the sheet to be stamped in a single operation.

Hans Lobsinger of Nuremberg invented a machine for the manufacture of ornamental metal strips as long ago as 1530. These strips found a ready market, which explains why absolutely identical reliefs turn up in the work of entirely different master craftsmen. Mechanically stamped and, later, punched sheets which could be simply set in or soldered on substantially reduced the time normally required to produce a vessel by hand.

The quest for originality impelled goldsmiths and silversmiths to evolve numerous different techniques, of which several were often embodied in the same work. A strong predilection for naturalism led, at the close of the sixteenth century, to an oddity which we meet again in our own day, this time in the form of galvanoplasty: the lifelike reproduction of leaves, beetles or lizards in gold or silver. For this purpose, small plants or insects were embedded in a casting material which, after its contents had been burned away, served as a mold.

In the case of articles which had to withstand intensive wear, chasing was soon replaced by casting, and as time went by craftsmen exploited the convenience of this process for other purposes.

Works in silver, especially those with a large surface area, were frequently gilded. Silver gilt of the highest quality is known as "vermeil." In this process, silver foil is coated with a mixture of gold and mercury. The mercury dissipates when heated, leaving a layer of pure gold on the surface of the silver. This method of hot gilding was already used in the ancient world.

One way of simulating the genuine, silvery vermeil produced by hot gilding is to use a galvanic process. The task of differentiating between the two kinds of gilding is very difficult and must be delegated to the expert.

A third method of gilding is the plating process, in which gold foil is rolled on to silver and soldered. This treatment can only be applied to certain types of work.

Just as silver can be gilded, so the external appearance of copper and other metals or alloys can be enhanced by silver-plating. Heavy pressure being enough to bond silver to a copper-based material without recourse to solder, the rolled plating method is the most durable. Galvanoplastic silvering is not as long-lived as silver-plating.

Precious metals were also used in combination. Rich ornamentation on articles of silver and gold was often "inlaid" in a combination of the two metals. This technique is also known as "damascening" because countless different examples of it occur on the weapons for which Damascus was famous.

In the nineteenth century, a Russian goldsmith succeeded in reproducing archaic styles to such perfection that his works were for years and decades regarded as undisputed originals from a civilization which had expired two thousand years earlier. Enormous prices were paid for them by governments and private individuals on the assumption that expert opinions are infallible.

The case of the so-called *Tiara of Saitaphernes,* a Scythian royal crown in three tiers, is, by its nature and the circumstances surrounding it, unique in the history of forgery. One of the *pièces de résistance* in the Louvre's collection of antiquities and long regarded as a masterpiece dating from the third century B.C., this crown was made by the Odessa goldsmith Israel Ruchomovski in A.D. 1880.

The *Tiara of Saitaphernes,* which might better be termed the tiara of Ruchomovski, won international acclaim. Of much greater interest to the connoisseur, however, are drinking cups in classical

Greek style, the *Achilles and Minerva,* a group sculpted in solid gold, and a necklace in gold relief with pierced ornamentation — all of them made by the same master craftsman from Odessa. The photographs in our illustrations convey some idea of his proficiency as a forger. Few gold- or silversmiths have ever rivaled his skill in the imitative field — or ever will, unless there comes a time when some other crowning glory of the goldsmith's art which has hitherto been admired as an undisputed original also turns out to be a masterly imitation.

The planning which went into the forgery of the tiara indicated that shrewd minds had been at work. So that the sudden appearance of this "ancient" work of art should seem more plausible, it was carefully pre-wrapped in a cocoon of legendary if not historical circumstance. In the third century B.C., so the story ran, prominent citizens of Olbia, a Greek colony situated at the confluence of the Hypanis and Borysthenes (now the Bug and Dnieper), decided to present the Scythian king Saitaphernes with a three-tiered golden helmet in token of their gratitude and loyalty.

After two thousand years of oblivion this treasure unexpectedly reappeared in Vienna, where a mysterious Rumanian offered it to the art collector Count Wilczek and to Baron Nathanael Rothschild, another patron of the arts. The crown, a unique work of art in solid gold and weighing about a pound, was richly ornamented and bore a raised inscription identifying it as a gift from the Olbiats to Saitaphernes. The Rumanian's asking price was 100,000 gold crowns.

Otto Bendorf, an authority in the archeological field, pronounced the tiara to be a splendid example of pre-Christian goldsmith's art and advised the two art patrons to buy it as a gift for the Austrian Museum of Arts and Crafts. The directors of the museum's department of antiquities, Leisching and Bucher, found it "peculiar and suspicious" that a work of art in pure gold more than two thousand years old should exhibit only superficial damage, none of which affected its sculptural relief. They deduced that the indentations had been made by artificial means and warned Count Wilczek and Baron Rothschild against purchasing it. Their advice was taken.

A few weeks later the mysterious Rumanian turned up in Paris with his royal treasure accompanied by a second man, apparently his brother. What had failed in Vienna succeeded in Paris. The Louvre, its experts having examined the tiara and found it to be genuine, bought it for 200,000 gold francs.

While certain doubts about the golden helmet were quietly and discreetly voiced from time to time, it did not become an object of open controversy until a Parisian jeweler alleged that an Odessa goldsmith had been commissioned to produce the *Tiara of Saitaphernes* from pictorial references by two Rumanian art dealers. What was more, he could name the men involved: the brothers Gauchman, and Israel Ruchomovski.

The ensuing debate between leading art experts was redoubled in intensity when, in May, 1903, the Parisian art journal *Les Arts* entered the lists with an article by André Falize, who devoted almost four pages to reaffirming the tiara's authenticity and casting doubt on the admissions of the goldsmith Ruchomovski, who had meanwhile come to Paris in person.

The art expert employed by the Ministry of the Interior, Clermont-Ganneau, conceded to his minister that he possessed "no especial competence in the field of ancient Greek art" and had established the tiara's authenticity at the time of its purchase on the basis of his "intuitive views." The 200,000 gold francs which the Louvre had raised by dint of a special overdraft was a high price to pay for this inexpert expert's intuition.

The same issue of *Les Arts* contained reproductions of a magnificently engraved golden chalice, a classical sculpture in solid gold portraying Achilles and Minerva, and a necklace, part of the Reitlinger collection in Paris, all of which the prolific Ruchomovski claimed to be his own work. Similarities between the figure work on the lowest tier of the helmet and that on the necklace proved beyond all doubt that they came from the same hand.

Such experts as still clung stubbornly to the theory that the tiara was genuine were finally silenced by yet another piece of testimony to the contrary.

It appeared that, as early as 1897, the director of the Odessa Museum had denounced the Hochmann brothers (known in Paris as Gauchman) for having commissioned work from the goldsmith Israel Ruchomovski, who plied his craft in a suburb of the city. They got him to execute "archaic" works of art by providing pictorial references for their figurative composition, such as *Antiquités de la Russie Méridionale* (Tolstoy, Konderhof and Reinach, Paris, 1891) and Weisser's *Pictorial Atlas of World History*. This material had served as Ruchomovski's references for his ornamentation and inscriptions. The champions of authenticity threw in the sponge when Ruchomovski, challenged to prove his avowed ability to imitate the composition and technique of pre-Christian goldsmiths' work, demonstrated it by producing an "Etruscan" piece — this time without pictorial references.

The fact that he made use of ancient models does not diminish the artistry of his work. From the technical aspect, Ruchomovski stood on the lonely heights of genuine ability.

The sense of shock with which the international art world greeted the news of Ruchomovski's fakes was heightened by recollection of another affair, only thirty years old. This concerned a bust of the poet Benivieni in early fifteenth-century style which had been acquired for 700 francs by a Count Novilos from the Florentine art dealer Giovanni Frappa and resold for 13,000 francs to

Count Nieuwekirke, then director of the Louvre. When Novilos declined to pass on a prearranged share of the profits to Frappa, the latter revealed that what "originated at the beginning of the fifteenth century" and was "attributed to the school of the greatest masters of the Renaissance, Donatello, Verrocchio, Mino da Fiesole" was really a work executed by Giovanni Bastianini in the year 1864. As a model for the poet, of whom no portrayal existed, the great sculptor had used the foreman of a Florentine tobacco factory.

Bastianini was also the author of a "medieval original" (a bust of Savonarola) acquired by the Victoria and Albert Museum. Perhaps the finest imitative sculptor of all time apart from Dossena, Bastianini declared that he had accepted Frappa's commissions because he could not afford to turn down orders worth three hundred francs.

Just to deepen the cloud of misgiving which brooded over the authority of art experts, another and, from the scientific standpoint, far more important fake was discovered, this time involving the august French Academy of Sciences. Vrain-Lucas, one of the most proficient forgers of historical documents, had sold this erudite body the "original documents of Blaise Pascal," whose purport was nothing more or less than that the law of gravity had been formulated not by Newton but by Pascal, the French philosopher and physicist.

Unmindful of uproar in the art world and uncertainty in the art market, forgers continued to manufacture treasures and trinkets of every description. Some Etruscan slippers turned up in Kiev, spun from the finest gold wire and as supple as silk. In London a coin was put up for auction bearing the head of a Roman ruler who had never existed.

Many of these imitations were of an extraordinarily high standard, and it cannot be doubted that perfect copies of work from the classical periods of the gold- and silversmith's glorious art found their way into reputable collections.

One time-honored forger's practice is to raise the "status" of a work. Unidentified pieces are equipped with an artist's, inspector's or guild's mark to increase their salability; individual features are refashioned in earlier styles, crude work is increased in value by chiseling, beating, scraping, engraving or embellishing; old-seeming enamels are inlaid in added recesses. In short, forgers seize every opportunity of transforming genuine but unimpressive works into masterpieces.

At the beginning of the nineteenth century, some excellent forgeries of Etruscan and Roman works in gold and silver were produced in Rome by Alessandro and Augusto Castelani, who had acquired the requisite technical skill from their father. Their fakes are among the best imitations of early works of art in precious metals.

Far from confining themselves to the production of work which was merely genuine in style, the two men also copied undisputed originals with the utmost accuracy. In the use of materials, too, they faithfully followed the early masters. It is very difficult to recognize a Castelani fake. Both the brothers and the excellent chiselers and engravers who worked under their instructions came as close to the original article, in proportion, decor and composition, as was technically and stylistically possible.

After Augusto's death, Alessandro got into difficulties arising from political intrigues. Accordingly, he packed up and moved to Paris, where he tried his luck as a singer. But fortune smiled less kindly on his larynx than on his hands; he turned his back on Paris and once more settled down in Naples, where he began to deal in antiquities. Whether the early examples of the goldsmith's art which formed part of his stock in trade were really genuine or included some of his own efforts must forever remain in doubt.

The admiration and esteem accorded to the goldsmiths and silversmiths of the Renaissance is matched by the prices paid for their work. A splendidly engraved and richly ornamented heavy silver dish by Renato Brozzi fetched £700 in a London sale before 1914. This, so it seemed, was unquestionably a work by "a great Italian silversmith of the sixteenth century, one of Benvenuto Cellini's contemporaries," who rivaled the latter as closely in technique as he did in power of creative composition.

A diligent search of technical literature and ancient Italian chronicles yielded no mention of Renato Brozzi. Then word came from a certain Ferruccio Brasi at Parma. Renato Brozzi had apparently been one of his apprentices. The "master craftsman of the *cinquecento*" had taken the silver plates which he had been given to finish off in the course of his daily work and transformed them into Renaissance masterpieces.

SEALS

There is a satisfying harmony of artistic and historical interest in the remarkably attractive collector's field which concerns itself with seals and crests. Very large sums are paid for signets of especial beauty or historical significance.

Only one seal of unquestioned authenticity survives from the first millennium, the signet of Emperor Lothair I (d. 855), engraved in crystal and preserved in the so-called Lothair Cross, which belongs to Aachen Cathedral.

Both secular and ecclesiastical authorities used to have accurate replicas made of their worn signets. These duplicates are not forgeries, but neither are they originals in the strictest sense of the word. It is almost impossible to draw the line between originals and facsimiles in this field.

If the first indubitably genuine seal dates from the tenth century, the earliest surviving forgery dates from the beginning of the eleventh. Carved in ivory by monks of the monastery of St. Maximin, it was used to seal the "Dagobert Parchments" — also forged by them — which were greatly sought after, being the records of the last of the Merovingians, a son of Clotair II. This seal is now in the possession of the Brussels Museum.

Forgeries of medieval crests in metal usually took the form of cast replicas which were afterwards finished by hand.

Signets carved in stone, particularly those from the age of richly decorated escutcheons, won a special place in the hearts of collectors. As a consequence, the "golden signet ring of Duke Jean de Berry" came up for auction no less than four times in the space of a few years.

It would burst the covers of a book designed to deal with the art of forgery only in outline if every special or secondary province were accorded the same detailed treatment as that devoted to the principal themes. For this reason, only brief allusion can be made to the forgery of greatly sought-after trinkets which do not fall directly within the scope of gold- and silversmith's work but constitute a field of their own.

ENAMELS

Skillful enamelwork has been remarkably popular in every period. The technique of manufacturing enamels by staining vitreous paste and of affixing the delicate material to a metallic ground has passed through a number of stages. Contemporary techniques have been imitated at every period, and cellular, inlaid, relief and Limoges enamel may be encountered in forgeries of varying date. Shape and external features may deceive the eye, but even old imitations lack the elaborate and intricate workmanship which characterizes the handiwork of a true master of the art. The medieval craftsmen who produced Venetian gold enamel used to apply tiny pieces of gold foil to the enamel before it had set. In imitations, this effect is achieved by subsequent painting or cementing on. Forgers of our own day are unequal to the technical demands of enamelwork and incapable of reproducing the original materials.

The collector should beware if a piece displays the deposits of verdigris which indicate slight defects in the union between enamel and metal ground, normally copper, or small bubbles resulting from scorification of the enamel in its molten state. Almost all fakes are "aged" in this manner.

The fragility of enamel, which cracks easily, explains why well-preserved antiques are so remarkably rare. It also explains why the forger finds it profitable to restore damaged enamels of only moderate age. However, the fact that genuine old enamel will not fuse with new makes it necessary for restorers to replace damaged sections with substitutes ranging from simple, colored resinous lacquers to materials of extreme complexity. Its great adhesive powers, which are effective with metal and other surfaces, make pre-colored dental cement a useful foundation. This is afterwards coated with lacquer of an appropriate color, and the whole mass serves to fill out the damaged portion of the work under repair.

PRECIOUS AND SEMIPRECIOUS STONES

Artificial precious and semiprecious stones belong in the province of industrial production. They are without exception identifiable by their specific gravity, which varies considerably from that of genuine stones, and by spectral analysis. Art forgers use them occasionally, and whenever an old piece of jewelry proves to contain one or more synthetic precious stones the authenticity of the whole should be regarded with the gravest suspicion.

Gold-ornamented works in lapis lazuli, greatly prized by a large number of collectors, have been imitated from very early times.

Gold being too expensive a material to use on large articles, it was often replaced by gilded bronze. Candlesticks, brackets and vases in lapis lazuli, in particular, enjoyed great popularity at various times. Many purportedly Renaissance works originated in the Roman workshop established in 1900 by Augusto Valenzi. J. Pierpont Morgan, well known as an experienced collector, acquired two gold-embellished lapis lazuli columns in high Renaissance style. They, too, came from Augusto Valenzi's forger's workshop. Morgan placed them in the drawing room of his New York house on either side of a magnificent stove with colored embossed tiles which he had acquired in France. When winter came and the stove was lit, the precious columns began to wilt. Valenzi had not only carried out the ornamentation in gilded bronze instead of gold but had substituted another stone for the solid lapis lazuli which should have formed the core of the columns themselves and covered it with thin plates of genuine lapis lazuli invisibly cemented together. Unfortunately for him, the stone, the outer skin of lapis lazuli and the adhesives all had such dissimilar coefficients of expansion that the whole structure disintegrated.

ORNAMENTAL BOXES

An extensive and remunerative field of activity for the forger is that of ornamental boxes. Starting from modest beginnings in the fifteenth century, these delightful collectors' pieces attained a peak of artistic composition in the sixteenth and, more especially, in the seventeenth and eighteenth centuries. *Tabatières* of polished and later decorated silver, brass and tortoise-shell were joined by gold snuffboxes of great value. Equipped with small feet, they ceased to be utilitarian articles which were carried in the pocket and became ornaments suitable for the display cabinet. As early as the sixteenth century, craftsmen were mounting them with precious stones. Originally an oval receptacle, the snuffbox now appeared in a variety

23. Perugino, *Wedding of the Madonna:* Musée de Peinture, Caen

24. Raphael, *Wedding of the Virgin:* Pinacoteca di Brera, Milan

RAFFAELLO SANZIO
• URBINO 1483 • ROMA 1520 •
Lo Sposalizio della Vergine

of guises: round, round-cornered or angular, shell-shaped or swol-
len-bellied, embellished with precious stones, enamel, lacquer, miniatures, delicately punched patterns, guilloches and engraving. Some
supreme examples of this art display a wealth of sculptural ornamentation made even more effective by the use of gold of varying
shades.

With the introduction of porcelain into Europe, the famous
Meissen porcelain manufacturers started to produce splendidly
painted boxes in that material, and almost all the leading manufacturers followed suit. Far Eastern influences gave birth to lacquer
boxes, usually embellished with gold, whose pictorial decoration at
first imitated Japanese motifs but later adopted those of the West.

Of intrinsic as well as artistic value, the snuffbox eventually attained the status of a royal gift, there being absolutely no limit to
the ingenious forms it could assume.

Snuffboxes had already become collectors' items in the reign of
Louis XIV. Frederick the Great balked at no financial sacrifice to
get the most gorgeous of these little works of art into his possession.
Of those that have survived, many of them extravagantly set with
diamonds, some are in the Louvre and others in the Wallace Collection in London, while still others belonged to the estate of the late
Kaiser, Wilhelm II. Two magnificent specimens formerly in the
Prussian king's possession came on the market a few years ago and
were auctioned at Sotheby's in London because King Farouk of
Egypt had been forced to part with them. Several others fell into
the hands of burglars during a raid on Hohenzollern Castle.

The masterpieces made by the great snuffbox makers of the
seventeenth century were not exempt from the attentions of contemporary imitators. The excise laws of the time prescribed that
articles in precious metal must bear a *"poinçon"* or punch-mark
enabling the amount of duty to be calculated according to gold or
silver content, and, since trading in untaxed jewelry and orna-

ments was subject to severe penalties, imitators stamped their fakes as conscientiously as honest craftsmen did their originals. The official *poinçon* is therefore only a very limited guarantee of authenticity. It may, provided it is genuine, indicate place, date and fine metal content, but it does not identify the workshop.

In France, classical home of the trinket, the Frenchman's pronounced sense of individuality very soon gave rise to the craftsman's practice of signing his own work. Indeed, the identifying marks of the men who had created these little masterpieces in precious metal and stones soon became an emblem of quality in general. Logical as ever, forgers began to use craftsmen's symbols as well as official *poinçons*. For all that, the snuffbox maker's craft was a combination of so many complex technical and artistic elements that forgeries of the period are lacking neither in form ornamentation, pictorial charm, skilled treatment of metal nor any other important feature.

Henry Nocq (*Le Poinçon de Paris*) and L. Carré (*Les Poinçons de l'Orfèvrerie Française du 14ᵉ Siècle jusqu'au début du 19ᵉ Siècle*) give a general survey of French marks and emblems. Anyone requiring precise information about the origin of a piece of French silversmith's or goldsmith's work is recommended to consult these two works — always assuming that the hallmark in question is genuine.

MINIATURES

The pictorial miniature, which received fresh impetus from the snuffbox maker's art, enjoyed enormous popularity in its time. It is a branch of painting which was practiced in the so-called New Kingdom of Egypt as early as 1600 B.C. The term "miniature" has nothing to do with size but is derived from the Latin *minium,* meaning native cinnabar or red lead, which was used in the early Middle Ages principally by monks and later by lay painters for illuminating manuscripts and embellishing initial letters, ornamental borders and small decorative motifs. In the course of time these little minium pictures or miniatures were enhanced by the use of gold-foil overlays and every kind of paint. This technique may be seen at its best in the various Books of Hours.

The course of this art form's development led from small paintings in Egyptian papyrus rolls and "books of the dead," via isolated illustrations or *rotulae* in early Christian documents, to Byzantine, Merovingian, early Romanesque, Gothic and later medieval book paintings, and culminated in the miniatures proper of the sixteenth to nineteenth centuries. Any works of this sort which date from after 1680 should be regarded as the product of archaistic tendencies.

Miniatures are distinguishable from panel pictures not only because of their different paints (the miniaturist used gouache or water color rather than tempera or oils) but, far more importantly, in respect of the brush as an implement and the brush stroke as medium of expression.

One vital factor was the introduction into miniature painting of thin plates of sawn and polished ivory. These lent water colors an appearance quite unlike anything known before. An additional fillip was provided by the invention of enamels by the French painter Leonard Limousin (also called Limosin), who accomplished marvels of the enameler's art in the years around 1570.

Nearly a century passed before it was discovered how to bind a homogeneous layer of enamel firmly to its metal base. The painter employed stained vitreous paste which, upon completing his pictorial composition, he baked into a durable mass. Enamel miniatures attained a gloss which had hitherto been an exclusive feature of painted porcelain.

In quite early times, many miniaturists were already copying works of larger format, a practice reminiscent of the modern reproduction of paintings on a postage-stamp scale for illustrative

purposes. Miniaturists of varied ability produced miniatures of very
varied quality. Because they are copies, they must be assessed on the
basis not of thematic composition but of optically correct and technically adequate execution. The concepts of forgery and imitation
are here invalid. The designation "contemporary forgery of a miniature" may be applied only to an imitation of a miniaturist's original copy. In this case, it is the copy of a copy which is a forgery.

In the years after 1650 the Flemish painter David Teniers the
Younger devoted several pictures to reproducing *en miniature* the
most famous paintings in Archduke Leopold Wilhelm's collection
at Brussels. We owe him a debt of gratitude for preserving this
collection if only in such a form.

Their small format made miniatures a favorite collector's item
and assured them a wide public, whether in the shape of portraits
or pictorial decoration on *tabatières,* souvenirs or miniature reproductions of famous paintings. During the eighteenth century,
miniaturists drew inspiration from the elegant and captivating
scenes painted by Watteau, Fragonard (himself a miniaturist),
Boucher and other contemporaries, and their work gained access
to the leading art collections of the day.

The miniaturist's art was practiced by such celebrated men as
Hans Holbein the Younger, Lucas Cranach the Elder and Moritz
Michael Daffinger, but it first reached its prime in early works of
the pre-Gothic and medieval periods and enjoyed a second golden
age towards the close of the eighteenth century.

Needless to say, book painting of the pre-Gutenberg era has no
connection with later portrait miniature, which began in the North
with Hans Holbein the Younger, lapsed for a long time, and then
developed into an art in its own right after 1700. During the
eighteenth century its especial home was France and England, but
after 1780 — and particularly during the Biedermeier period — it
flourished in Germany and Austria. Notwithstanding their highly

complicated technique, masterpieces of the miniaturist's art were faked with no mean skill.

Little masterpieces by Elisabeth Vigée-Lebrun, Jean-Baptiste Isabey, Frédéric Millet and the English exponents of this genre are still greatly prized and fetched high prices even during the lifetime of those artists. Any attempt to forge them is a near impossibility.

Contemporary fakes apart, miniatures are still being forged today. But the sudden appearance of a miniature which is not listed in the standard works on the subject, yet bears the signature of a celebrated miniaturist, signals the institution of such far-reaching inquiries that however skillful its imitation of style and materials, a fake will almost certainly be detected.

Outside the province of forgery lie the "miniatures" which are manufactured industrially by photomechanical means, mainly at Nuremberg. Initially reproduced in monochrome and later hand-painted, these are mass-produced articles whose price varies, according to quality, between three dollars and thirty — inclusive of frame.

The more expensive of these small mass-produced pictures are sometimes done on fossilized mammoth-bone, wild boar's tusk or even genuine ivory, and set in little frames of mother-of-pearl or rare wood. The backs are frequently pasted over with printed sheets from legal books of the eighteenth and nineteenth centuries, which can be bought by the pound.

These "miniatures" are not, however, designed to deceive the novice alone. When cleverly aged, mass-produced articles have often been sold to collectors, with a great show of secrecy, in the guise of heirlooms from some princely estate.

The latent but undying ambition of collectors and dealers to pick up valuable items at a ridiculous price has led, apart from frauds of a more routine nature, to some grotesque confidence tricks.

A leading American jeweler, visiting the Cairo Museum of Early

Egyptian Art in quest of attractive, original and intriguing pieces of jewelry for his main shop in New York and subsidiary concerns in other cities, once encountered an obliging attendant who, after sundry manipulations, cautiously lifted the glass lid of a specimen table, extracted a magnificent scarab, and offered it to the astonished visitor for a hundred dollars.

On his journey home, the American visited a leading firm of jewelry manufacturers at Pforzheim. Under seal of strictest secrecy, he showed the managing director his precious scarab and inquired if it would be possible to copy it. The copies would not, he assured him, be sold as genuine Egyptian antiquities but as high-class reproductions, mounted in gold and offered as "novelties." He declared himself ready to lend his scarab as a model, but only on condition that it was carefully safeguarded.

The German businessman examined the scarab from every angle and made a telephone call to his stockroom overseer. After a brief conversation, he offered his American colleague immediate delivery of ten gross gold-mounted scarabs quite as genuine as the original in the display case, which had also come from the Pforzheim warehouse.

It goes without saying that, where jewelry and ornaments are concerned, it is not always so simple to draw a distinction between genuine and fake. In Africa and the Near and Far East, more imitations of indigenous craftsmanship mass-produced in European and Japanese factories — chains, rings, figurines, talismans, coins, smokers' requisites and even "hand-woven" textiles — are sold than could ever have been genuinely produced. Precious jade, the classical nephrite, becomes at best an inexpensive stone of dark shade.

The manufacturer is no forger, for his wares are delivered complete with a certificate of origin and trade-mark. Industrially produced copies do not become fakes until the dealer in Tetuan,

Hong Kong, Beirut, Cairo, Dakar or Bombay has hammered the inscription "Made in England" out of a silver bracelet or copper tray. The smooth edges of metal articles immediately betray their mechanical origin. Handwork is always irregular.

TANAGRA FIGURINES

Quite different methods are adopted by imitators who attempt to deceive a more discriminating and financially powerful class of dealers and enthusiasts.

One of the most eminent collectors of the nineteenth century, Count Gregor Stroganoff, was able to give his passion free rein because he had almost unlimited resources at his command. When his original residence proved too small to hold his expanding collection he built a house on the Via Sistina in Rome and equipped it as a museum.

Augusto Jandolo, scion of a family of art dealers, inscribes in his book *Confessions of an Art Dealer* the innumerable treasures of the Stroganoff collection, among them twelve famous Tanagra figurines especially dear to the heart of the count, who was a connoisseur of this incomparable form of miniature art.

The Viennese archeologist Ludwig Pollak, who had devoted himself to the study of these small sculptures in Greece, examined the Tanagra figurines in the count's collection and reached the firm conclusion that all of them were fakes.

The count sent for the art dealer Tavazzi, one of his advisers and suppliers. Gathering up the figurines with a broad sweep of his arm, he presented them to the antiquarian on condition that he never resold them.

When, some time later, Stroganoff asked Tavazzi where they were, the latter admitted that he had handed them all over, as a gift, to the young Augusto Jandolo, who had just opened his own shop.

Because Jandolo refused to guarantee their authenticity to any potential buyer, the figurines remained permanently in stock, greatly though his shaky financial position would have benefited by a good sale. Then Tavazzi hit upon the idea of asking the count to certify merely that the twelve Tanagra figurines came from his collection. Stroganoff scribbled a few lines and added his signature. The note is dated Rome, August 15, 1895. It asserts neither that the figurines are fakes nor that they are originals: merely that they once reposed in a showcase in Count Stroganoff's house.

A few months later the collection was split between two major American museums. The purchase price assured young Jandolo's future, and the Tanagra figurines were pronounced by leading American experts to be uncontrovertible originals.

It is still uncertain who was right, the archeologist Ludwig Pollak or the American art historians. Stroganoff himself, having originally paid 40,000 gold francs for the twelve figurines, now held them to be spurious. Was he really convinced or merely seeking consolation for a loss which he had deliberately brought on himself by giving away genuine Tanagra figurines because a single expert opinion had shaken his confidence? Whatever the truth, the twelve Tanagra figurines brought young Jandolo the first big stroke of luck in his business career.

If there was a conflict of opinion over the Tanagra terra cottas, all doubt was finally dispelled in the case of the so-called *tesoro sacro,* various items of which were also acquired by Stroganoff.

It appeared that, long ago, a noble *cavaliere* named Giancarlo Rossi had brought these ecclesiastical treasures to Rome from distant lands and presented them to a bishop as a mark of his devotion. Magnificent examples of early Christian goldsmith's work, they were unearthed, apparently by accident, in the bishop's tomb when that worthy man's remains were being reinterred. Eager archeologists at once took charge of the ceremonial vessels and pronounced them to be rare works of great importance. They were hastily acquired by Count Stroganoff before the Papal Chamber of Art had time to appropriate them — a danger which was repeatedly stressed by the owners.

Glowing accounts of the find appeared in the press and space was devoted to extensive articles on the subject in art journals. Then Hartmann Grisar modestly pointed out that the inscriptions and ornamentation on the vessels belonged to a period separated by several centuries from their alleged date of origin. Since the presence of early medieval lettering and pictorial motifs on early Christian work was explicable only in terms of some anachronistic miracle, the splendid items in the *tesoro sacro* were, beyond a shadow of a doubt, fakes.

FANS

Any survey of high-priced *objets d'art* of the Renaissance and rococo periods must include the fan, which appears in innumerable shapes, often of a gorgeous and exotic nature. This article, which came into use in about 1520, may be identified in paintings as early as the sixteenth century, constructed of ivory and mother-of-pearl and decorated with gold and silver. Fans were an integral part of the noblewoman's and courtesan's equipment, but were used by the lords of creation as well. Initially modest affairs of stretched silk, they were soon embellished with delicate paintings, while the fans of the age of gallantry were adorned with precious stones, rare lace, enamel and inlays. By the nineteenth century, far less attention was lavished on this adjunct to feminine beauty. The circle of collectors, never very large, is constantly decreasing, and fan forgeries are now extremely rare. More frequently, simple contemporary fans are falsified by the subsequent addition of inlay, pictorial decoration or forged lace.

WALKING STICKS, HANDLES, PAPERWEIGHTS, SAND CASTERS, QUILLS

These items also provide a somewhat out-of-the-way field for the collector, although the nineteenth century, in particular, saw an upsurge of interest in pipe-heads of richly carved clay, meerschaum or carved amber.

Walking sticks and pipes are occasionally faked for the benefit of the few collectors who are interested in the personal relics of famous personalities. "Historic" walking sticks, stick-knobs, pipes, quills and writing implements are usually accompanied by forged documents or spurious personal dedications. More cane-handles belonging to Frederick the Great have reached the market than he ever possessed during his lifetime!

GLASS

The art-conscious Maecenas of the Renaissance, having discovered the beauty and unique charm of old coins and trinkets, was likewise attracted by the miraculous shapes and colors of early glass from the Hellenistic and Roman artistic world. The fragility of glass vessels, which were originally manufactured for personal use, soon encouraged people to collect them as a form of ornament. The few surviving pieces of authentic early glass were quickly absorbed by the collections of wealthy men, and forgery was enlisted to repair the deficiency.

Coloring, etching, grinding, cutting, polishing and — a practice introduced in very early times — "spinning" with decorative filaments, all enhanced glass in an infinite variety of ways. It was not until very much later that artistic perfection gained full expression in the stained-glass windows of Romanesque and Gothic cathedrals, which blended the arts of painting and staining into a unified whole. The "shimmering gold" of the old glassmakers has never since been reproduced.

The fragility of glass provides a logical reason for its extraordinary scarcity and the high artistic and material value set on all glass vessels, from nearly pre-Christian times, via the days of classical antiquity, to the golden age of Venetian glass manufacture. Murano, the glass town near Venice which has once more become famous for its magnificent creations, was already supplying the Renaissance connoisseur with glassware of unique splendor. At its date of origin this glassware served a genuinely utilitarian purpose despite — or perhaps because of — its richly imaginative ornamentation. As yet unbanished to the showcase, it was as great an adjunct to the joys of conviviality as the hand-engraved silver goblets and bowls with their gilded interiors. Paintings of the time illustrate the diversity and magnificence of contemporary table requisites.

It was only natural that the extraordinary wealth of shape, color and ornamentation from which the Venetian glass industry derived its renown and success should inspire imitators. The glass industry at Altare near Genoa operated as a competitor of the glass factories in the city of lagoons, yet so strong was the latter's influence that the Genoese workshops tended to gravitate into the Venetian orbit, use related techniques and produce related designs.

From time to time, immigrant Italian glassmakers produced similar work in the lands beyond the Alps, making it uncommonly difficult to identify dates and places of origin. As early as the middle of the sixteenth century a glassworks established in Antwerp on the Venetian model undertook the manufacture of fine glass which, though made by specially recruited Italians using native techniques, never quite matched the incomparable creations of Venice either in delicacy of material or beauty of design. German, French, Spanish and English glassworks evolved different types of glass and individual designs which make it impossible for the expert to confuse them either with indigenous or with Antwerp Italian. Of course, there is always a chance that mistakes may be made in borderline cases because the work both of individual craftsmen and competing glassworks frequently coincided, a fact which allows the forger some scope for stylistic errors.

By the fifteenth century small works of art in glass were already being pictorially decorated. Early ringed cups, *Passgläser,* Maigelein beakers and other receptacles were painted in enamels and cut or etched with pictorial representations. Glass engravings done with a diamond cutter range from purely technical exercises in craftsmanship to genuine works of art whose creative designs played a role in the formation of contemporary styles.

Engraving was also executed on rock crystal until, at the close of the seventeenth century, Bohemian glassworks succeeded in making ordinary glass look so like rock crystal by the addition of chalk that it might almost be regarded as an example of industrial forgery. Real crystal was largely replaced as an item of common use by the new material, which looked like rock crystal but was considerably easier to work with. This was one of the first instances in which an industrial substitute captured the market.

Whatever form cutting takes, and it may vary widely from simple stylized lines to imaginatively conceived designs, both genuine and synthetic crystal present a brilliant and effective appearance. Among the most famous styles is the "Baccarat" cut.

Artificial crystal produced by molding may give the impression of having been cut, but it lacks the sharp edges which only cutting can achieve. Shrewd and unscrupulous glass cutters sometimes take molded replicas of especial beauty and richness of design and go over their edges with a carborundum disk, producing results which may easily be mistaken for the genuine article.

The surface of decorated glass displays a variety of different techniques. First, the pictorial design was scratched into the surface, and this engraving formed the basis on which raised or recessed patterns of considerable plasticity were later carried out.

The execution of a picture in glass produced results similar to those of a woodcut. Special effects were made possible by the simultaneous use of cameo and intaglio techniques, while gold overlays provided an additional means of ornamentation. On a still higher plane came the *Zwischengoldglass* or "gold sandwich glass," for which two perfectly fitting glass beakers had to be made. The decorative charm of this technique derived from gossamer-fine pieces of gold foil which the craftsman cut accurately to shape and applied to the exterior of the inner glass shell.

Convincing forgeries of such high-class glassware are very few and far between because they are not a remunerative proposition. Specimens of the glassmaker's art can be dated to within narrow limits, but it is difficult and sometimes impossible to distinguish with complete certainty an original from a contemporary imitation. Opinions based on stylistic criticism are also subject, in such cases, to the element of uncertainty which is a feature of every really skillful old copy. More commonly encountered is the falsification of old and genuine but unadorned glassware by treating its surface with cutting tools or etching acids. A monogram or crest added in this way can effectively increase the value of a piece.

Unlike porcelain, glass only rarely bears marks of identification. There are, in fact, no "glass marks" in the same sense that there are porcelain marks. Only close familiarity with an artist's or a workshop's working methods will permit one to gauge the origin of glassware. In cases where richly decorated glass is called in question, attention should be paid chiefly to stylistic purity and the harmonious interplay of specific techniques with the designs for which they were commonly used.

The restoration of damaged glassware is possible only within strictly circumscribed limits because the effects of refraction will betray even the most skillful repair. Restorers usually content themselves with grinding off the splintered remnants of ornamentation or working up defective engraving. Since intervention of this sort modifies the harmony of the original composition, the expert should be able to recognize breaks in stylistic continuity even when the features they replace are no longer visible in tangible form.

Were a list to be compiled of all the examples of classical glassware ever bought from a dealer or at a sale, from Phoenician jars to guild cups, Renaissance goblets and fragile gems of the rococo, Empire and Biedermeier styles, their very profusion would demonstrate that, even at the most liberal estimate, imitations far outnumbered authentic specimens. Glassware dating from pre-Christian times is still being discovered today, but it immediately disappears into museums and collections. Items supposedly acquired "on the side" find their way into the hands of glass collectors, but most of them are later identified as fakes. Vessels with elaborate serpentine patterns or glasses in Roman style with embossed portrayals of chariot races or circus games are usually betrayed by their crude technique, for few imitations can achieve the amazing delicacy of execution and unity of composition which mark an original.

The delightful iridescence which is so characteristic of old glass may be due to a number of factors: uneven coloring of material, the effect of metallic residua, or prolonged interment in earth containing vegetable acids.

Iridescence caused by metallic oxides is a feature of late Roman glassware. The scientist Franchet succeeded in reproducing these by adding resin-bound metallic oxides to molten glass.

Other effects are easier to simulate. The simpler an imitation, however, the simpler its detection. The forger normally roughens the exterior of a glass by treating it with acid or imparts a slightly matte texture by means of sand blasting. The retentive surface thus produced is, in contrast to smooth glass, receptive to paint.

Minute quantities of aniline dyes are enough to produce iridescent effects as light passes through the glass. To protect the aniline dyes, which are easily soluble, and summon up the pristine luster of the glass, the coarsened surface is sprayed with a hard-drying fixative. The technique certainly produces some beautiful iridescent effects, but any high-gloss coating can be detected with the aid of a solvent.

The irisated glass now manufactured industrially both for daily use and for display can render the forger useful service — not as a finished article but as raw material. By melting it down he obtains a supply of genuine irisated glass for blowing or molding into archaic shapes.

The soft yellowish tone of old glass is attributable not to age, the color of glass being immutable, but to oxidizing compounds left in the original material by men who were not as yet sufficiently conversant with the technique of chemical decolorization.

To simulate the appearance of great age by imparting this yellowish tone is not a task which presents the forger with any serious problems. He adds metallic oxides to the molten mass, fashions the glass in correct period style over his flame, then cuts it and adds gold filigree in the archaic manner.

When imitating painted glass the forger coats his paints with fixatives to prevent rapid discoloration of the pigments and protect them from wear. These high-gloss resins and synthetic films react to a wide variety of solvents. Panes of fake bull's-eye glass are bound together with strips of lead "kneaded" in the medieval fashion.

Fakes which have been carried out with especial regard for medieval style and technique should always be submitted to chemical and spectral analysis.

If the material under inspection contains manganese, this signifies unquestionably that it is a latter-day imitation. The presence of pigments which were not yet in existence when the glass is supposed to have originated is clear evidence of forgery. Traces of antimonic acid lead, too, are an infallible sign that artificial toning has taken place.

The dissolving of metallic alloys in lead glass produced some remarkably effective results. After repeated heating, silver assumed a shimmering golden shade, while copper gave a luminous red.

During experimental attempts to extract gold artificially in the Potsdam glassworks at the close of the seventeenth century, the alchemist Kunkel succeeded not in manufacturing that precious metal but in inventing the ruby glass which has retained its unrivaled reputation to the present day.

Ruby glass, which was extremely expensive in former times, is now manufactured on a large scale. The alchemist's original process has been superseded by a method of coloration based on copper compounds. Spectral analysis readily distinguishes between the varied range of materials present in genuine old ruby glass and those used in the modern version, and microscopic examination will reveal the telltale presence of colloid solutions.

Glasses whose translucency has deteriorated under the influence of chemical change and, in particular, humidity are said to have fallen prey to "clouding." Many glasses start to go "blind" in tropical regions or in sea air of high iodine content. Anyone who tries to remedy such damage is operating in the no man's land between falsification and forgery.

Because this clouding process begins on the exterior surface and works inward, it is possible to grind away only those "cloud formations" which have not penetrated too deeply. But, however carefully the clear, newly obtained "skin" is polished, this procedure reduces the volume of the glass and, by modifying its external form, betrays the fact of interference.

Repaired and treated glasses are coated with a protective film which is invisible to the naked eye but can be detected by means of solvents or a small knife. Its presence is always a signal for caution.

LACE

For almost four centuries, specimens of the famed Italian needlepoint and Flemish bobbin lace produced during the Middle Ages were highly prized and assiduously collected. With the decline of lace making into a professional handicraft and later into an industrial process, the major collectors' interest in it waned. New techniques were evolved in areas where labor was cheaper and the market was flooded with fine handmade lace produced by operatives working in their own homes. General demand was satisfied by machine-made lace. Just as genuine pearls suffered a fall in price when vast quantities of cultured pearls arrived on the market, so the demand for genuine old lace declined as supplies of the substitute increased. Not even the finest Alençon lace of aristocratic pedigree was spared the effects of this commerical invasion, although changes in taste also played a certain role.

In 1905 at a sale in the Hôtel Drouot — then the leading Paris auction house but now bereft of much of its pristine aura — a splendid piece of Alençon lace formerly in the possession of Marie Antoinette fetched a sum roughly equivalent to three thousand dollars in modern terms. Only a hundred years earlier, this fine work was valued at many times that figure.

Lace can be divided into four major categories: *point à l'aiguille* or needlepoint; *dentelle à fuseaux* or bobbin lace; *crochet;* and *tissé au métier* or embroidery-frame lace. The latter constitutes an imitative form.

Extremely high prices were paid for fine lace during the sixteenth century. A garniture consisting of ruff, jabot and wrist frills cost over seven thousand dollars in modern money. It took one woman a year to produce a piece of Chantilly lace eighteen inches long and eight inches wide — and very few years to impair the eyesight of the girls and women who practiced this craft.

By the close of the sixteenth century, imitations of these delicate works of art in hand-worked thread had already appeared. They are distinguishable from original work only by somewhat less exacting standards of inspection.

From the eighteenth century onwards, imitation of the very finest lace ceased to be remunerative. The taste and *expertise* of purchasers imposed such high standards that the substantial sum which an imitation might fetch was disproportionate to the time spent in producing it.

Imitations of classical lace deviate from the genuine article in constructional detail. The mobile, elastic and variable nature of the material makes it almost impracticable to copy the finest motifs. Goldsmiths, painters and sculptors create firm shapes with firm materials. Lace does not achieve its pictorial effect until there is a complete harmony of individual detail.

The subject of lace had already gained a literature of its own by the sixteenth century. Matteo Pagan published the first work on lace in 1558, while a treatise on lace by Caesare Vecellio, a relative of Titian, appeared at Venice in 1591. At Paris in 1594, Vinziolo dedicated a book on lace design, profusely illustrated with woodcuts, to one of the most enthusiastic and knowledgeable of contemporary collectors, Catharine de' Medici, Queen of France.

One sure sign of genuine lace is the "change-over." Since no lace maker could work uninterruptedly for more than a few hours at a time, a piece was produced by several women working — to use a modern term — in irregular shifts, and the points at which fresh hands took over are clearly discernible. Background, filling and figure work were sometimes carried out by specialists. Furthermore, it is possible to see where one group stopped and another started. Careful scrutiny will reveal such individual and recurrent characteristics that lace which is obviously the work of a single pair of hands and remains consistent from beginning to end cannot have been produced in the celebrated workrooms of the sixteenth to eighteenth centuries. The opposite is true of the so-called Rosaline lace, which originated in convents. These little works of art in relief were sometimes the output of a single nun and therefore lack the signs of collective endeavor.

Mechanically produced lace is so perfectly regular that it can never be used for fraudulent purposes. Artificially induced irregularities, too, occur at regular intervals and do not disguise their mechanical origin.

Imitations of every conceivable type of early lace-making technique are still being produced today by skilled exponents in Italy, Spain and, more particularly, in the Spanish and Portuguese islands of the Atlantic, but they can be distinguished both by their materials and manner of execution.

Modern handmade lace is harder, less flexible and more bulky than genuine old lace. To proof it against the eye and hand of the expert collector the forger boils it repeatedly in chalkless water, sometimes adding a weak oily emulsion. The pale shade characteristic of old lace is achieved with the aid of weak colorific additives. Painstaking forgers evaporate a few drops of indanthrene cream to produce the correct *teinture* and guard against the risk that the toning will disappear when washed.

The most famous lace-making centers were at Alençon, Argentan, Bruges, Brussels, Chantilly, Cluny, Genoa, Le Puy, Lille, Lunéville, Malines, Milan, Paris, Sedan, Valenciennes, and Venice. They were the home of the noble and masterly designs which patient hands created out of fine gold and silver thread, silk, and hand-twisted linen yarn.

The lover of fine old lace will find valuable examples and technical information in the Museum of Industries and Crafts at St. Gallen in Switzerland, which incorporates the Jacoby-Iklé collections. Fragile masterpieces of the sixteenth to nineteenth centuries and a collection of nineteenth-century white embroideries provide the visitor with a unique survey of the subject.

7

❧❧❧❧❧❧❧❧❧

Ceramics

THE potter's art ranges from the primitive and utilitarian vessels of dim prehistoric times and regions to the refined clay vessels of the Far East, and from the masterpieces of Meissen, Sèvres and other famous factories to the creations of artists employed by manufacturers operating on the scale of organized craftsmanship or industrial production.

A field of infinite richness and variety, ceramics fall under two main headings: crude ceramics or stoneware, and fine ceramics or earthenware. The first category may be omitted from present consideration because it embraces, fundamentally, building materials of the most varied types.

The term fine ceramics comprises every sort of refined and baked earthenware, such as utensils, tiles, baths, insulators and — last but not least — vases, sculptures and other *objets d'art.*

Forgeries occur in the sphere of crude as well as fine ceramics, but the imitation, forgery or falsification of fine ceramics is all that will concern us in the present treatment. Past and present imitations of early or prehistoric earthenware affect only museums and the very limited circle of collectors who specialize in this field.

As with nearly all other artistic creations, the forgery of refined earthenware ensued immediately upon the appearance of originals. In doubtful cases it is profitable to distinguish whether one is dealing with a contemporary, later or modern imitation.

At about the turn of the century, pieces of earthenware by the potters of Moab, Ammon and Basan were unearthed in the rubble of Palestine's holy places and found their way into museums in Paris, Berlin and London. It was not until some years later that experts had perforce to identify them as imitations, though of superb quality. The Roman antiquarian Schapiro declared that he had acquired them "on the spot," but the spot in question was a forger's workshop in Apulia.

However industrious and hard-working, the Apulians could never, during their two hundred years of ceramics manufacture, have produced a ten-thousandth part of the antique vases which reach the market every year. Because some imitators do not even take the trouble to transmit original designs to the surface of the clay by photomechanical means, these small-scale works of art display "original marks" which never existed at all and have become increasingly modified and distorted in their transference from one piece to another. Nevertheless, the fact that genuine Apulian works of art were done in only three colors — black, brown and red — makes the forger's task relatively simple. August Demmin notes in his *Guide de l'Amateur des Faïences* that "an erstwhile employee of the factory of Villeroy & Boch at Wallerfangen near Saarlouis . . . made Arretine earthenware which even insinuated its way into museums." These "Arretine works of art" must have surpassed the imitations of Italian forgers in every respect, being betrayed only by variations in density of materials and an inconsistent arrangement of figured decoration.

Scientists have evolved a very practical, if extremely complicated, method of identifying hand-finished imitations in molded clay. This is based on the assumption that the potter's clay is adulterated with ferruginous substances. Because they remain mobile in the soft damp clay until it has set, the position of these minute particles of iron permits inferences to be made about the age of the material used. Just as the needle of a compass indicates the direction of the North Pole, so the metallic particles in the soft clay become arranged in relation to the earth's magnetic field. After much extremely painstaking and laborious research, the scientist Folgheraiter tabulated the magnetic variation peculiar to each century. In the first century B.C., for example, the bearing in the Arezzo district was 61° 3′, while that of Pompeii at the date of its destruction was 66° 5′. If, therefore, clay is tested with a freely swinging magnetic needle, the result will enable its age to be computed with at least some measure of accuracy. Methods of chemical analysis suitable for clay were developed by Le Chatelier, and form the basis on which all the Louvre's projected acquisitions of earthenware are tested before purchase.

Thus, disregarding stylistic examination, which is not always exempt from error when shapes have been molded or outlines stenciled, the expert may base his judgment on metallographic tests of material, chemical analysis and — yet another method — the spectral analysis of particles of pigment. It goes without saying that only very important pieces justify the employment of such complex methods of research.

Since the degrees of hardness peculiar to the materials used in the manufacture of almost all early pottery have been tabulated, a piece may be tested by being scratched in an unimportant place —

usually beneath the base. Specific gravity, too, may be informative.

Many and ingenious though the methods used by forgers are, almost every fake has its Achilles' heel. The plaster cast from which a forger makes his basic shape is coated with milk or a thin film to prevent paints from seeping into the porous material. Having sealed the pores of the article with a matte varnish, the forger is at liberty to decorate it with water color or gouache. Figured representations are transferred to the surface with stencils, a method which can produce remarkably convincing results even on the cheapest hackwork. Other forms of paint-receptive priming entail the use of colorless size, stearic amalgams, petroleum zinc paste, natural varnishes and synthetic lacquers.

A well-developed sense of smell will detect all these substances a long time after their application, and laboratory tests will readily reveal their presence. The inexperienced purchaser should always bear in mind that the most tempting bargains are usually the most disappointing — and this often applies to items acquired *in situ.*

Spurious glazes and firing effects which have been obtained by brushing or spraying-on natural varnishes, or, what is much more common these days, synthetic resins, are sensitive to alcohol, benzine, ether and turpentine. Purely artificial resins will dissolve under a single drop of nail-polish remover. Genuine old fired clay resists these solvents so stoutly that scarcely any damage will result from such a test.

It is hard to detect repairs which have been skillfully carried out on genuine old earthenware or imitations of very early date. Where paints are concerned, improvement or fraudulent modification can be identified by exhaustive chemical tests, but only at the risk of damage. Spectroscopic tests and the ascertaining of an article's specific weight may make it unnecessary to run that risk.

Forgers obtain a convincingly hard surface by transforming magnesite into rocklike magnesium oxyhydrate. This will resist normal solvents almost as efficiently as a genuine fired glaze. Only where the glaze accumulates around the rough edges of the base or on ledges will there be any perceptible variation, for these deposits differ substantially in cross-section from the results of genuine firing.

No less than original pieces, fakes vary considerably in quality, from the aspect both of workmanship and materials. The forger who manufactures imitations for a wider and more gullible market will concentrate on cheap mass-produced articles appropriate to the potential returns. His colleague who concentrates on a smaller and more discriminating market will exert every care and economize neither on materials nor detailed workmanship.

Thus Tanagra figurines, for example, being destined for pampered tastes, are forged in genuine fired clay. Because of their tiny format and the extremely laborious workmanship involved, a high percentage of unsalable rejects has to be destroyed. Even so, the genuine fired clay of an imitation is differentiated from that of an original by its coarse granulation and cloudy red color. When seen in a false light, the black tones of one of these little works of art tend to assume a deep brown shade, while those of an imitation become either pitch-black or blue-black. Even superlative forgers find it impossible to plumb all the secrets known to craftsmen of the past.

Among forgeries with greater pretensions to quality, certain Roman terra cotta lamps make high demands upon the imitator's skill. The existence of innumerable cheap imitations of simpler models has meant, for a long time now, that only lamps decorated in relief are still remunerative. "The world's most comprehensive collection of rare terra cotta lamps" could once be admired in the Pesaro Museum. Shortly after the turn of the century, exhaustive research revealed that all the major items in this collection were forgeries. One lamp, "adorned with splendid miniature reliefs," proved to bear an inscription which was irreconcilable with its apparent date of origin, a circumstance which invited closer examination. Curious as it may seem, these and similar symptoms of forgery, though rudimentary and obvious in nature, have often passed unnoticed for decades or even centuries.

An "early Christian lamp in the shape of a large fish, holding a smaller one in its mouth and bearing Christ's monogram on one side and a cross on the other" was long regarded as an early example of symbolic design. The piece was not unmasked as a fake until very much later. What was more, it turned out that several museums prided themselves on possessing the same imaginatively designed lamp, among them the Berlin Museum, as can be gathered from the *Official Reports of the Royal Art Collections*, 1913-1914. The forger's convincing handiwork had apparently been reproduced in quantity.

Forgeries of early works in clay are not, however, confined to the West or the Near and Far East. Clay cult vessels and sculptures by the Incas, Aztecs and other pre-Columbian inhabitants of South and Central America have also found excellent imitators. It is indicative of the superior quality of these fakes that a large proportion of the Louvre's Mexican treasures turned out to be imitations.

For centuries, scant attention had been paid to the works of art of pre-Columbian South and Central America. It was not until European mercenaries brought home thousands of intriguing sculptures after the execution of Emperor Maximilian in Mexico that the interest of scholars and collectors was aroused. The year 1870 saw the first organized excavations in Central America, with American millionaires filling the role of sponsors and purchasers. And, as always, growing demand encouraged forgers to work overtime.

Apart from the imitation of genuine works of art, a brisk trade developed in simpler types of clay utensil also purporting to date from before the advent of Columbus. For a time it became almost a social obligation to possess clay gods, bowls and sacrificial vessels from the early days of Latin America.

To prevent the total exhaustion of genuine finds, the governments of Central and South America imposed a strict embargo on exports which could be circumvented only by dint of considerable financial outlay. But, since very little was known about the originals, the new-born market readily accepted the authenticity of portrayals of gods and mythical creatures which had originated only in some forger's fertile imagination. Because even scholars were at first ignorant of the significance and material composition of these strange-looking works of art from alien civilizations, the market became flooded with earthenware cult vessels which originally existed only in stone. Native craftsmen naturally found clay much easier to handle than stone, and, to the men who paid them, time was synonymous with money. In this way, much genuine Mexican stoneware was cast and fired in clay.

There is room here only for a fleeting glance at the many forms of Chinese and Japanese ceramics and their forgeries — a field of almost inconceivable variety and one which embraces thousands of years. This province of art sometimes presents even the specialist with almost insoluble problems of stylistic criticism, because copying went on, with a certain degree of legitimacy, from the very outset.

European forgeries of Far Eastern ceramics can be recognized even when they are the most slavish of copies, whereas imitations produced in their country of origin by superlative craftsmen may deceive even the most experienced collector.

The first pure examples of Chinese porcelain, a development of stoneware, were manufactured during the T'ang Dynasty, between A.D. 618 and 906. The earliest T'ang porcelains display white Hsing-yao and celadon-green glazes. Imitations were in existence shortly after the year 1000, and there are vast numbers of fakes dating from the eighteenth and nineteenth centuries.

Prehistoric Chinese earthenware, mainly unpainted, ranges in shade from gray to dull red. Isolated examples of crude ornamentation in black and reddish-brown appeared at a very early date. The transition from purely utilitarian to artistic and decorative earthenware is marked by century-long lacunae which correspond to the waxing and waning of the major cultural periods.

Far Eastern ceramics are supposed to exhibit countless features which enable sure identification. The vase form of the T'ang period, for example, is characterized by a flat base, tapering sides and the absence of a ring around the foot. Decorative motifs testify to Hellenistic and Near Eastern influences. Every period has its own demonstrable characteristics, but it is fallacious to assume that these are known only to art experts. The Oriental forger of such works of art is equally familiar with them and, having a unique and quite un-Western attitude towards time, brushes aside more mundane considerations and devotes himself wholeheartedly to perfecting his imitations.

Fraudulent alterations carried out by expert hands constitute a field of their own. Genuine but undecorated vases, for instance, are enhanced with additional decoration. Periods which are more sought after and bring higher prices are simulated by means of added coloring, while artificial *craquelure* is often used to increase the age of a piece by a century or two.

The much-quoted "rule" by which genuine old Far Eastern ceramics can be recognized from the patina which appears after a very prolonged sojourn underground has only very limited validity. Oriental forgers command the ability to reproduce the patina characteristic of genuine archeological finds with startling success. Laboratory tests carried out on this patina *may* render chronological differentiation possible, but reliable evidence is hard to secure.

Generally speaking, the forgery of ceramics is always established if they prove to contain substances which did not exist at the ostensible date of origin. There are instances where clay has been found to contain impurities which did not become known until centuries after the date simulated by the forger.

European porcelain originated independently of the Far East. The potters of Venice did not know what to make of the stories about Chinese porcelain brought home by the Venetian explorer Marco Polo at the close of the thirteenth century. It is uncertain when Chinese porcelain appeared in Italy for the first time. Isolated examples were probably known during the fifteenth century, but it was not until the opening of the sea route around the Cape of Good Hope that Chinese porcelain gained a foothold in the Western market, which it did in the middle of the sixteenth century.

The burgeoning trade in genuine Chinese ceramics and the inception of European manufacture inspired forgers to produce fakes, unconvincing though they at first were.

The decorative glazed dishes in bright and attractive colors named after the French potter and author Bernard Palissy were already being copied during the lifetime of their creator, who was working for Catherine de' Medici as early as 1570. Palissy's work was fetching such high prices by the seventeenth century that even distinguished artists like Clerice and Guillaume Dupré started to produce figurative sculptures in his style. During the nineteenth century, Palissy's style and working methods were brilliantly imitated by Alfred Corplet, who originally specialized in the restoration of enamels.

The widespread belief that European porcelain was invented by Johann Friedrich Böttger at the turn of the seventeenth and eighteenth centuries runs counter to an assertion, made by an Italian monk in the year 1470, that a certain Antonio di Simone

had succeeded in manufacturing "transparent ceramics." Half a
century later a Venetian mirror-maker named Leonardo Peringer
claimed that he had discovered the secret of manufacturing Chinese porcelain.

In about 1530 there were produced at Florence the translucent
ceramics which, under the name "Medici porcelain," have survived
in a few examples to the present day. In 1620 Cosimo II made the
potter Nicolo Sisti an allowance so that he could "continue his
attempts to manufacture genuine porcelain in comfort." All the
ceramics produced during these experiments differed from Far
Eastern importations both in substance and finish. The finish was
very far from perfect, and pieces were glazed twice to enhance
their appearance. A Florentine Medici dish of about 1580, ornamented with blue toning after the Chinese manner, bears the
distinguishing mark of all Medici porcelains, namely a Florentine
dome and a horizontal "F." All these works exhibit Chinese,
Persian and Italian motifs, the latter borrowed from majolica ware.

The first European to manufacture porcelain in the modern
sense of the word was Johann Friedrich Böttger. Born on February
4, 1682, this latter-day rediscoverer of what had been invented in
China some thousand years earlier wanted, like so many alchemists
of his day, to unearth the secret of manufacturing gold. At the age
of fourteen he was apprenticed to a Berlin apothecary named Zorn,
and early developed a taste for mysterious experiments. The word
soon went around that he knew how to manufacture gold, but
before the matter could be put to the test by royal command,
Böttger fled to Wittenberg in Saxony. However, wild rumors of
his prowess as a gold-maker had reached Dresden, and Augustus
the Strong, Elector of Saxony and King of Poland, decided to
secure the benefits of synthesized gold for his privy purse by keeping the "apothecary's apprentice and alchemist" in safe custody.

Böttger experimented. He failed to manufacture any gold, but he did discover the secret of porcelain. It is probable that the chemist and glass painter Ehrenfried Walter Tschirnhaus put him on the track leading from glass to porcelain in about 1708. Fine examples of the new material appeared in large numbers at the Leipzig Fair of 1713.

Since 1707, Böttger had been producing hard red stoneware comparable with the so-called *buccaro* of China by means of a casting process. Owing to the twofold shrinking phenomenon described elsewhere in this section, these imitations were considerably smaller than the originals.

The influence of German goldsmiths was responsible for a Europeanization of design, painting and decoration which never quite stifled the influence of the Far East. *Chinoiserie* retained its popularity for a long time.

The extraordinary success of the new material and the manifold uses to which it could be put led to the establishment of numerous porcelain factories, particularly at the princely courts. The factory founded at Meissen was followed by others at Vienna, Berlin and elsewhere.

In France, Louis Poterat of Rouen had received the royal privilege of manufacturing "porcelain in the Chinese style and faience after the manner of Delft" as early as 1673. By 1696, Pierre Chicanneau was producing "articles of use from porcelain-like material" at St. Cloud. However, the great age of French porcelain arrived with the masterpieces emanating from the factory at Sèvres in the neighborhood of Paris, which by 1750 mustered more than a hundred employees. Louis XV contributed a quarter of its capital of 800,000 gold francs.

The establishment of factories in Italy and Spain resulted in the uninhibited imitation of the great by the small, though even the great had little respect for copyright. With their sometimes superb craftsmanship and material, these contemporary imitations, whether intentional or unintentional, can deceive even the genuine connoisseur.

Today, forgers employ every modern chemical and technical aid to make their "originals" as convincing as possible. The decoration, house-marks and delicate brushwork of the original is transferred to surfaces which have been sensitized with albumin. Forgers of earlier times were compelled to use comparatively large kilns and found it no easy matter to achieve the high temperatures needed for porcelain manufacture. The modern electric kiln takes up little space and can be adjusted so as to give any degree of heat required.

The difficulties of imitating earthenware diminished considerably under the impact of technical progress. Mediocre stoneware made smaller demands upon the forger, the necessary material being always at his disposal. The actual shaping was done by kneading the work or using a potter's wheel or lathe. As always, heat was provided by charcoal so that subsequent examination should not reveal telltale residues left by some other fuel.

Nevertheless, insoluble problems are posed by the contraction of any object molded from clay and hardened by firing. The clay decreases in volume, first, when its moisture begins to evaporate in air and, second, when the process is completed by firing.

In order to manufacture a copy of correct proportions a forger would have to start with a mold which allowed for the subsequent twofold loss in volume. However experienced he may be, the copyist will find it beyond his power to counteract the factors of reduction by prior enlargement, even to an approximate degree. This forces him to produce "creative" work which is merely suggestive of originals, and the resulting errors in design, style and decoration will betray its fraudulent nature to the art historian.

It is virtually impossible to conduct experiments on surface treat-

25. Carlo Maratti (1675-1713), *Madonna and Child with Angels*. Ordinary photograph, taken in sunlight. The painting was subjected to examination by four different techniques, as a result of which it was found that certain things had been superimposed.

26 *a*. Under X-ray, the face appears broader and the layers of colour more solid.

26 *b*. Under infra-red, the signature (top left) appears, and the face is further altered.

26 *c*. Under quartz rays, the surface appears mottled and the signature has almost disappeared.

26 *d*. In a combined test, using transverse irradiation, some marks disappear and others are revealed.

27 a. Rembrandt forgery, derived from the genuine *Portrait of Hermann Doomer:* Metropolitan Museum, New York

27 b. The same painting, with a part of the top layer of colour removed, revealing one eye, locks of hair, and the arm and hands of the original.

28. X-ray photograph of the Rembrandt forgery shows the original 18th-century painting underneath; it is a portrait of Johann Georg Muller.

ment, painting, glaze and firing without damaging the piece in question. In the majority of cases, therefore, investigation must be confined to the use of optical aids.

Some experts of long standing can detect certain differences between a piece of genuine porcelain and a fake, however skillfully aged, by testing the surface with their fingers. Spectral analysis may reveal the nature of any damage and repairs.

To distinguish genuine from spurious in the sphere of porcelain, provided one is not dealing with crude imitations, demands great experience and an intimate knowledge of materials.

The vulnerability of porcelain, especially porcelain figures, means that the older it becomes the greater likelihood there is of damage. A broken finger, smashed ruff or missing fiddle bow distracts the eye and considerably diminishes the market value of a piece. Defects are remedied by skillful restoration. There are some experts in this field whose work can pass almost undetected, and should the slightest suspicion attach to an expensive piece of porcelain it ought at least to be tested with a spectroscope. (It must be added that a method of carrying out repairs so that they escape detection by this means has been in existence for some considerable time.)

The restorer attempts to hide cemented cracks under ornamentation. A missing hand is remodeled and given a natural or synthetic glaze. The two raw surfaces where wrist meets arm are joined together with a quick-drying porcelain adhesive or very fine dental cement. When the superfluous adhesive which has been extruded around the edges of the joint has entirely dried, it is scraped off and the fracture camouflaged, perhaps with a finely executed gilded bracelet. Similarly, the place where a missing finger has been replaced may be masked by a ring.

Another remunerative, if fraudulent, occupation consists in changing low-priced manufacturers' marks into ones of higher value. Skilled forgers have transformed the perpendicular device used by the Berlin factory for porcelain made about 1870 into that used between 1763 and 1837. It is equally profitable to adorn unnamed porcelain with the mark of a leading manufacturer.

The crossed swords of Meissen passed through six stages during their evolution from the clumsy affairs of 1724 to the slim blades of today. Here, too, the forger exploits every available opportunity. The simplest method, of course, is to paint-on the requisite mark by brush. This crude form of fake will not deceive even a good magnifying glass, so the practiced forger grinds away the whole base or internal concavity — whichever is appropriate — to which the existing mark has been applied, and thereby obtains some remarkably convincing results.

Reputable manufacturers naturally put modern trade-marks on authorized reproductions of their early works because they have no desire to mislead purchasers. To forgers, however, these copies of precious old pieces represent a heaven-sent opportunity, for the fact that they have been glazed by a genuine firing process and correspond to the originals both in technique and artistry makes them a fairly easy subject for falsification.

The whole base or a sufficiently large portion of the surface bearing the new trade-mark is removed with the aid of a fast-rotating carborundum disk which is capable of abrading the hardest materials. The use of instruments equipped with flexible power transmission and tiny drills — similar to those used by dentists — makes it possible to remove the glaze from any desired surface, even when the trade-mark is situated on the internal rim of the base.

After the mark has been removed, the coarsened surface is filled with paste and semi-polished. At this stage the forger takes time off to paint-in the old manufacturer's mark. The paint penetrates the still porous ground, thus producing the somewhat blurred outlines characteristic of an original trade-mark. The surface is then gently polished and coated with a genuine or synthetic glaze which fuses with the original so efficiently as to be invisible to the naked eye. Where a base has been entirely reglazed the forger's work will pass undetected even under a powerful magnifying glass, for the lines of demarcation between new glaze and old will merge with the original rim.

The small defects indispensable to genuine old porcelain are obtained by inflicting a judicious amount of damage and then repairing the defects so crudely that a prospective buyer cannot fail to notice them. Like the cracks which are artificially induced by a brief and controlled application of pressure, they serve as evidence of authenticity.

Fraudulent copyists frequently commit gross blunders by following what, in their ignorance, they conceive to be originals but which are really nothing of the sort. The end product of their labors testifies with particular eloquence to the stylistic distortion peculiar to forgery at second hand.

Freely devised imitations seldom achieve a harmony of form and decoration sufficiently effective to deceive the critic of style.

Many early forgers betrayed their efforts because a *folie de grandeur* impelled them to use scarce trade-marks from greatly sought-after periods on pieces which were patently unworthy of them. It is far from uncommon to find figures which bear the Meissen mark, for instance, but have been put together from components made by entirely different manufacturers.

The fact that eminent authorities on porcelain are sometimes quite as prone to error as experts in any other province of art is illustrated by the case of a vase with a royal blue background, bearing the mark of the Sèvres factory, which was long regarded as one of the showpieces of the Jones Collection of porcelain housed in the Victoria and Albert Museum. It unfortunately turned out to

have been faked from a model produced by the Coalport manufacturers.

The sale of undecorated white rejects by the Sèvres factory in
1848 was responsible for temporarily flooding the market with
falsifications. Suitably enhanced, these genuine Sèvres pieces sold
like hot cakes. Although the makers later stamped their rejects
with a special mark to prevent abuses, they continued to reappear
in a new and richly decorated guise. There was no great difficulty
about filling in the stamped impression with cement, and the
task of forgery was made considerably easier because the legend
"Décoré à Sèvres" was originally applied to genuine Sèvres products on top of the glaze. Not until after 1897 was the mark applied
beneath the glaze, making it more difficult for the forger to tamper
with.

Similarly, the remarkably high prices paid for faïence by specialist collectors resulted in the imitation on a truly professional
scale of pieces by all the famous old manufacturers. As early as
1735, a ceramics workshop belonging to the Marquis Ginori at
Doccia near Florence specialized in the forgery of rare Tuscan
faïence.

Colored reliefs by Luca della Robbia and other masters occur in
countless reproductions, but the real expert will detect a fake by its
general "tonality." However convincingly the early forger succeeded in reproducing original colors, a natural harmony between
form and color eluded him.

Scientific examination of faïence is unusually difficult because
the removal of particles of material, however careful, is liable to
cause severe damage.

Painted trade-marks may also be bleached out. Once glaze and
paint have been dissolved with fluoric acid and the resulting surface made good and polished, a new and more valuable mark takes

the place of the old and unimpressive one. The patch is then coated with natural or synthetic glaze.

Artificial *craquelure* is produced by spraying pieces with a calcareous film and afterwards glazing them. This results in a convincing network of fissures.

The widely varying "ring" of ceramics can sometimes provide an experienced examiner with useful information. Whether clear, medium or dull, light or heavy, it may not itself be an absolute indication of the genuine or spurious, but it can prove informative if there is any conflict between volume, shape and decoration.

Shaping procedures, too, provide the observer with a further means of identification.

Every potter's wheel leaves its own pattern of grooves, and the microscopic comparison of an indisputably genuine article with one of dubious origin will permit the establishment of either identity or deviation.

Fremersdorff, an authority on ceramics, used handprints left on lamps by the potters of ancient Rome to detect fakes on which, under favorable circumstances, forger's handprints were similarly detectable.

It can also prove informative to ascertain the exact temperature used when firing. Any substantial difference in the degrees of heat to which an indisputably genuine piece and a dubious piece have been subjected may well be indicative of forgery.

Still further valuable information can be derived from tests for hardness and density of material, although such complicated methods of research are justified only where unusually rare pieces are concerned.

As is almost invariably the case, the main attraction of forging ceramics reposes in the potential rewards. Majolica, faïence and porcelain of the rarer kinds all fetch very high prices. At a sale in

April, 1959, an eighteenth-century group by Kaendler was knocked down at 12,400 marks (about $3000).

It often happened in the past that owners of valuable ceramics were forced to dispose of their treasures. Sometimes, in order to keep the sale a secret, a purchaser contracted to supply the seller with accurate reproductions.

The Counts Branitschki kept a magnificent collection of Delft faïences at Wilanow Castle near Warsaw. When a careful inventory was taken after the Second World War, it had to be conceded that these pieces of fine blue Delft were fakes manufactured by a team of French specialists. The last of the Branitschkis had sold the originals to a Parisian dealer named Seligmann on condition that perfect copies were placed at his disposal.

It turned out, shortly afterwards, that the Titians, Rembrandts and Veroneses in the castle's picture gallery were also copies.

It is not known where the originals are today.

8

❧❧❧❧❧❧❧❧❧

Textiles

THE first textiles date from the late Stone Age and were hand-plaited from fibers. From about 2900 B.C. onwards, the Egyptians wove cloth with the aid of spindle and loom. The number of people interested in these very early plaited or woven materials is very small. Moreover, they possess so thorough a knowledge of their narrowly circumscribed subject that forgeries have little prospect of success.

A larger circle of people collect woven silks, of which the earliest originated in China some two thousand years before the beginning of our era. Once again, convincing imitation is out of the question. Such attempts at forgery as have come to light look clumsy in the extreme when compared with the genuine article.

By the early Middle Ages technical progress had made it possible to weave cloth of rich design, and the late Middle Ages saw the start of large-scale production in Italy and Flanders. With the increasing replacement of hand-weaving by mechanization in the middle of the eighteenth century, genuine old hand-woven cloth rose in price.

From the point of view of forgery, principal attention centers on the copes, hangings, stoles and altar cloths which represented long years of devoted work by pious monks and nuns who derived their decorative and pictorial inspiration from the Byzantine and Gothic styles of painting. The influence of these ancient exemplars can be detected even in later fabrics, for the formative effects of painting of more recent periods made themselves felt only gradually.

To imitate such works of art presupposes not only outstanding manual dexterity but superlative artistic ability, not to mention supplies of suitable material, which are extremely difficult if not almost impossible to obtain. Even fine imitations will rarely deceive an expert. This view was expressed before the turn of the century by Justus Brinckmann, an expert who regarded medieval cloth as "forgery-free" because "apart from the difficulty of reproducing the old colors and gold, only manufacture on a large scale would . . . bring the forger a profit." The faking of figured tapestries and Gobelins required an expenditure of time and material which was out of all proportion to the potential rewards, quite ignoring the fact that to copy a splendid work produced in the service of the Faith demanded the selfless devotion which only animates those who work in quiet seclusion to the greater glory of their God and Church.

Compared with early medieval cloth, even the finest of our modern textiles seem little less perishable than a soap bubble when we reflect that the Oriental *casula* worn by Bishop Bernwand of Hildesheim at his burial in the year 1020 was found to be almost intact on his reinterment hundreds of years later. Emperor Charlemagne's burial robe, too, exhibited no pronounced signs of decay when his tomb in Aachen Cathedral was opened in the last century.

Whereas contemporary forgers still had the correct materials at their disposal, the modern forger cannot even procure gold and silver thread, except of a quality whose machine-made origin is only too easily detectable. This alone is enough to give a fake away, for machine-drawn thread is entirely regular, and any attempt to distort its diameter in order to reproduce a hand-made finish will be equally self-evident.

The hand-copying of precious old ornamented and figured tapestries inevitably founders on the difficulty of maintaining the original technique consistently throughout. Nor can a forger plausibly reproduce either the hand-spun threads and special dyes or the feel of tapestry woven on the primitive looms of long ago. He will thus concentrate less on forgery than on the falsification of genuine old cloth with additional decoration in order to simulate a more remunerative date of origin. Because the pictorial sections of old tapestries were often added to the foundation separately, forgers sometimes "dignify" a genuine old fabric by adding small medallions which do not require an inordinate amount of handwork. The resulting rise in value — of an illuminated stole, for instance — will well repay any expenditure of time and energy.

When testing the authenticity of old cloth, the expert begins by scrutinizing the threads of which it is composed. Old thread, unlike the machine-made version, is completely irregular and characterized by variations in thickness. Whereas the twist of mechanically produced thread remains almost constant throughout its length, hand-spun thread will, within the space of a few inches, exhibit marked variations attributable to the irregular drive imparted by a spinning wheel.

Examination of cloth with a thread-meter will likewise reveal any differences with great clarity.

Since the breaking point of genuine old thread has been established, tests conducted on a single strand with the aid of a specially designed, highly sensitive instrument can provide proof of authenticity or the reverse. Examination of dyes may also yield valuable information.

Even the finest repairs to cloth show up under spectral analysis, although the value of rare old cloth does not invariably depend on its state of preservation. Defects inevitably occur in very old material which has been exposed to varying climatic conditions for long periods of time.

The touching-up of faded colors must unquestionably be regarded as a fraudulent modification. There is a widespread belief that the dyes used in early times were almost exclusively of a mineral type. This is inaccurate. Vegetable dyes were also employed, and thread treated with vegetable dyes frequently loses its color. If touching-up is carried out with sufficient care it will be detectable only by scrupulous chemical and optical examination.

What applies to rare cloth of ecclesiastical origin applies equally to that of secular manufacture, including brocatelle, lampas, satin, velvet and silk from the great age of textile manufacture in the sixteenth, seventeenth and eighteenth centuries.

All imitations lack the charming irregularities which testify so eloquently to the deliberation or impatience of those under whose deft hands the cloth of earlier times took shape.

During the sixteenth century, Brussels had gained a leading name for carpet manufacture. Antwerp manufacturers not only copied the "B" which appeared on the famous products of that city and the "BB" which identified those of Brabant but also adorned their wares with the trade-marks of the two centers.

In 1619, after years of wrangling, Antwerp ceased to use borrowed trade-marks but calmly went on copying the various weaves. "BB" weaves were produced in Holland, too. The Dutch factory of Schoonhoven claimed that there was no question of forgery because "BB" stood not for Brabant but for *"bon-bon."*

Despite the manifold difficulties involved, imitations of Gothic weaves occasionally turn up, although they are never of recent date. An ostensibly late Gothic portrayal of King Frederick III and Pope Pius II was based on a woodcut in the Nuremberg Chronicles of 1493, but the two figures grouped to left and right of the protagonists betrayed the forgery, conclusively if very belatedly. The figure on the left, described as the *"Marchio Brande"* or Margrave of Brandenburg, wore a Saxon coat of arms, while that of the Count Palatine on the right was a pure figment of the forger's imagination. It is not absolutely certain to what period this Gothic-style tapestry belongs, but it can hardly have originated earlier than 1700.

Gobelins, other forms of wall hanging and, in particular, Oriental carpets are a subject for the well-versed expert, and each of their numerous subdivisions represents a field in itself. Nevertheless, as we have seen, genuine and fake can be distinguished with vastly greater certainty in the case of textiles than in that of paintings and sculptures.

Mistakes can arise only from crass ignorance, but it is advisable never to acquire a Gobelin or a rare carpet without consulting a reliable specialist. Details scarcely perceptible to the layman will reveal not only age but origin to the true expert. A Persian carpet with a Turkish Ghiordes knot is just as suspect as a Turkish carpet with a Persian Senné knot.

In the case of Gobelins, the criteria upon which any decision between genuine and fake must be based are weaving technique, materials, and artistic design.

The earliest Western tapestries date back to the eleventh century. These exhibit a strong relationship to ecclesiastical book illumination, although secular themes were also exploited, if only in rare

instances. The Bayeux tapestry of the eleventh century and the
Scandinavian Baldesholtaeppet of the thirteenth both testify to
their authors' ideological independence.

The factories at Arras, Tournai and Paris played a leading role
in the development of tapestry. From the fifteenth century onwards,
Brussels and other cities entered the lists against them. One name
which remains permanently associated with the noblest works of
this particular art is Aubusson, a small township in the French
department of Creuse.

A form of fraud which can cost the inexperienced buyer dear is
the transformation of cheap but genuinely well-designed Persian
rugs into rare collectors' items. There are excellent, mediocre and
inferior examples of almost every design and origin. The difference
lies not only in the type and fineness of knot, but also in material
and workmanship.

Selecting a mediocre or cheap specimen whose decoration and
general design approximate that of a rare piece, the forger first
modifies its colors to match those which are such a salient feature
of valuable old rugs and then mercerizes it. This process, originally
evolved by J. Mercer, beautifies fabrics and imparts a wash-proof
luster with the aid of caustic alkali applied under tension. Thanks
to modern developments in this technique, mercerized textiles
acquire an almost silken sheen, and in recent years treatment with
synthetic substances has evoked a similar appearance even in cotton
fabrics. By means of these processes, the forger can now turn a
cheap rug into a "genuine silk Kheshan" of far greater value.

But, though the eye may be deceived, a single thread taken from
the fabric will suffice to disillusion the would-be purchaser. Even if
shaved down to the core, genuine silk remains what it is: genuine
silk. A strand of cotton or other material which has been treated to
resemble silk grows dull as soon as its glossy exterior is scraped off,

and threads steeped in synthetic additives shrivel when burned, whereas genuine silk thread merely glows.

The genuine Oriental carpet always exhibits a genuine fringe (one that grows naturally out of the terminal knots), while the fringe on a machine-made carpet is attached separately — a feature which provides sure means of recognition. Closer scrutiny will also reveal a painfully obvious contrast between the regularity which springs from mechanical production and the unique and charming irregularity peculiar to manual work.

9

❦❦❦❦❦❦❦❦

Furniture

FROM the forger's point of view, there is scarcely a more lucrative or extensive field of operations than that of antique furniture. The wish to surround oneself with old furniture may often be prompted by a subconscious belief that fine old pieces provide unobtrusive but tangible evidence of family background and tradition. It is undeniable, too, that there emanates from the fine workmanship of old cupboards, heavy tables, solid chests and armchairs an aura of calm and dependability which is especially welcome to those who live amid the bustle of modern times. However, the demand for works of art by the cabinetmakers of past centuries can hardly be attributed to the aesthetic sense alone — not, in any case, where old pieces are acquired rather than inherited.

The purchaser of any antique furniture, especially pieces of particular beauty or value (the two do not invariably go hand in hand), should ask himself to what degree they originated in the period to which they are ascribed. Certainly, no other province of art or craftsmanship includes a higher percentage of fakes and falsifications than that of old furniture. These include:

(1) The complete fake, a piece of period furniture which looks old but has been newly built in its entirety. Copied by hand from an old original, often with consummate skill, carefully aged by specialists and apparently complete with all the characteristic features of old cabinetmaking, this is insinuated into the market as a piece of genuine antique furniture.

(2) The professional or even industrial manufacture of period furniture from old wood.

(3) The reconstruction of a dilapidated but genuine old piece using additional components, made of old or new wood, which are adapted to the original members and artificially aged.

(4) The fraudulent embellishment of a plain antique, whether wholly or partially genuine, with inlay or ornamentation to simulate an appearance of greater value.

(5) Falsification with the aid of genuine old stylistic elements, such as the addition of so-called "noses" to unadorned Frankfurt cupboards. These and other forms of "improvement" are used in order to disguise date and place of origin. A similar purpose is served by replacing the tops of commodes or tables with slabs of marble, for the age of a marble slab, especially if it has been skillfully treated, is extremely hard to establish.

Because in France, true home of the individualist, the great cabinetmakers (*maîtres ébénistes*) used to sign their works, fakes based on such originals are adorned with the appropriate craftsman's cipher. The stamp is reproduced in metal and driven into the wood, heated or unheated, a much simpler matter than trying to add a convincing imitation of a signature to a picture. The indentations left by the stamp are then deliberately soiled and given a patina which matches the surface of the surrounding wood.

A furniture forger finds it easier than a picture forger to snap his fingers at the critic of style. The piece of furniture to be copied is photographed full face and profile so that accurate enlargement will give the exact geometric and cubic volume of the original. All that remains, given a supply of "period" wood, is cabinetmaker's work.

Furniture sustains a variety of hard knocks in the course of daily use, and even more extensive damage can result from removals. Many purchasers view these defects as a sign of the genuine antique. But, while it is true that genuine antique furniture almost always shows signs of damage, whether obvious or disguised by repairs, its presence is no guarantee of authenticity, for the forger makes a special point of simulating these outward marks of antiquity in unimportant places and then "repairing" them, sometimes in a crude and obvious way. Other pieces reach the market in a purposely dilapidated condition so that dealers have a chance to point out defects and suggest that they be remedied by expert treatment. Instead of accepting this as a token of the seller's honesty, the purchaser would often do better to regard it as a shrewd stroke of psychology.

The polishing of furniture, formerly a manual operation of the utmost drudgery, constitutes a field on its own. The hardwood surface was first smoothed very carefully and then polished, inch by inch, with a pad soaked in spirit. This work is now done mechanically, and a power-driven rotary polishing pad takes the place of thumb, forefinger and palm. Scrutiny of technical execution and polishing materials will distinguish with near certainty between new polish and genuine old polish which has merely been retouched.

Many apparently trivial details are worthy of close attention. A deep mirror, for instance, will display less shine on the lower portions of its frame than on the upper because the latter, not being so readily accessible, will have been less frequently polished and dusted over the years. A meticulous forger takes this circumstance into account and refrains from giving his mirror-frame a consistent polish.

No expert will be duped by the high-gloss surfaces achieved with a modern spray gun and cellulose lacquers.

Other things are much harder to detect: for example, the fact that an attractive little Empire table has been repaired with a reproduction leg. When making the new leg (out of old wood, of course) the forger had three existing legs to work from — although, had positions been reversed, one genuine old table leg would have provided just as adequate a guide, in respect to design, technique and proportions, for the reproduction of three missing legs.

Some forgers specialize in the manufacture of fake fittings, notably the flat plates which serve to embellish and reinforce keyholes. These are normally carved in metal and copied from an original, a fairly simple task. The scratches which always appear in the vicinity of keyholes are equally simple to reproduce. However, modern forgers work with electric saws which leave marks readily distinguishable from those made by hand-operated tools.

Particular attention should be paid to metal fittings such as hinges, locks and carrying handles. In the case of a very valuable piece, practical tests are advisable, for any doubts that may exist will usually be dispelled or confirmed by the removal of hinges, keyhole guards or interior door fittings. With utilitarian pieces of only moderate value, forgers will not bother to fit their substitutes too meticulously into the recesses left by old plates and ornaments of iron, brass or copper. For that reason, new "antique" fittings are simply made a little larger, to mask the original indentations. If they are removed, old nail or screw holes will be clearly visible, even when these have been filled in with a cellulose primer. The presence of fake metal fittings is enough to cast doubt on the authenticity of an entire piece.

Painting and lacquer-work is effected by the photographic transfer of decoration, ornamentation and pictorial motifs. If the imitator relies on his own imagination, obvious discrepancies between the piece of furniture and its decoration usually result.

The joints in furniture can be very illuminating. Tongue-and-groove joints were not introduced into cabinetmaking until the middle of the eighteenth century, so a piece which purports to be of earlier date but evinces this technique cannot be genuine. Laboratory tests on glue can also provide valuable information, and hand-wrought nails not only differ entirely from the machine-made article but are chronologically informative as well.

It should, however, be stressed that, as all these distinguishing features are known to the forger as well as the expert, old glue and handmade nails are far from an absolute guarantee of authenticity.

In this respect, the results of accurate research into the tools employed in cabinetmaking carry very much more weight. Electrically driven circular and band saws leave fairly conspicuous marks on wood which will preclude the possibility of its having been cut by an early cabinetmaker, for scarcely any mechanical planes or electric drills were in existence before the beginning of this century.

Masterpieces by the cabinetmakers of very early times, linen presses or Renaissance chests of the sixteenth century, buhl commodes, early Gothic folding chairs, baroque console tables or furniture of other early periods are just as susceptible of forgery as Chippendale or even Biedermeier pieces. However, the discriminating collector can console himself with the fact that celebrated cabinetmakers such as Leleu, Riesener, David Roentgen, Benemann and many others were possessed of greater craftsmanship and artistic ability and could spend infinitely more time on perfecting their creations than any modern forger.

It sometimes happens that professional furniture forgers turn out work of such outstanding quality that the market happily absorbs their output of brand-new antiques for decades. In a book of memoirs entitled *Au Pays des Antiquaires* (Paris, 1935) André Mailfert openly admitted that, while working in Orléans between 1908 and 1930, he took daily delivery of at least ten wooden beams removed from old houses in process of demolition and turned them into antique furniture. In all, he produced no less than seventy thousand "rare old pieces."

The majority of fake antiques occur in the medium, inferior or lowest price ranges. Generally speaking, lovers of old furniture seldom command enough practical or stylistic knowledge to enable them to distinguish the fake or falsification. Embarrassment tends to stifle the mild doubts which they may sometimes entertain. To them, the external appearance of a Georgian wine cooler, baroque commode or or even Gothic chest is all-important, and what percentage of a wing chair or corner cupboard is truly antique has little significance compared with the ocular impression made by the piece.

To satisfy the demand for antique furniture with antique furniture would be beyond the bounds of possibility. As the number of potential buyers increases, so the craft or business of faking antique furniture from every period gains in scope.

One of the simplest forms of fraud consists in adding dates like those carved by craftsmen of former times not only on door lintels but on furniture as well. Although the price of an old piece of furniture does not by any means depend solely or even principally on its age, materials and execution being far more important factors in determining value, dates usually exercise a quicker and more persuasive effect on the prospective buyer. On the other hand — and there's the rub — they also make it easier for an expert to detect the fake. Any stylistic incongruity between the piece as a whole and the date which has been carved into it or sculpted on it in bas-relief will give the game away. One can only wonder at the carelessness of the numerous experts who have failed to notice such inconsistencies. Before the First World War, the furniture section of one London museum proudly displayed a "Renaissance chest *de dato* 1526" which was later identified by the art historian Robert Schmidt as a Hamburg peasant chest — *de dato* 1826.

Considering that forgers of Gothic carvings find it hard to satisfy even their comparatively small requirements of old wood in the appropriate dimensions and quality, furniture forgers are confronted by a seemingly insoluble problem. Supplies of old wood hardly suffice for the frontal portions which are directly exposed to observation.

Fraudulent cabinetmakers make up this deficiency in genuine old wood with material which has been artificially aged. Spacious drying kilns compress years and decades of natural air-drying into a period of days. In numerous stages, the wood's surface is carefully treated with alkaline solutions and dilute acids. Subsequent drying in a kiln causes the detergents and acids, which will have impregnated the wood to a depth of several centimeters, to evaporate. Mechanical scouring, too, produces effects very similar to those caused by many years of natural cleaning.

When the surface of the artificially aged wood has been treated with lye and acid, dried and scoured, it is ready for staining. The most reliable method of toning down the color of wood is to use potassium permanganate, which becomes wedded to the fibers by a process of chemical decomposition. Having acquired a light, medium or dark shade, the wood must be left in the air to dry for a few days if chemical changes are not to make its surface unsuitable for polishing. Only then may kiln drying commence.

Further aging of material is effected with the same aids as are used in the case of picture panels, mounts and frames.

The technical execution of the cabinetmaker's work is governed by the nature of the piece to be reproduced. Our knowledge of the regulations observed by members of the old cabinetmakers' guilds is fairly detailed, and working methods can usually be dated to within a few decades. No piece which displays glued edges can be genuine medieval guild work, for the rule was that all contiguous boards should be jointed. The treatment of interior boards, supports and battens was likewise clearly prescribed, and an expert can draw useful conclusions from all these details.

Wood which is coarse-fibered or pierced by many knots is an almost invariable sign of the fake, for guild inspectors would not allow their members to use inferior timber.

In doubtful cases it is advisable to file off a little wood where it will not be noticed, say from the reverse side of a board, and burn it on a glass or china dish. Unstained natural wood will be reduced to light gray ash; timber stained with permanganate of potash leaves a darker residue.

The chemical examination of polish is of only limited importance because there are hardly any early pieces of polished furniture which have not had to be repeatedly restored in their time. Ignoring the few museum pieces which are subjected to constant and careful attention, genuine old polished furniture normally exhibits at least some dull patches. The fact that these are continuously spreading makes it necessary to restore and preserve the brilliance of the original polish. Surfaces which have been carefully stained with nut oil and darkened with polish over a longish period of time give a convincing impression of antiquity.

An expert can derive valuable information from the marks left on a piece of furniture by the tools employed to build it. Every period had its own particular manual techniques and implements. Often, even in imitations which have been manufactured with every due care, figures or ornamentation are produced as separate components instead of being carved out of the solid wood (small pieces being much easier to work with) and glued onto the main body. Again, decorative features are sometimes routed out of the solid wood by machine, but traces of this process are still detectable even when the appearance of the work has been enhanced by means of a superficial hand-finish.

Fake gilding is effected with the same technique as that used by the enchaser of sculptures. Instances of this can be detected by using the methods already prescribed in the case of enchased figures and frames.

Genuine old inlay differs from the modern fake both in substance and method of attachment, many materials being expensive and difficult to work with. The forger replaces genuine ivory with a substitute which is cheaper, softer, and more easily cut and fitted. For genuine tortoise-shell he uses plates of a synthetic substance which can be cut without trouble and is not so liable to split as the animal product. In place of the rare woods needed for marquetry decoration he employs cheap and readily available substitutes. Since these normally have to be stained, the presence of chemical coloring agents is a fairly reliable indication of forgery. In the case of wood staining (not to be confused with wood painting) the piece of wood must be impregnated at least to a depth of several millimeters in order to withstand smoothing and polishing. A superficial film of stain would be destroyed.

The speckled, lightly stained appearance of wood on the interior surfaces of cupboards and chests of drawers can be reproduced with the aid of ultraviolet and infrared rays, which leave no traces.

By means of hot and cold compressed air, wood inlays can be fitted together, expanded, and, after gluing, dried out at the same time as the surrounding mount.

The introduction of synthetic glues heralded a new age in cabinetmaking. Artificially manufactured out of urea-formaldehyde compounds, these glues were adhesives of a strength hitherto unknown and allowed pieces of wood to be "sweated" together. When two pieces of wood are clamped together, the chemical union of glue with wood welds their fibers into a unified mass. Thin sheets of genuine old wood can be mounted on heavy boards of new wood under pressure and their edges smoothed off.

The only practical method of detecting this is to drill a small hole into the wood. Minute quantities of sawdust from the internal lamination are enough to provide chemical evidence of synthetic resin, but especial care must be exercised in the selection and handling of the drill. Since the rapid rotation of an electric drill produces torsional vibrations which may easily cause the metal shaft to snap, the drill must be a short one. Drilling should be done as slowly as possible and frequent pauses be made to allow time for cooling. It is essential to calculate the permissible depth of the borehole in advance to avoid fracturing the external surface. It also goes without saying that drilling must be carried out only in an inconspicuous place.

Some experienced furniture forgers go to the lengths of exposing their finished "antiques" to the concentrated smoke of a low wood fire.

Complicated though the forger's subterfuges may be, they are all vulnerable to chemical and physical examination. However, enthusiasts and collectors utilize these facilities all too seldom, despite the fact that they would banish any uncertainty and very often eliminate the risk of financial loss.

10

❦❦❦❦❦❦❦❦❦

The Limits of the Forger's Art

THE forger's most powerful foe is time.

Even if chemical or physical processes successfully reproduce external and internal changes which would otherwise have taken centuries to appear, by compressing them into the space of days, weeks or months, the final effect is only specious. The artificial curtailment of a lengthy natural process may well simulate the outward effects of that process but it will seldom if ever eliminate the danger of detection. Even if, despite the inadequacies which a fake will normally exhibit when compared with an original work of art, it cannot be detected as such on purely stylistic and aesthetic grounds, differentiation by empirical means will still be possible in the majority of cases.

A forger may simulate the elapse of decades or centuries when producing an imitation, but even the most subtle tricks achieve only a limited degree of pseudo-antiquity. The dust which he rubs into the artificially engendered fissures in his paints possesses, after all, the attributes of twentieth-century and not nineteenth- or eighteenth-century dust. Modern, highly developed methods of research can not only detect artificial *craquelure* but accurately establish the age of particles of dirt which are meant to give a fake an appearance of authenticity. For all that, identification becomes correspondingly more difficult the closer a fake is to the period of the original or the more "genuine," in the temporal and chemical sense, are the artificial aids used in its manufacture.

The answer to the hackneyed but valid question of how it is possible for leading authorities to certify the authenticity of works of art which are later proved by the use of scientific methods of research to be forgeries runs as follows:

While the human eye can be deceived, scientific methods of research will, except in extremely rare cases, shed light on any forgery, and practical experiment can prove whether a work of art is a fake. The fact that it exhibits no outward symptoms of forgery does not in itself constitute evidence of authenticity, any more than it is proved that a doctor must be a first-rate physician because he is not a surgeon.

Expert opinions which are purposely fallacious must, of course, be excluded from the present discussion. Far from furnishing genuine information, they further the ends of fraud.

It is doubtful whether any artist of our own day can produce a work of art in the spirit, style, atmosphere and context of past centuries and still be termed as "creative" as the contemporary painter or sculptor. A true artist is more intimately linked, in spirit and sentiment, to his own time and environment than any other mortal. A work in the manner of an age long past may successfully reproduce the style but can never be begotten of nor sustained by the spirit of that age — a requirement which the true work of art invariably fulfills. An Apollo in the classical Greek manner becomes transformed, under the hands of a *cinquecento* sculptor, into a creative copy, separated from the original by an unbridgable chasm of spiritual and temporal incompatibility. The Byzantine saw his own time through his own eyes, just as the medieval artist embodied his own period in his own work. The artist of the late eighteenth and early nineteenth centuries saw and experienced, suffered and enjoyed differently from the artist of our own day. Different surroundings, problems, hopes, disappointments and successes all receive different expression in every field of art. A Bach cantata could probably be imitated today in that a modern composer might do his best to arrange some notes as though they were by Bach, but he would not be arranging them as Bach not only could but was probably compelled to arrange them. Even if an artist were capable, in some transcendental sense, of transferring himself to an earlier period he would still be, in an inherent sense, a prisoner of his own period, and his work, while wearing the garb of another century, would never possess the same intellectual and spiritual content.

Nevertheless, the ability to distinguish an intellectual and objective conflict between form and content, material and spirit belongs only to those who can pick their way without flinching along the vertiginous ridge between actuality and appearance.

An X-ray photograph seems to distinguish readily between a genuine van Gogh and a fake, yet a forger could object to such a finding on the grounds that, in view of van Gogh's various painting techniques, radiography may conceivably have demonstrated no more than a similarity to or discrepancy from certain of van Gogh's works. The factor of uncertainty would persist. Titian, Rubens, Rembrandt, van Eyck and many other painters changed their technique, implements and materials so radically that works from different stages in their creative development cannot always be identified with absolute certainty, either by simple practical tests or with the aid of chemistry or physics. In 1587 Armenini wrote of the "new, toilsome, dry and unpleasant work" which had resulted when van Eyck went over to pure oil paints. In Titian's early days, so we are informed by Vasari, he painted with such remarkable diligence and delicacy that his pictures were "equally effective at close quarters as from a distance," whereas he later "applied his paints broadly," so that "the picture looked complete and the figure alive only when seen from a distance." There is strong evidence that the bold brushwork and disregard of detail which characterized his later pictures were associated with farsightedness, a possible characteristic of Titian in his later years. Were one to base a scientific and technical examination of a very late work by Titian on the features typical of one of his very early pictures, the result might cast doubt on the authenticity of one or the other.

Scientific methods of research cover so wide a field that their detailed description must be reserved for specialized literature. The potentialities of modern laboratory tests are occasionally over- as well as underestimated, even by experts. Guy Isnard, a senior officer in the Paris police who devoted his life to detecting art forgeries and bringing to book those responsible for them, claims in his eminently readable *Les Pirates de la Peinture* that one simple and often conclusive method employed by experts when making practical tests on a picture is to probe its layers of paint with a pin: if the pin sticks in and stays there, this proves, apparently, that the picture in question was painted only a fairly short time before; if the pin penetrates the mass only with difficulty or not at all and the paints disintegrate under pressure, it may be assumed that the picture is an old one.

This claim is wholly untenable. Any forger with even a moderate degree of technical know-how can harden his paints artificially in such a way that the primitive pinprick test will reveal nothing. The classical example of this is Hans van Meegeren.

Of greater and more abiding importance are the facilities for scientific research afforded by numerous branches of photography, from close-ups of detail to enlargements, shots taken under various forms of doctored light, illumination and transillumination with sundry kinds of "ultra" rays, and X-ray photography of surface or substrata. Research into the use of X-rays for examining pictures conducted by Dr. C. Wolters for the Doerner Institute of Munich has produced some authoritative conclusions.

While never forgetting that, on the one hand, all true research into art must be based on and proceed from the individual characteristics of the work of art in question, and, on the other, that the radiographic examination of a painting only assumes its correct significance when used in close conjunction with every other facility for scientific research, it is important to note that X-rays show up two features in a painting with especial clarity:

(1) The use of white lead, which enables inferences to be made about a picture's light-construction. X-rays clearly bring out plastic and spatial structure, which is usually far more informative than the layout of line and plane. Moreover, features which can be perceived without technical aids, though indistinctly, become conspicuous.

(2) The artist's method of procedure, which furnishes information unobtainable from the finished work.

An optical microscope permits the viewer to scrutinize tiny, translucent particles of matter under thousandfold magnification, while an electronic microscope does likewise, but boosts the image a hundred thousand times or more. Colors can be eliminated or intensified by means of various filters. Also among the aids provided by the exact sciences are the results of wave-length tests and spectroscopic analysis.

The comparison-microscope enables one to view details of the internal construction of two paintings simultaneously, i.e. those of an indisputably genuine picture and a suspect one. Careful comparison will go far toward eliminating uncertainty.

Apart from optical tests, scientists also have at their command various methods of chemical analysis. Highly developed forms of modern apparatus make it possible to investigate the composition of minute fragments of material. Where a forger has made every effort to reconstitute old materials accurately, definite evidence of forgery may be impossible to obtain. However, if chemical analysis establishes the presence of even one substance which did not exist at the alleged date of a picture's origin, the suspicion that it is a fake will have been largely confirmed.

"Svelature, trenta o quaranta!" Titian used to apply between thirty and forty coats of glaze, not uniformly throughout a picture but in accordance with the needs of particular sections. It is therefore impossible to obtain positive proof that a whole painting is Titian's own work, even by radiographic examination of its substructure. *Alla prima* painting was followed by the gradual application of undercoats and overcoats, partly of common and partly of special resin varnishes. Titian followed the advice which he gave to others, namely to "smear" paint in order to achieve special effects. The interaction of clear, bright individual colors and contrasting hues was an evolved technique which differed considerably from that of his early days. For this reason, the examination of two works widely separated in time will only yield conclusions whose validity is limited to one or other of them — and that within fairly narrow limits. It is this circumstance which casts doubt on the absolute reliability of radiological or other purely scientific methods. These objections naturally lose their force when X-ray photographs or other chemico-physical methods of research disclose subsequent

overpaintings or other structural features, invisible to the naked eye, which provide cogent evidence of forgery or falsification.

In the case of clumsy imitations, the experienced art historian's criteria of observation are good enough to allow him to form largely reliable conclusions without recourse to the exact sciences. The factor of uncertainty grows in proportion to the quality of a fake.

Differentiation between genuine and fake is easiest in the case of Gothic figures, which combine the techniques of sculptor and painter. Their plasticity does not gain full expression until they have been enchased, usually by a combination of paint and gilding. (Unpainted specimens are exceptional.)

Here, several alternative courses of action lie open to the forger:

(1) Forging an entire work.

(2) Falsifying an old work by stylistic alteration, e.g. changing a High Gothic into a Romanesque figure by modifying its carving.

(3) Remodeling certain vital features of an original, e.g. changing a portrayal of a bishop into that of an emperor by transforming his miter into a crown.

(4) Complete remodeling, in which only the material of an original is employed for fraudulent purposes.

(5) Falsifying a simple treatment by gilding it with a view to increasing the value of the whole piece.

Expert opinions which confine themselves to extolling the style and external features of a work of art prove remarkably unreliable when they concern superior imitations. Works by forgers, imitators or archaists like Dossena, Bastianini, Antonio dal Zotto, van Meegeren, Malskat, Weininger and others have been unhesitatingly accepted as originals. Serious blunders on the part of eminent art experts have brought opinions based on general impressions into

severe disrepute and have frequently led to civil and criminal proceedings.

For many years, the Bavarian National Museum at Munich exhibited a figure known as *Der Ritter Sankt Georg* which was alleged to be "a characteristic work by the Tyrolese school of *circa*
1480." Wilhelm Pinder stressed its importance in his work on wood
sculpture. In 1927, this Gothic masterpiece (registered in *Das Bay-
erland,* Volume XXXVIII, I, p. 35) was declared to be a crude and
obvious fake, based on a late Gothic reference of about 1480 but
actually dating from 1860. It accordingly went down to join the
numerous other forgeries in the museum's cellars. But *Der Ritter
Sankt Georg* did not spend more than a few years in exile. Re-
newed investigation cleared the stain on his honor and restored
him to his original place in the museum. "Incontrovertible evidence" had (once again) proved beyond all doubt that he was a
valuable wood carving of *circa* 1480. Which of the two sets of "incontrovertible" evidence was really incontrovertible?

The human eye is not infallible. Founded on a mixture of knowledge and intuition, the art expert's opinion is vulnerable to the
forger's skill. In doubtful cases, therefore, the last word must rest
with scientific research. Of course an inadequate interpretation of
the exact answers furnished by chemistry or physics can transform
absolute into relative, for even the most perfect instrument is de-
pendent upon the human being who makes use of and "feeds" it.
Where doubt prevails, however, scientific tests carefully conducted
by qualified experts should be given pride of place over opinions
of a stylistic, aesthetic and intuitive nature.

The guiding principle must be that only chemical and physical
research can, in the last resort, distinguish between genuine and
fake. If the results of exact research are in conflict with art experts'
opinions, the latter must reluctantly be regarded as the product of
human error. That an art critic should persist in his opinion when

29.   Raphael, *Leo X:* Pitti Palace, Florence

30. The copy by Andrea del Sarto in Naples

confronted with the results of scientific tests is understandable, but he will never be able to justify his stand in factual terms. Where feeling and knowledge are in conflict, the intangible must yield to the tangible. In view of the fact that it is now possible, by measuring radiation phenomena, to determine the age of prehistoric rock, primitive implements and complex geological formations with a startling degree of accuracy, it would seem that few limits are set on the scientific identification of works of art. And yet undetectable forgeries do exist, as the following simple case will show.

In 1959, the Austrian state mint was still minting golden Emperor Franz Josef ducats and silver Maria Theresa thalers, the latter being still in use in Abyssinia. The new coins bear different dates, it is true, but the two monarchs' profiles and the textual and marginal inscriptions are those of the originals.

Several original dies belonging to rare and early Roman, Greek and medieval coins have disappeared in the course of the past two thousand years. These have been used to mint "archaic" collectors' pieces such as tetradrachmae, gold staters, gold solidi, bracteates, sequins and gulden in gold and silver alloys corresponding to those of the originals. Forgers swap these fakes from hand to hand to simulate the effect of natural wear or put them in small leather bags containing coins of the period in question. The connoisseur may sense a fake, but he will not always be able to prove it. Some optimists hoped that the "atomic clock" would identify even the most perfect forgery, but (according to Dr. Werner Koch) this method can only be used on objects whose material structure contains carbon with an atomic weight of 14.

Enchased Gothic carvings require particularly thorough examination in every respect: wood, priming, proportions, paints, gilding, and exterior and interior surfaces. Different works of art demand the use of different methods, although the extent of any research undertaken is limited by the value of a piece, especially if it is privately owned. In criminal proceedings which may have far-reaching consequences, the question of how much expenditure is justified must be determined from the juridical aspect.

A figure which has been newly made in its entirety is the easiest type of fake to detect. Specimens of wood obtained by drilling an inconspicuous hole in the base, concave back, or any deep recess will enable the age of the material to be identified with certainty. Where brand-new fakes are concerned, no artifice on the forger's part can seriously hinder their detection by analysis. Wood that has been treated with alkaline solutions or acids or buried in earth or mud for a considerable period becomes impregnated in a manner quite unlike that caused by genuine aging, and where fibers have become decomposed or stained they exhibit a uniformity which bears not the remotest similarity to the irregular structural changes which occur naturally in wood during the course of centuries.

If wood has been thoroughly impregnated with chemical solutions the surface becomes corroded or decomposed to such a degree that it can usually be detected with the naked eye. Even when subsequent washing and baking has taken place, the chemicals employed will not have been entirely removed. Fraudulent methods of achieving a spurious antiquity can be detected with the aid of simple reagents.

The use of genuine old wood makes detection of a fraud rather more laborious but never really difficult.

Where a forger has obtained his wood from the beams or supports of an old building, the process of carving, which removes the surface in part or whole, creates a "young" outer skin. In a genuine old work the surface and interior are of equal age, from the farthest projections to the deepest grooves and most concave areas.

For the forger, the prime requirement is that he should work, solely by hand, in the technique of the period and style of the artist to which he intends to ascribe his fake — a task to which only a

master of his craft can aspire. More than that, he must try to invest
his work, in its proportions, in the smallest detail of a fold of drapery and in the unity of its total effect, with the feeling of originality which is the natural attribute of any genuine work of art. He
will be lacking in the spontaneity which a truly creative artist of the
past derived from the spirit and experience of his age. The wood
carver of the fifteenth century got the inspiration for his saints
from the faith which animated him as a man of the Middle Ages;
the imitator of A.D. 1960 cannot hope to emulate him in this respect.
Disregarding the problem of material, it is this conscious attempt
to reproduce what is alien to one's nature which forms the chief
barrier to perfection of the forger's art.

A forger prefers to obviate the difficulties inherent in creating an
"old" composition of his own by adopting the simpler course of
imitating an old original, even though this will expose his work to
a greater risk of being recognized as a latter-day imitation. The old
masters did occasionally produce replicas of their work, so that
there are instances where two or more almost identical originals
exist. However, all such cases should be approached with the utmost caution because many replicas are only pupils' work.

Apart from the actual imitation of a work, the forger has many
smaller but nonetheless significant problems to overcome. An object of true antiquity displays many forms of patina, especially if it
comprises a variety of materials. Old wood becomes worm-eaten;
metals change, particularly on the surface; ivory grows discolored;
old textiles vary in fragility according to their thread; paints
darken; varnishes crack, shrivel or develop fissures. All these
symptoms must be reproduced by the forger.

Woodworms, for instance, are extremely inconvenient creatures.
In an old carved figure, their holes and tunnels correspond to the
sculptural design. Where a figure has been newly carved out of an
old beam or rafter, they tend to appear in unnatural positions.

When whole layers of wood have been cut away, they turn up in all the wrong places because the timber has assumed a totally different shape.

Some forgers attempt to provide worm-free wood with artificial wormholes. No modern forger worth his salt makes use of that old-time favorite, the small-caliber shotgun pellet, for this method can be readily detected by probing the holes with a needle. Not even a fine drill, auger or similar instrument can successfully reproduce the tunnels made by a genuine woodworm. The latter does not follow a straight course but eats his way round corners. Also, being a mortal creature, he leaves physiological traces. His tunnel becomes his tomb, and to fake a dead woodworm would overtax any forger's powers of ingenuity. Moreover, since worms die embedded in the wood fibers, it is no use trying to remove larvae and deceased worms from genuine holes and blow them into artificial tunnels, as some painstaking forgers have done.

Examination of the entrance itself will reveal whether a wormhole is genuine, for the woodworm's extraordinarily neat and efficient biting equipment produces an almost circular opening which leads straight into the tunnel without any abrasion of the external edges. Openings effected with the aid of drills, awls, pins or shot all exhibit edges characteristic of these forms of artifice. Attempts have been made to produce entirely circular holes and curving passages by heating bent needles and forcing them into the wood. This method certainly produces circular holes and curving passages, but it also leaves traces of carbonization which are visible with a magnifying glass of only moderate power.

The above applies to all forgeries in which wood is used: panel pictures, wooden sculptures, candlesticks, frames and furniture, to name only some.

The remarks about worm-eaten material apply in an even greater degree to enchased carvings, whose substrata of priming and painted surfaces make it considerably easier to test wormholes.

In an old enchased figure, wormholes do not run straight through the wood and emerge vertically. On reaching the layer of priming, a woodworm changes direction. Priming and paint are not to his taste, so he avoids the surface and bores farther into the wood, which is his natural food. That is why surfaces from which portions of decoration have disappeared often look like veritable labyrinths. Beneath the chalk, the wood has been riddled with crisscross furrows made by woodworms seeking a means of escape. It is this circumstance which prompts the forger to heat his work until it cracks in places and then adorn those places with artificial wormholes. Passages which have been made with some form of tool differ so substantially from natural passages that they can usually be detected with the naked eye. Furthermore, woodworms leave excrement and mortal remains in their escape trenches just as they do in the tunnels which run through the interior.

The chemical composition of paints and substances used for priming can be positively identified with the help of microscope, spectroscope and chemical reagents. The chemical nature of substances and their volume may also be ascertained by means of visible and invisible rays, which means that they can be compared both quantitatively and qualitatively with those of works known to be genuine. The combined use of complementary methods of research helps the expert to track down a fake. Even if the forger mixes his paints and priming according to medieval formulas and imitates the working methods of the old masters, he can never fully reproduce the natural changes which occur in substances during the course of centuries. Even if he ages his painting and gilding artificially, damages them, rubs them away down to the priming in some places, masks the gold in deep recesses with mud colors, warms the whole piece and, after drying it, glazes it with additional paints compounded of various substances, rubs the whole piece down again, covers it with dust, varnishes it, adds *craquelure,* and employs as many further artifices as his shrewd and inventive brain can devise — even if he does all these things to perfection, his very thoroughness will expose the fraud to chemical and physical examination, for each phase harbors a corresponding risk of detection.

Craquelure is particularly treacherous. A forger can reproduce this phenomenon, which is especially characteristic of old pictures painted on canvas, by any one of three methods:

(1) By scratching the surface varnish with a very sharp needle and rubbing dirt into the resulting fissures.

(2) By subjecting the surface to intense heat for a short period.

(3) By applying a coat of special *craquelure* varnish.

The latter, which is commercially obtainable, consists of two fluids, one of which dries more rapidly than the other: as hardening proceeds, the less volatile fluid bursts its faster-drying companion, thereby causing *craquelure.*

None of the artificial *craquelures* can withstand scientific investigation. Dust which has settled in genuine *craquelure* in the natural course of time is much more varied in composition than the "elementary" dust, soot, powdered pigment or plain dirt which the forger rubs into his artificial cracks, and chemical analysis of particles removed from these will determine whether it is young or old. Dust varies from century to century: fifty years ago, for instance, the air was innocent of diesel fumes.

In *Graphice,* a work which appeared in 1658, William Sanderson related that the painter Lanière of Paris had evolved an ingenious method of giving his pictures an appearance of age. Having completed a painting, he rolled it up, causing minute fissures on its surface which made it look like a genuine old original. So the secret of producing artificial *craquelure* by means of hard, quick-drying paints which cracked when rolled was already known by the middle of the seventeenth century — although there is strong evidence to suggest that fakes had been aged by similar devices much earlier than that.

The "flyspecks" on fake sculptures and paintings are usually reproduced by spraying them with a solution of powdered asphalt and turpentine. Investigation will immediately show, however, that these spots are deficient in the substances with which flies usually immortalize themselves!

New gilding which has been treated to resemble old is equally susceptible to expert examination. Medieval craftsmen did not roll their gold leaf in a modern precision press. Even the thickest of today's gold foils is much thinner than the finest medieval overlays. What is more, gold was alloyed differently in the Middle Ages, which offers a second means of detection.

Inspired by a painting by Simone Martini (1283-1344), Dossena sculpted a life-sized *Annunciation* in wood. Art experts were amazed at the sudden appearance of a group sculpture by the painter Simone Martini, but the true magnificence of the work triumphed over their initial uncertainty and it was acknowledged to be an original, despite the fact that careful scrutiny by an expert — a cabinetmaker would have done — would, without any scientific aids and instruments or even a magnifying glass, have demonstrated just how absurd it was to ascribe this work to a fourteenth-century artist.

Without any fraudulent intent, Dossena had obtained the wood for his monumental work by sticking several old blocks of wood together with commercially produced glue of a type which did not come on the market until after 1880. The very fact that its components were glued together in the modern manner proved that the work was not of the early Gothic period, since the contemporary practice was to attach separate components with wedge-shaped pegs, using bone-glue for additional strength.

What applies to the forgery of sculptures also applies, suitably modified, to other forms of imitation.

In the case of a picture painted on copper, the principal object of scrutiny should be the degree to which metal surface, paint and priming have become fused. Because time naturally produces markedly different degrees of porousness in the paint-covered copper on the picture's face and the bare metal on the reverse, this in itself facilitates an approximate assessment of its age.

Paintings on canvas should be submitted first to physical and then to chemical examination with reference to paints and layers of priming. Further tests will establish the character of the textile threads in a canvas and the extent to which they have become fused with priming and pigments. If these tests are carefully carried out, the possibility of error is negligible.

A forger often tries to disguise the nature of his canvas by *rentoilage,* or mounting the original fabric on a new canvas or wooden panel, ostensibly to strengthen it. Microscopic examination or chemical analysis will usually determine whether an old painting has been remounted in order to preserve it or solely to further the forger's ends.

In the case of drawings, whether of early or recent date, scientific differentiation between genuine and spurious is more difficult. The paper or cardboard on which they have been executed can always be reproduced in its original form, while the composition of lead, graphite or ruddle can also be imitated with a high degree of success. Once again, scientific investigations — particularly of a spectroscopic nature — furnishes valuable help in this much-favored province of forgery. Only where technique and intellect go hand in hand will an "ideal" conformity between the methods employed in a modern fake and those of earlier times create the essential conditions under which that fake will exhibit a convincing unity of material and form, composition and inspiration. When a fake does fulfill these requirements, the casting vote must go to the art historian or true expert on art.

Sculptures in stone or cast metal give scope for definite conclusions in the sphere of modern research, although the lines of demarcation become less distinct in the case of an imitation dating from the same period as the original or a little later. A work dating from the first century and based on an original from the first century cannot be identified by scientific means alone. Only searching examination and stylistic comparison by an art historian will determine the probable relationship of the two pieces.

The greater the lapse of time between original and imitation, the greater the chance of detecting a fake by means of exact science and stylistic knowledge. Patina, both in the symbolic and chemical sense, can be plausibly reproduced. But what deceives the human eye will not escape detection by sophisticated instruments.

Forgeries of goldsmiths' and silversmiths' work are almost always detectable, if only by dint of lengthy experimentation, nor will the stamping of forged or falsified works with genuine old dies prevent their being recognized for what they are.

Genuine and spurious can be distinguished with equal assurance in the fields of coinage, postage stamps, ceramics and the almost infinite range of antiquities in general.

Counterfeit money would be identified as such even if it had been manufactured by forgers' workshops which had access to all the technical facilities available to a firm of banknote printers operating under official aegis. During the Second World War, for example, German forgeries of English banknotes, though convincing enough to look at, were weeded out by the Bank of England's laboratory technicians.

Fake woodcuts, fake copperplate engravings, fake philatelic rarities, fake faïences and fake sarcophagi all serve to disturb the market, but this fact pales into insignificance beside another: namely, that modern methods of identification make it possible to detect forgeries. Anyone who wishes to assure himself that his collection of paintings or antiques is genuine should avail himself of these facilities — though many collectors are frightened of knowing the truth.

Scientific progress is alone responsible for the fact that increasingly accurate and reliable methods of identification are constantly diminishing the forger's field of action. A few decades ago, paint tests required the removal of quite large amounts of pigment from the picture under examination. Today, a few hundredths of a gram, whose removal will cause no damage, are quite sufficient for the purpose. The synthetic paints Prussian blue and Chinese white have been in existence only since the eighteenth century; synthetic ultramarine, cobalt blue and cadmium yellow since the nineteenth. Pictures containing these pigments cannot, therefore, have originated earlier than the eighteenth or nineteenth centuries respectively.

Excellent fakes of fifteenth- and sixteenth-century works whose paints, materials, brushwork and aging all exhibit skillful treatment have often been positively identified because X-ray photographs showed that the canvases were attached to their frames with machine-made nails. Since the old masters used handmade nails (no others yet existed) and nailing coincided with the completion of painting, evidence of mechanically produced nails is usually enough to settle the question of authenticity beyond dispute.

We are familiar in outline with the essential features of the technical methods employed by great exponents of the classical periods and possess a detailed knowledge of the working methods of many of the great painters of the nineteenth and twentieth centuries. W. F. Burger has the following to say about Ferdinand Hodler's Maloja landscapes: The Swiss painter used only eight colors: madder lake, light ultramarine blue, oxide of chromium brilliant, cadmium lemon, light ocher, dark ocher, vermilion and white. He began by making a brush drawing, dark areas in blue and light areas in madder lake, going into considerable detail. Next, thinning his colors with petrol, Hodler painted realistically on top of this underpainting. He then took his palette knife and removed all but a thin layer of paint, submitting even the center of his canvas to this treatment, but tending to leave a thicker layer round the edges. Following that, he did some more brush drawing with thinned color, then painted opaquely over it, and finally scraped it off again with his knife.

Such exact knowledge of a picture's construction and the colors and type of brushwork employed makes it very much easier to differentiate between genuine and fake. However painstaking he is, a forger seldom commands the knowledge and scarcely ever the patience to imitate another man's technique perfectly in all respects.

PART THREE

The Forger's Interests

11

❦❦❦❦❦❦❦❦❦

Dossena, the Human Anachronism

THE First World War flooded the international market with major art treasures from a variety of sources, some known and others obscure. Valuables of every sort changed hands. Aristocrats who had fallen on evil days turned their collections into ready cash, and countries parted with showpieces from their national collections which they would never have dreamed of selling once upon a time, often under the pretext that they were duplicates. Many acquisitions of illicit origin found their way onto the black market and into the collections of men who asked no questions because their lust to possess the hitherto unobtainable overwhelmed every other consideration.

Supply was matched by an equally brisk demand as growing inflation triggered off a flight into tangible assets. There were few safer or more compact methods of salting away large sums of money than the acquisition of masterpieces by great artists.

In 1918 there appeared in Paris several sculptures, formerly

Italian-owned, of such high quality that the question of their origin was discussed with bated breath. Collectors, art historians and dealers all paid homage to these treasures, which gave evidence of true greatness. In accordance with their relative merits, they found new homes in famous museums and private collections.

These works of art were followed by others of equal quality. They came from Rome. Was the Vatican parting with items from its vast store of treasures, or did they hail from a private collection which was being disposed of, for some unaccountable reason, through discreet and reliable middlemen?

Judging by the number of sculptures involved, they were closely guarded items from a very extensive collection, for the magnificent works which were being offered for sale were as unknown as their artistic merit was obvious.

The various items dated from such unrelated periods that no sort of case could be made out for their having originated in a collection built up on historical lines. They varied in material, too, from marble and terra cotta to wood. If they had indeed shared a common origin, their very diversity pointed in the direction of museum ownership. The absolute discretion preserved by leading antiquarians and the avoidance of sale by auction, which would have been the normal procedure in such a case, seemed to confirm this. Many authorities expatiated upon their knowledge of the masters and schools to which they unhesitatingly ascribed these sculptures.

Of unique importance from the art historian's point of view was a sculpture by Simone Martini, the painter, who had never been known as an artist in wood or stone before. Two reliefs, *The Virgin with St. Anthony* and a *Madonna and Child,* numerous portrait busts, an *Annunciation* in wood and a marble fountain portraying the Madonna afforded art experts a new insight into the creative activity of great masters of long ago. The prices paid for these works of art during the next decade exceeded five figures in almost every case.

The magnificent sculptures which caused such a sensation in the market between 1918 and 1928 — brilliant examples of the creative art of two millennia, from archaic masterpieces like the Greek *Athene* and *Attic Warrior* to noble Gothic carvings and Renaissance terra cottas — were all the work of a single man who worked in a small workshop by the Tiber, not far from the Castel Sant' Angelo. His name was Alceo Dossena.

The story of how the simple craftsman Alceo Dossena became the stonemason of the century has now passed into legend. The Roman art dealer Jandolo has given an enthralling account of the beginning of Dossena's connection with the art world.

On Christmas Eve, 1916, Alceo Dossena arrived in Rome as a private soldier on leave from the garrison at Poggio Mirteto. Although his meager pay had not run even to a modest present for his family, he was putting his faith in the *Madonna,* not the one to whom he prayed so devoutly but the wooden one which he had carved in relief. He was hoping that the sale of this little work of art, which had gradually taken shape under his hands during off-duty hours, would provide the money for his Christmas presents. Weary, he dropped in at the Frascati wineshop on the Via Mario de Fiori, concealing under his military cloak the newspaper-wrapped parcel which contained the figure. After he had drunk a Chianti he carefully laid the parcel on the table beside him. Before long, the inquisitive landlord wanted to know what his customer had in the parcel. With some hesitation, Dossena showed him the *Madonna,* but the landlord had plenty of religious knickknacks already, and was not interested. On the other hand, he was never averse to doing a little business, so he went and fetched the goldsmith Alfredo

Fasoli from his workshop across the way. Alfredo knew something about art, and the landlord nudged him as a sign not to forget him if a bargain was struck.

Fasoli hemmed and hawed. He asked where the carving had come from. Dossena told him that he was selling it for a friend who was on duty over Christmas.

Fasoli at once recognized the merits of the figure and assumed that the soldiers had "found" it in an old chapel somewhere. After a certain amount of haggling he bought the *Madonna* for a hundred lire. The soldier was as delighted as the goldsmith, who thought he had made a real bargain.

Later, on examining the sculpture more closely, Fasoli realized his mistake. It was a beautiful piece of workmanship and had obviously been made by a master of his craft. There was only one snag: it wasn't old. It merely looked old. Fasoli was immediately struck by the thought that the hands which had fashioned this relief could make something even more convincing, more deceptive — more lucrative.

Quite by chance, Fasoli bumped into the soldier again. He talked him into producing more of the same kind of work, this time properly aged and technically more perfect.

Alceo Dossena listened. He didn't know whether he was good enough. Still, the man had paid him a hundred lire for the *Madonna,* and he had only been able to spend a few hours of his spare time on it. Given a little peace and quiet and better working facilities, he might be able to produce something better. He agreed.

After his release from military service, Dossena started regular work as one of the artist craftsmen in which Italy abounds. They live unpretentiously, a job well done being their one source of satisfaction, contentment and peace of mind.

The first sculpture supplied by Alceo Dossena was a figure in medieval style. Fasoli sold it without difficulty for 3000 lire, of which almost 2000 came in gold. Inflation had begun to gnaw at Italy's monetary stability.

Dossena received 200 lire. He was worried. He hoped that Fasoli was not losing on the deal: 200 lire was a lot of money!

Evidently, Fasoli could not keep his secret, the secret called Dossena, to himself. Either that, or other people must have found out about the stonemason by the Tiber, for his clientele grew and orders flowed in.

There is absolutely no evidence to suggest that Dossena ever knowingly defrauded a third party. He merely supplied work which had been ordered from him exactly as his customers wanted it: archaic, Roman, Gothic or Hellenistic. Middlemen of every complexion buzzed round the honeypot.

There was no problem in finding purchasers, but potential customers of the more discriminating kind became increasingly curious about the origin of such first-rate works, and many of them would not be satisfied with enigmatic hints alone. Accordingly, dealers had to manufacture pedigrees so that buyers who wanted something more concrete than a discreet allusion to the Vatican, a princely house or museum could be provided with documentary evidence.

Anyone who sold one of his fake Greek goddesses took the trouble to provide it with all the requisite documentation. But, as an artist craftsman, Alceo Dossena had absolutely nothing to do with these subterfuges.

Dossena's work was hewn stone, carved wood, fired terra cotta. Anything else lay beyond the horizons of a world which encompassed only his workshop, home and family. The fact that he spent long spells of time "on the loose," tasting the delights of sun-kissed wine and sun-kissed maidens, was consistent with an Italian temperament which combined the weary round of daily toil with hours devoted to *dolce far niente* and intoxicating sensuality, a har-

mony of opposites which found expression in the varied nature
of his work.

Meanwhile, the leading art dealers grew more demanding, and
Dossena's clients switched their attention to pieces of even higher
quality and greater rarity. Almost effortlessly, Dossena adapted his
work to meet their more ambitious requirements.

From a well-known dealer in Florence came an order for an
early Renaissance tomb in the style of Mino da Fiesole. The inscription, he suggested, could be made to refer to the Savelli family,
for there was evidence that a tomb belonging to this house had once
existed. When Dossena had successfully completed the work, it
could be conveniently discovered in a suitable place.

Dossena produced a work of art in the requisite style and a
conscientious scholar unearthed the patrician family's last resting-
place in a dilapidated little church standing on land which had
once belonged to them. After centuries of oblivion, the *Tomb of the
Savelli* emerged in all its High Gothic splendor. Even more miraculous was the discovery of a receipt signed by Mino da Fiesole
himself in which he acknowledged payment by the Savelli of a fee
for stonemason's work. A work of art of the *quattrocento* AND
a contemporary document indicating it to be the work of one of the
greatest sculptors of the period! It was almost too good to be true.

After passing through many hands, the *Tomb of the Savelli* was
eventually acquired for six million lire, a very high price, despite
the inflationary conditions prevailing at the time. Dossena received
25,000 lire for his work.

Another commission from the same quarter required him to
produce an *Athene*. Dossena fashioned this work, belonging, as
it did, to a cultural sphere fifteen hundred years earlier than his
Savelli tomb, with complete mastery and conviction.

The *Athene* was just over 5 feet 6 inches tall. Its classical beauty
makes it worthy of comparison with the *Apollo* of Vei and other

superb examples of ancient sculpture, while its movement, miraculously captured in stone yet retaining its animation, puts the eye of the beholder under the same spell. Tangible form and spiritual content combine to produce a harmonious unity.

Dossena did not confine himself to creative work alone. He also gave his sculpture a faintly luminous patina of the correct texture by treating the stone with a liquid paste which sank deep into its pores and, when dry, left the surface rock-hard and faintly discolored. Dossena took the secret of this paste to his grave. All we know today is that he immersed his archaic sculptures in the mixture, usually more than once. A large cement-lined pit in the workshop of the house on the Tiber shows us where he used to lower and raise his statues with the help of a winch.

Two things occurred to change the life of Dossena and the people who lived around (and on) him. First, he got into severe financial straits because of his wife's death, and, second, he caught wind of the enormous sums which were being paid for certain of his works.

Hitherto, he had not worried about the dealers' profits. He was a craftsman and, as such, unaffected by the profit margins of those who commissioned his work. They bore the potential risk of being left with the pieces on their hands, so he let them take what profit they thought fit. This mentality was fully in accordance with the spirit of the old guilds, from which only those who deserted the craftsman's society and milieu and rose to be free-lance artists in their own right could ever be free.

When Dossena, armed with the knowledge of the fantastic sums which had been fetched by his works, sought out the Roman antiquarian who had sold his *Madonna and Child* for three million lire and paid him fifty thousand for it, he received a rude awakening.

He needed some money to pay funeral expenses and asked the man for an advance. He was refused. Let him first bring along a marketable sculpture, said the dealer, and some money would then be forthcoming—not a day sooner. Dossena returned home in a thoughtful mood. After brooding for some days in the silence of his deserted house, he came to a decision. He would go and see a lawyer.

The legal position was clear. He had never sold a sculpture under false pretenses. His clients, on the other hand, knew that the sculptures they bought from him were all his own work. What they paid him was no more than the normal price for good contemporary work. He supplied what was ordered without fraudulent intent, without being party to any deception and without deriving any financial gain from the fact that his creations were resold as medieval or classical originals.

It is quite possible that Dossena's major works would still occupy a place of honor today, had not excessive greed and ill-advised meanness finally impelled the artist to air the whole sordid business. Of course, doubt might have been cast on one or two of his works as time went by, particularly the sculptures in wood, whose technical treatment of material betrayed their very recent origin and could scarcely have resisted close examination indefinitely. But the large works were never in question until Dossena's own deposition showed them for what they were: works of art of the *quattrocento* and *cinquecento,* made in the twentieth century by a man who lived not only in his own time but in the fourteenth and fifteenth centuries and in the early Christian world as well.

Dossena's revelations triggered off an explosion which shook the art world as it had never been shaken before.

Many men of international standing were hard hit by the news. The first to react was the Paris antiquarian Jakob Hirsch, who at once traveled to Rome. The *Athene* had passed through his hands.

For him, more was at stake than a few million francs. His own name and the reputation of his firm were in jeopardy.

Hirsch had at first dismissed the story as a tendentious rumor put about by competitors and maliciously inclined dealers, experts and collectors who felt that he had passed them over. The *Athene* couldn't, mustn't be a fake. The stone goddess was as genuine as the six-carat diamond on the little finger of his left hand.

Face to face with Dossena at last, the Paris antiquarian, with an outward semblance of calm, put the fateful question. The answer was a crushing disappointment.

Hirsch expostulated. He went over to the attack. There was little doubt in his mind, he said, that Dossena, a nobody, a penni-less stonemason who had spent his life in squalid surroundings, was laying claim to the authorship of such superb masterpieces only because he imagined that the publicity would help him to escape from the obscurity of his daily life into the glamorous sunshine of success.

Dossena smiled, went into a neighboring room, rummaged about among some rubbish in a corner, and came back with a fragment of stone: the fingers missing from the *Athene's* hand. There was no mistake about it. Dossena told Hirsch that he had "amputated" them because his client wanted it so. Like all ancient sculptures, the *Athene* had to exhibit visible signs of age. All genuine old sculp-tures got knocked about a bit, he pointed out, and two thousand years was a long time . . .

Dossena had supplied conclusive proof that the *Athene* was his own work. It was as though the creator of the Venus di Milo had produced her missing arm as evidence of authorship.

Jakob Hirsch knew what was involved. It was not principally a question of incurring financial loss, but — and this was far more important — of forfeiting the confidence of art enthusiasts in every

corner of the world. The international trade in art and the reputation of leading art historians were endangered. What happened to
Hirsch would happen to other antiquarians, large and small.

There was only one chance of saving what remained to be
saved: to insist that all the works of art whose authenticity had
been impugned by Dossena's allegations were genuine. The most
that might be conceded was that Dossena had carried out restoration
work on them, which would explain his detailed knowledge of the
pieces in question. He was, in fact, nothing more or less than a
craftsman turned megalomaniac.

The experts who had certified Dossena's work to be authentic
hoped that this plan of campaign would save both their honor and
their reputation as authorities on art.

All the art historians who had ever uttered doubts about the
sculptures sunned themselves in their newly confirmed wisdom,
prevision and infallibility. Those whose opinions had fallen upon
deaf ears now pointed with ruthless logic to the crude symptoms
of forgery in Dossena's work. How far these crushing attacks
were inspired by deep moral conviction, a quest for truth and desire for enlightenment it is difficult to determine.

The Dossena case not only developed into a scandal of the first
magnitude but presented the art world with some highly unusual
problems.

Dossena's activities were not confined to works from a single
period. They covered a span of time whose beginning was dominated by the spirit of the ancient world and whose end was steeped
in the spirit of the Renaissance. He had not merely imitated originals within the narrow confines of a few decades, but recreated
work in stylistic and artistic forms which were fifteen hundred
years apart in time. The former task should not present an efficient
copyist with any undue difficulty; the latter, considering the variety
and range of Dossena's original work, presupposes true greatness.

While the imitation of differing stylistic forms might seem to the superficial observer to be only a matter of technique and craftsmanship, any art historian will realize what really insuperable problems are posed by the task of lending shape and expression to spiritual opposites. The contrast between archaic sculpture, which captured the human form in repose, and late medieval sculpture, which expressed life and motion in a solid medium, is as great as the intellectual and spiritual heterogeneity of the cultural backgrounds, separated by fifteen hundred years, from which they sprang. Under Dossena's hands, both received genuine expression.

A whole literature grew up round Dossena and his oeuvre. Art historians who had once described many of his sculptures as magnificent works now wrote them off as worthless fakes. They would have been wiser to define them as archaistic but creative works, thus conceding that the experts had been guilty of an interpretative error but not exposing them to the charge of having acknowledged fakes to be genuine.

Other authorities sought refuge in the word "copyist," but found themselves unable to point to a single original which Dossena had reproduced. Accordingly, a paraphrase was devised: there are copies which have no single original, but single copies which an imitator bases on several different originals.

A final attempt to explain away the Dossena phenomenon was made by those who claimed that he had found substantial inspiration for many of his ancient sculptures in the *Goddess Enthroned*.

This *Goddess Enthroned* was a fine example of archaic Greek sculpture and regarded as one of the greatest treasures in Berlin's Museum of Antiquities. The fact that it had been described by the Italian art historian Galli as a late medieval forgery did not discourage the champions of this theory from tracing certain details in Dossena's sculptures back to an original which was not unanimously recognized as such.

Dossena was neither copyist nor forger nor imitator. Just as he reproduced Simone Martini's skill as a painter in sculptural terms by re-creating a two-dimensional Madonna in three dimensions, so he also worked from incorporeal "pictures" visible only to his inward eye. He succeeded in projecting the world of long ago into his own time and giving it tangible expression, far surpassing the archaist Giovanni Bastianini in the spiritual content of his work.

Zadikov, the Berlin sculptor who worked in Paris, told Adolph Donath, editor of the *International Art Review* and chief adviser on art to the *Berliner Tageblatt,* of his visit to Dossena's Roman studio in the year 1930. He saw a kneeling angel in Gothic style made out of old, worm-eaten wood, and near it two completed Renaissance busts in marble, models for reliefs, bronze statuettes in High Renaissance manner, and archaic heads.

"I felt that I had seen it all before, yet it was all strange in some way. In one of the marble fragments of the hand I recognized a genuine piece, probably a model. But, when I questioned him about this, Dossena was particularly emphatic that it was all his own work. I was far from satisfied, however. The very dissimilar treatment displayed by the various pieces struck me as suspicious . . . I couldn't reconcile the Gothic angel and the more austere pieces with Dossena's appearance and character. After all, there is an inward link between an artist and his work. One can recognize a man's handwriting even in imitations."

Zadikov, cited by Donath as a "master," went on to claim full confirmation of his surmise that excellent forgers' schools had existed in Italy for centuries. "Dossena was the head of one of these. But his especial skill lay in the fact that his works were never straightforward copies but new creations, each of which was based on some well-known style."

There is no factual basis for the assertion that Dossena was a leading light in the schools of forgery which had flourished in

Italy for centuries. All that is worthy of note is the expert sculptor's admission that he had not been able to reconcile "the Gothic angel and the more austere pieces" with Dossena's appearance and character. So they were of alien character and appearance — but whose and what sort? And how Zadikov was able to recognize the authenticity of a fragment of stone at a glance remains his personal secret.

Adolph Donath, one of prewar Germany's leading experts on art, declares in his book *How Forgers Work* that "Dossena's work leaves us unmoved." Since he can hardly be using the royal "we," this presumably refers to art experts in general. In that case, why did eminent members of that fellowship lavish superlatives on Dossena's work before he designated it as his own?

A mere four sentences later, Donath compares the manner in which Dossena aged his sculptures with that used by Michelangelo when he buried his freshly sculpted *Sleeping Cupid* to give it patina, adding, however, "with the difference that Michelangelo was Michelangelo" — a qualification which is as broad as it is long. Forgery by means of artificial patina remains forgery, whoever the perpetrator.

Experts who had fallen over each other to pay tribute to Dossena's sculptures and ascribe them to Donatello's circle, the early Gothic Pisano family, Verrocchio's studio or other early sources now dismissed them, from one day to the next, as obvious examples of the forger's art.

Anyone who tries to be analytically and intellectually fair to Dossena will at once meet a drawback which is always in evidence when well-knit facts contradict the best-knit theories.

As a human being, a craftsman and an artist, Alceo Dossena poses three questions which must be answered before any discussion of his personality or activities can take place.

(1) What explanation is there for the fact that an artist of his ability spent fifty years of his life in complete anonymity, to emerge into the glare of international publicity only because of circumstances which lay beyond the artistic sphere?

(2) How was it that a man of Dossena's creative powers declined to base his oeuvre on personal experience of his own environment, rejected contemporary subjects, and drew his inspiration from periods which lay centuries in the past?

(3) How could a man of the early twentieth century perform with equal facility and conviction in the style of the pre-Christian era and of the fourteenth and fifteenth centuries, exhibiting such spontaneity that his work seemed, in a fundamental sense, empirically genuine?

Of all the vast band of archaists, imitators, copyists, forgers and falsifiers who have marched parallel to the straight and narrow path of the creative artist from the earliest times to our own day, none has ever emerged as a phemomenon far beyond the norm save Alceo Dossena, for he represented — and this may be the way to enlightenment — a link between the twin worlds of actuality and appearance.

Just as important but controversial figures in history have become distorted by the hatred or indulgence of their detractors or partisans, so portrayals of Dossena's character range from the rough sketch to the harshest of black-and-white treatments. He has been described as a genius, a fraudulent genius, a handicraftsman, a fraud. If insanity is the brother of genius, its cousin may well be stupidity — but never rascality.

Let us attempt to find the answers to our three basic questions.

Until the day when he made his deposition, Dossena was unknown. He belonged to the mass of Roman craftsmen who turn their inherited abilities to the pursuit of a trade which ensures them a livelihood, usually a fairly slender one. They are their own masters, work when they think it necessary, loaf around when they feel like it. In short, they are free agents.

Rome's great and overwhelming past is at once a curse and a blessing. No one can ever shake it off, whether he engraves golden cups, glues broken windows together, repairs the gilt on wooden candelabras or restores the ancient patina to copper vessels which some well-meaning servant from the Campagna has polished in error. Only very occasionally does an exuberant temperament burst the bounds of this little world and open like a flower in the sun.

No smooth passage awaits this blossoming desire for fame and recognition as it does for the artist of the North. The handicraftsman, whatever his advantages, lacks the means to realize his art in freedom. Hence, like Dossena, he finds satisfaction in work for its own sake and disregards the chances of success on a wider scale.

His work, though creative, derives its thematic and formal sustenance from archaic and medieval classicism. He is imperceptibly steeped in the environment of the present, which has become merged with that of the related past to form a single stream.

The answer to the question of how a modern man can give the same visual expression to what is long past as an artist who experiences it in the present can be sought only in an admission that exceptions do exist: namely, creative beings who are so intimately tied to the past that they live not in their own period but in others. This, however, conflicts with the general validity of the hypothesis that it is impossible for a man to produce creative works of art outside his own period.

The Dossena case shows — and it is impossible to escape this conclusion — that there are no absolute rules or norms in the domain of art.

Whether Dossena's original motives for producing archaic and medieval sculptures were of a materialistic nature, as the case of the

Madonna carved during respites from military duty would seem to suggest, or arose from sheer joy in his work and an inward compulsion, in which case financial gain took second place to artistic performance, remains an open question.

Is it so improbable to suggest that Dossena, activated by forces of a metaphysical nature, worked from inner compulsion in a manner which was at once his own and that of others? His works were forgeries in a material sense but, in an immaterial sense, creative originals.

None of this is affected by the objections of art historians who regard the artificial aging, patinating, splitting, cracking and breaking of Dossena's works as evidence, if not of deliberate fraud, at least of a predisposition in that direction.

There is a more plausible explanation of this. If an artist of Dossena's rank expresses himself creatively in archaic or classical terms because of some inward compulsion, he will not be fully satisfied until the completed work is genuine, in his own estimation, down to the last detail.

This is fundamentally different from the motive which inspires imitators or forgers, who age their work to make it sell better and more readily. Dossena had no such intention. Had he been in league with the men who exploited his efforts he would undoubtedly have demanded fees much higher than those which he actually received. In fact, they bore little relation even to the manual labor involved.

It is worth mentioning that Dossena was not alone in his predilection for artificial aging. For instance, although Lenbach did not personally age his own paintings, he did not object to people darkening them or imparting a *craquelure* to their varnish, because it made them look more like paintings by masters of former times.

Dossena said of himself: "I was born in our time, but with the soul, taste and perception of other ages."

Dr. Hans Cürlis, Director of the Institute of Cultural Research at Berlin and maker of the film on Dossena, sheds light on the whole problem with the following description of the Roman stone-mason's technique:

We watched Dossena modeling for a long time before we filmed him. He was working on a life-sized clay group of three mourning women for a war memorial at Cremona. His technique was scrupulously academic. The figures were first modeled accurately from the life, a pair of large wooden dividers being frequently used to measure length of limb, head and distances on the model and transfer them to the clay figure. Later, Dossena draped a robe over the model and did the same in clay to his nude figures. . . . As if for relaxation from this arduous work, he then spent days modeling fourteen reliefs of the Stations of the Cross which he had been commissioned to execute for the Vatican.

And here we witnessed the most amazing example of a sculptor at work. Unhurriedly, but in the space of a few minutes and without any plastic or two-dimensional sketch, figures in high and medium relief came into being. Everything happened so quickly and unexpectedly that we could scarcely get the camera into position in time. The ancients must have exercised a like facility when they improvised stucco decoration for the ceilings and walls of castles and churches. With equal unconcern, Dossena modeled daring and imaginative architecture, city gates and walls whose large plane structures projected from the background in bold perspective.

We were naturally very keen to see Dossena at work on an archaic statue. When he inquired what he should make, I asked him for a Greek goddess. He offered us the choice of a standing or seated figure, and, while we were deciding on the former, had already selected a few pieces of wood and was building the armature. Half an hour later we were looking at an Attic goddess, some two feet tall, modeled in clay with the captivating beauty which springs from the only slightly relieved rigidity which we admire in the best genuine pieces. It is noteworthy that this work, without more of a pause than it took to utter our wishes, ensued directly on the Passion relief described above. The goddess, too, was first modeled in the nude and then draped in her robe. The head took shape with equal fluency, and quite suddenly a smile dawned on the face of a woman to whom the Greeks had prayed two thousand five hundred years before. We filmed Dossena working with mallet and chisel on the reclining figure of an early Greek warrior, complete master of his technique and entirely unconcerned about the final result. We also filmed him drawing a head of Christ crowned with thorns, which he conjured up in light and shade with charcoal on a dark stumped ground.

We watched Dossena for many days. He worked with a complete lack of affectation and mystery, from time to time singing an air from an opera or smiling at us in friendly fashion. In fact, the abnormality of his work became so natural that it only later occurred to us that we had witnessed the reincarnation of a Renaissance master and an Attic sculptor. To an art historian, at least, but also to me, this is at once an alarming and an enthralling thought. One of the fundamental laws governing our attitude to all art seems to have lost its meaning, the law according to which a work of art can only originate once, at the point where certain temporally determinate causes intersect. It is as though causality has been suspended and its dogmas cut adrift from the safe anchorage of experience.

Nor is the matter sufficiently explained by the fashionable "state of trance" theory. Certainly, no such conclusion can be drawn either from Dossena's personality or his working methods. In unscholarly terms: we should be glad that our age was so flexible that Alceo Dossena, a true child of that age, could work where his inclinations lay.

The fact that none of Dossena's works was a copy and each one an expression of its period was acknowledged by many leading authorities such as Wilhelm von Bode, Swarzenski, von Hadeln, Loeser, Moll, D. B. Groves, Perkins, Parson and others.

The Boston Museum of Fine Arts acquired a "sarcophagus by Mino da Fiesole" for $100,000, New York's Metropolitan Museum a "Greek goddess," and the Cleveland Museum of Fine Arts a "Madonna and Child by Pisano." All three masterpieces were the work of Alceo Dossena. It has been estimated that the works by

31.   Albrecht Dürer, *St Eustace*, from the Paumgartner altar (1494), after restoration: Alte Pinakothek, Munich

32.   The same picture before restoration, showing the additions of Johann Georg
Fischer, made in 1614.

33. Sir Joshua Reynolds, *The Misses Payne*: Lady Lever Coll., Port Sunlight, Ches. One of the masterpieces of 18th-century English painting has been tampered with, as the following illustration shows.

34. The same picture after cleaning. The previous restorer has painted out the figure of the mother, regarding it as an intrusion which disturbed the smooth harmony of the work. Reproduced by kind permission of the Trustees of the Lady Lever Collection.

35. A pastiche alleged to be the work of Holbein. From each of the two pictures shown here, the forger used one half — the upper half of the first, the lower half of the second. The present location of the work is unknown.

36 *a*. Hans Holbein the Younger, *Portrait of a Man of 54*: Deutsches Museum, Berlin

36 *b*. Hans Holbein the Younger, *Portrait of a Man of 28*: Kunsthistorisches Museum, Vienna

Dossena which found their way to the United States fetched a total sum of more than half a million dollars.

In 1928, Dossena brought an action for fraud against the agent Alfredo Fasoli and the art dealer Romano Palazzi. Fasoli tried to save himself by political means and accused Dossena of anti-fascist agitation, but the so-called "stonemason of the century" met him on his own ground by engaging Farinacci, secretary of the Fascist Party and one of Mussolini's intimates, to defend him. Neither case came to anything.

Dossena died in a paupers' hospital at Rome in the year 1937. And Farinacci, the man who had defended him against Fasoli's dangerous allegations, was executed by partisans on April 28, 1945, together with Mussolini, Clara Petacci and fifteen of the Duce's companions.

12

🌷🌷🌷🌷🌷🌷🌷🌷🌷

Thirty van Goghs in Search
of a Painter

BERLIN in the years after the First World War was a place where people were all out for what they could get. The value of life had been debased by the death of millions. Anyone who could made up for lost time. The night clubs were as overcrowded as the doss houses, the mark a worthless scrap of paper. Fortunes were made and lost overnight. Money could buy anything — even the most forbidden of fruit.

It was in this hectic atmosphere that a male dancer named Olindo Lovaël, whose lithe and supple body was surmounted by an undersized, degenerate head, nightly displayed his charms.

When the Rentenmark threatened to put a stop to all this riotous activity, the proprietor of the establishment whose best parlor had been used for Lovaël's esoteric performances reverted to the role of respectable boarding-house keeper, while Olindo Lovaël the erotic

dancer once more became Otto Wacker, joint owner of Kratkow-
ski's, a Berlin taxicab firm.

The Wacker-Kratkowski partnership was not destined to last for
long, and in 1925 the two associates split up. We know that Wacker
derived an income from other sources which have never been satisfactorily identified, but it has never been ascertained exactly what
he did during the next two years.

In 1927 he once more entered the public gaze when an art gallery
bearing his name opened in the Viktoriastrasse, an old and digni-
fied street in Berlin. As a subsidiary line of business, the firm also
planned to publish books on art history.

At the opening of the Kunstgalerie Otto Wacker, guests and art
critics found themselves confronted by a considerable number
of mediocre prints and paintings. However, there were also some
pictures which aroused genuine interest. These comprised an unusually large selection of works by Vincent van Gogh. The proprietor of the gallery hinted that they hailed from some nobleman's
estate.

Collectors and dealers were interested in pictures by the Dutchman, whose work was rising in value because he was considered to
be the exponent of an art form which had superseded Impres-
sionism. Vincent van Gogh was not only a safe but a profitable in-
vestment, and the margin between purchase and resale price was
growing with a rapidity unusual even in the art trade.

The extent of van Gogh's total output was unknown, but it was
assumed that there must have been some pictures produced either
in the high noon of his genius or in the gathering twilight of
his mental derangement whose fate no one knew. It was common
knowledge, too, that piles of van Goghs had been removed
from attics and lumber rooms, loaded on to carts and sold like
wastepaper — signed and unsigned, begun, half-finished, and completed.

The Dutch art historian Dr. Baart de la Faille had been working for years on an oeuvre catalogue of van Gogh, and was assiduously collecting material from widely scattered sources. He was effectively assisted in the task of compiling an authoritative work on van Gogh by Otto Wacker, who placed thirty paintings by that artist at his disposal. De la Faille showed his gratitude by consenting to incorporate Wacker's pictures in his book. The authenticity of the van Goghs in Wacker's possession was automatically corroborated by this token of acknowledgment on the part of a leading van Gogh expert, for it implied that the Galerie Otto Wacker dealt only in authentic pictures.

New paintings at once took the place of the first van Goghs in Wacker's establishment, which sold briskly. No one found it either remarkable or suspicious that for every van Gogh sold by a lately opened gallery belonging to a hitherto unknown art dealer a new one appeared on the wall. Collectors and dealers were happy to accept de la Faille's expert opinion. Questions about the pictures' origin were satisfactorily answered by vague allusions to a former owner of noble birth — satisfactorily because the interested parties *wanted* to be satisfied. The van Goghs from the Galerie Otto Wacker had acquired a status in the international market.

Autumn 1928 saw the publication of a standard work, *L'Oeuvre de Vincent van Gogh, Catalogue Raisonné,* by Baart de la Faille. It contained, among others, the thirty paintings by van Gogh which could be traced back to Otto Wacker — and no further than Otto Wacker.

"The editor of the Oeuvre Catalogue of van Gogh, Dr. Baart de la Faille, finds himself compelled to append a supplement to his work designating thirty works, described in the Catalogue as genuine, to be dubious forgeries. Dr. de la Faille has arrived at this conclusion only after exhaustive study, and acknowledges his error with deep regret."

The expert's laconic announcement threw collectors and dealers into a state of uproar. Everyone who owned a van Gogh waited impatiently for a precise statement as to which works had been established as fakes, and uneasiness increased with every new rumor that circulated, both in interested quarters and in public. People remembered the Dossena case only too well. Sudden announcements were always having to be made, with varying degrees of reluctance, describing this or that work by some great artist as a fake. So intense did the general uncertainty become that the administrators of the Berlin Museums were obliged to state publicly that "the Attic goddess acquired from the Altes Museum in 1925 for one million marks is an original work, definitely not an imitation by Dossena nor any other type of fake."

Having at last penetrated the veil of secrecy which surrounded the details, the Amsterdam *Telegraf* published a complete list of the thirty fakes which Dr. de la Faille had unmasked (see page 272).

Picture No. 421 reached the Gildemeister collection via the Berlin art dealer Hugo Perls, the same route as was followed by the *Cypresses* (Nos. 616 and 741) and the *Cornfield* (No. 823). The *Olive Tree* (No. 713) was acquired by Kommeter, the Hamburg art dealers, and resold to M. J. Gildemeister.

It is noticeable, even on superficial examination, that the above list contains several pictures dealing with the same theme. This fact alone should have put collectors and dealers on their guard. It was astonishing enough that a collection of thirty van Goghs had found their way into the hands of one gallery, and a young one at that, but no one should have been credulous enough to accept the fact that it contained four "self-portraits," four "cypresses" and three "olive trees."

The spurious van Goghs
in the Oeuvre Catalogue

*(The following are proved to have been in the prior possession
of Otto Wacker.)*

Oeuvre Catalogue Number	Subject	Owner	Origin
383	Self-Portrait	M. Silverberg, Breslau	Wacker
387	Still Life with Roll of Bread	M. Thannhauser, Munich	Wacker
418	Seascape near Ste. Marie	Galerie Wacker	Wacker
421	Ste. Marie	M. J. Gildemeister	Wacker
521	Self-Portrait	Thannhauser, formerly Abdy	Wacker
523	Self-Portrait at the Easel	Chester Dale, New York	Wacker
539	The Zouave	Dr. Otto Kramer, Holzdorf	Wacker
577	Garden	Galerie Wacker	Wacker
614	Cypresses	Galerie Wacker	Wacker
616	Cypresses	B. E. Wolff, Hamburg	Wacker
639	Alpine Path	M. Thannhauser, Munich	Wacker
685	Peasant (after Millet)	Galerie Wacker	Wacker
691	The Sower	Matthiesen, Berlin	Wacker
705	The Sower	Kunsthandel Hugo Perls	Wacker
713	Olive Tree	Gildemeister, Hamburg	Wacker
729	Sunlit Landscape	Matthiesen, Berlin	Wacker
741	Cypresses	Kunsthandel Hugo Perls	Wacker
812	Fields	Galerie Hodebert, Paris	Wacker
813	Fields	Kunsthandel Hugo Perls	Wacker
823	Cornfield	Dr. Otto Kramer, Holzdorf	Wacker
824	Trees in Landscape	Kunsthandel Hugo Perls	Wacker

(No documentary evidence. Must be regarded as having come from Wacker.)

418a	Small Boats, Ste. Marie	Private Collection, Switzerland
527a	Self-Portrait	Private Collection, Switzerland
539a	Portrait of a Zouave	Private Collection, Switzerland
625	Rising Moon	Unknown
681	Vase of Flowers	Private Collection, Switzerland
710a	Olive Trees	Private Collection, Switzerland
715a	Olive Trees	Private Collection, Switzerland
736	Haystack	Private Collection, Switzerland
741a	Two Cypresses	Private Collection, Switzerland

What could have impelled Dr. de la Faille to acknowledge so grave an error? At first, no one knew the answer to this question. It was true that, for some time now, rumors had been going about that the van Goghs sold by Wacker included some extremely suspect pictures, but nobody had made any concrete accusations because of the risks involved. A long and often thorny path stretches between an allegation and proof of its accuracy. It can also be expensive: loss of good will, direct or indirect prejudice, damages in respect to lost or canceled contracts, slander, defamation . . . Nobody dared go further than vague hints. Had some of them reached the ears of Dr. de la Faille?

Kriminalrat Uelzen and Kriminalkommissar Thomas from the Alexanderplatz headquarters of the Berlin police had, on the basis of first reports, instituted an inquiry — but in the strictest privacy, since no pretext for official intervention yet existed. There was no injured party — or, at least, none had so far come forward. The fakes had been announced by the same expert who had two months earlier certified them to be genuine. In short, there was no basis for legal action. The police did not even possess a *corpus delicti*.

Nevertheless, almost as though they could scent the banner headlines that were to come, the two police officers quietly went about their preparations.

The first move was to clarify Dr. de la Faille's motives. Something must have been very seriously wrong for an expert of his international repute suddenly to announce that thirty paintings which he had previously acknowledged to be genuine were fakes. As it transpired, the exposure of the van Gogh forgers' network rested on an episode which was known only to a few initiates.

At about the turn of the century, the art dealer Paul Cassirer had established his picture gallery in spacious premises on the ground floor of Number 35, a fine old house in the Viktoriastrasse. In 1901 he exhibited the first works by Cézanne. Little more than two and a half decades later, the same street housed the Kunstgalerie Otto Wacker and its van Goghs.

Paul Cassirer belonged to a family of some standing. Two of his brothers owned a cable factory. Dr. Richard Cassirer was known as an eminent neurologist. Bruno Cassirer ran a publishing house. Ernst Cassirer had devoted himself to philosophy. Paul himself was married to the celebrated actress Tilla Durieux, whose portrait, painted by Renoir when he was an old man sitting semi-paralyzed in his wheelchair, had won international acclaim. Paul Cassirer was a name to be conjured with in the art world. It was associated not only with the first Cézanne, which fetched all of two hundred and fifty marks, but with the priceless Renoir.

After Paul Cassirer's death, Dr. Feilchenfeld and Dr. Grete Ring carried on the gallery in the spirit of its founder.

In 1927 the Galerie Paul Cassirer held a van Gogh exhibition. The art dealer Otto Wacker, also of the Viktoriastrasse, contributed four paintings by van Gogh which were to be exhibited and sold if an adequate offer materialized.

Dr. Grete Ring examined the four pictures and gained the impression that they were crude fakes. She then asked Dr. Feilchenfeld for his opinion without telling him her own. He, too, came to the conclusion that they were poor imitations and that there could be no question of including them in the exhibition.

The pictures were returned to Otto Wacker. Nothing more happened. Having identified them as forgeries and declined to accept them, the administrators of the Galerie Paul Cassirer naturally felt that their responsibilities were at an end. It would have been beyond the scope of their interests and competence to pursue the matter further. Besides, they had made no secret of their views to Otto Wacker, but told him flatly that his van Goghs were fakes.

Strangely enough, Wacker paid no apparent heed to the opinions of two such reputable members of his profession.

Ears remain closer to the ground in the art business than in most other commercial fields. In short, people caught wind of the affair, among them Dr. de la Faille. He became uneasy as more and more doubts were voiced. Finally, after an extremely thorough re-examination, he published his extraordinary admission.

On the way to this painful conclusion, de la Faille encountered the views of experts whose international reputation as authorities on van Gogh were in no way inferior to his own. Meier-Graefe, art reviewer for the *Frankfurter Zeitung,* whose works on van Gogh were held in almost religious awe, espoused the authenticity of the thirty dubious van Goghs in unqualified terms. The art historians Rosenhagen and Blumenreich and the art critic Bremmer followed his lead. What was more, Bremmer, in his capacity as adviser to the well-known Dutch collector Mme. Kroeller, suggested that she should buy one of Wacker's van Goghs, and the lady decided to do so, even though the painting in question had been positively identified as a fake by Dr. de la Faille. Meanwhile, other voices were raised in support of the van Goghs from the Galerie Otto Wacker.

Despite this, Kriminalrat Uelzen and Kriminalkommissar Thomas became increasingly convinced that it was only a matter of time before the "Wacker case" would find its way into the courtroom reports in the daily press. They continued to gather material, sounded the views of foreign police organizations and sifted the conflicting expert opinions which would — in the event of a concrete accusation — form the first obstacle to criminal proceedings.

The fact that some prominent art experts had unreservedly condemned the paintings struck the police as a promising sign. Herr Krenz, for example, Managing Director of the Kestner-Gesellshaft in Hanover, declared that on being recommended to accept

some pictures from the Galerie Wacker for a van Gogh exhibition
he had immediately recognized them as fakes. This applied particularly to the paintings which had been submitted to him by Meier-
Graefe and other experts. He further claimed that any remaining
doubts had been dispelled by comparison with the originals exhibited at Hanover, most of which derived from the van Gogh
family itself. However, Krenz added, even when faced with this
clear confrontation of genuine and spurious, the art experts had
still insisted that the imitations were authentic.

At last, purchasers started to come forward demanding their
money back. Matthiesen's of Berlin and Thannhauser's, the Munich
art dealers, took back their pictures without demur and refunded
the purchase price in full. That dealt with the first 150,000 marks,
of which some 90,000 had found their way into Wacker's pockets.
Perls, another firm of art dealers, declined to take their pictures
back, maintaining that they were genuine. They based their stand
on expert opinions by de la Faille, Meier-Graefe, Bremmer and
others. Perls took the view that de la Faille had erred not when he
certified the van Goghs as genuine but when he pronounced
them to be spurious.

Otto Wacker sent the press a statement in which he announced
his intention of suing Dr. de la Faille for having alleged that the
van Gogh paintings in the Galerie Wacker were fakes. At the same
time, he proposed to sue for damages anyone who spread this allegation. He also sought a temporary injunction prohibiting publication of the corrective addendum to de la Faille's oeuvre catalogue,
invoking expert opinions by Meier-Graefe, Bremmer, Rosenhagen, Blumenreich, and others. Finally, to cap it all, he announced
that he was at once setting off for Holland to assemble all the
evidence needed to prove the authenticity of the van Goghs
handled by him.

True to his word, he traveled to The Hague. No one could stop him, for the "affair of the fake van Goghs" was as yet no more than a sensational newspaper feud. How Wacker managed to get nine of the suspected paintings across the German-Dutch border was a mystery. That he succeeded in doing so could not be denied, for he showed them at The Hague — to the experts who had already acknowledged them to be genuine. Their opinions remained unaltered.

On the day after Wacker's departure came the first serious move in the direction of an official elucidation of the affair. The Association of German Art and Antique Dealers decided, at a committee meeting held by its Berlin branch, "to prefer charges against the art dealer Otto Wacker through the Galerie Matthiesen, a member of the Association."

At long last, public prosecutor, examining magistrates and police could intervene. The first interrogations were held, the first statements taken from expert witnesses of both persuasions, and the first of the injured parties came forward, hesitantly, as if reluctant to expose themselves to ridicule.

Wacker wrote letters from Holland.

At police headquarters in the Alexanderplatz, a detachment of the fraud squad was installed in a special office with express orders to clear up the Wacker case.

The Dutch art world was even more intimately involved than its counterpart in Germany. After all, van Gogh was *the* representative contemporary Dutch painter, and trembling in the balance were the reputations of de la Faille and Bremmer, both of them Dutch art experts. Where the author of the oeuvre catalogue was concerned, people were just as enraged by the apparent carelessness with which he had compiled his work as by the admission that he had been mistaken about thirty of the van Goghs included in it. That he now appeared to believe in the authenticity of five of the van Goghs which Wacker had smuggled into Holland merely added fuel to the flames. As for Bremmer, it was alleged that the art critic had encouraged Mme. Kroeller to acquire a definitely suspect picture merely in order to save his face.

Mijnher de Wilt, a restorer whom Wacker called in to give expert testimony on his behalf, regarded the dubious pictures as genuine because, according to him, they had been painted more than thirty to thirty-five years earlier, i.e. at a time when no one was faking van Goghs. Even though their age had not been scientifically established and there was as much evidence for van Gogh's having been faked during his lifetime as against, this assertion gained a measure of acceptance.

Bundling together all the favorable reports he could find, Otto Wacker returned to Berlin, forgetfully leaving his nine would-be van Goghs behind at The Hague. He arrived in Berlin on October 3rd. It was a Saturday, but that did not prevent Kriminalrat Uelzen from requesting an immediate interview and reading him the charges which had been preferred by the Galerie Matthiesen.

Invoking the favorable reports which he had brought with him, Wacker declared that all contrary opinions were erroneous and represented the whole affair as a squabble between experts in which professional rivalry had played a substantial role.

Pressed to reveal where and from whom he had acquired the pictures, Wacker dished up his old tale about a Russian *émigré* of noble birth, but this time condescended to supply more details. The family in question was related to the Tsar's house, and any mention of names would mean certain death for those members of the family who still lived in the Soviet Union. Quite apart from that, said Wacker, a man of honor never breaks his word.

The police officer suggested that Wacker and he should take a trip together to Switzerland, where the blue-blooded Russian apparently lived. Both the police and the public prosecutor's office gave an assurance that no names would be divulged.

Wacker declined, but said he was prepared to visit his Russian client in the company of Meier-Graefe, the art historian. He explained that he trusted Meier-Graefe, which was why he had shown him the original of a letter from the Russian some time before.

Uelzen was already aware of this incident. It was true that Meier-Graefe had been shown a letter purporting to be from the mysterious aristocrat, but Wacker had studiously concealed the signature and address. When the police officer drew attention to this circumstance and added that anyone could have written a few lines on a sheet of paper without a letter heading or signature, the accused man agreed, but said that to show it would not have been consistent with "the actions of a man of honor."

The interrogation closed with the signing of a long statement which meant precisely nothing. It had neither been established that the pictures sold by Wacker were forgeries nor could it be proved that, even if this were so, he had known of their fraudulent nature when he sold them. Wacker was released and went home.

On arriving at his gallery on Monday morning, Wacker found himself preceded by police officers who wanted to look round the premises. They found two paintings bearing the signature "van Gogh," but there was no legal justification for their seizure.

An examination of the Galerie Wacker's books gave food for thought. The books were kept by a friend of Wacker's, a salesman by the name of Renkiewitsch who acted as his secretary, but since they consisted merely of occasional entries in summary form, loose scraps of paper and bills, neither purchases nor sales could be ascertained with any accuracy. Only a few isolated sales were entered in a proper fashion, but whether the figures tallied was another matter, for no bank statements were available. Similarly, only a few isolated purchasers could be identified, and these, when questioned on the telephone, said that they regarded their van Goghs as originals and wanted nothing to do with any police inquiry.

The secretary, who admitted that he had been responsible for the clerking, apparently knew of only four van Goghs that had been sold, two of which had been dispatched to New York. A self-portrait had fetched 65,000 marks and a smaller picture 30,000 or 35,000 marks. He didn't know the purchasers' names. As to the origin of all these pictures, he only knew what Wacker had told him in confidence: it seemed that a Russian aristocrat in Switzerland . . .

Considering how hard the police had worked, the results seemed meager. However, when these were added to the outcome of confidential inquiries into Otto Wacker's personal background, the conviction that his van Goghs were fakes was considerably strengthened.

Otto Wacker was himself a painter. Otto Wacker's father was an artist and restorer in Düsseldorf, and was regarded as an extremely good man in his own field. Otto Wacker's sister likewise plied a paintbrush with some success. Slowly but surely, the file marked "Otto Wacker" grew.

All attempts by the police to find the previous owner of the controversial paintings came to nothing.

Instead of clarifying the situation, tests by art critics led only to violent clashes of opinion. Professor Justi, director of the National Gallery at Berlin, asked all present owners of Wacker's van Goghs to release them on loan so that the pictures could be examined during preparations for a van Gogh exhibition to be held at the Kronprinzenpalais. He met with nothing but refusals.

From the United States came a file of reports on the van Gogh *Self-Portrait* sold by Wacker to the Chester Dale collection. The main report, which had been given by Baart de le Faille in July, 1927, pronounced the picture in question to be "an authentic and characteristic work by van Gogh painted by him while at Arles in 1888." A second report bore the signature of Meier-Graefe who, in March, 1928, had described the *Self-Portrait* "not only as an authentic but as one of the most typical and important of van Gogh's works." A third report came from Bremmer and called the painting "one of van Gogh's best works." Yet another expert opinion by Rosenhagen employed the same words.

Kriminalrat Uelzen returned from an investigatory trip to Holland without any material evidence. A similar journey to The Hague by Kriminalkommissar Thomas was destined to be equally unrewarding.

On January 29, 1929, the *Vossische Zeitung* published a full-page article by Professor Justi in which he made a detailed examination of the work of the "experts" (he put the word in quotation marks) in the Wacker–van Gogh case, using a tone considerably more acid than is customary in the field of artistic criticism. Justi was convinced that he could prove the falsity of all Wacker's van Goghs on the basis of exhaustive critical examination.

After the publication of this view, which amounted to a sentence of death, Otto Wacker traveled back to Holland. On the day after his arrival in Leyden he was found lying unconscious in the corridor of a house. He was taken to the hospital and his luggage and incoming mail sequestrated by the police.

The police report stated that "the proprietor of the house in which Wacker collapsed unconscious was the sister of the art historian Bremmer."

Discreet inquiries conducted at the hospital in Leyden revealed that Wacker's condition was regarded as very serious and that there

282 THE FORGER'S INTERESTS

could be no question of a speedy recovery. It could not be ascertained from the brief report exactly what complaint the patient was suffering from.

During the weeks that followed, the Wacker–van Gogh case disappeared from the columns of the daily press.

On August 8, 1931, the subject was reopened by a report on "the affair of the fake van Goghs" in the *Vossische Zeitung*. It appeared that the case had been shelved because there was insufficient evidence for an indictment. Almost two years had passed since the Galerie Matthiesen had filed charges against Wacker. The case seemed to have died a natural death.

It was not until September 4, 1931, after three years of intermittent investigation, that the public prosecutor's office at Berlin announced that an indictment had been filed against the artist Otto Wacker "for persistent fraud and breach of contract." According to the charge sheet, Wacker had "between the years 1925 and 1928 sold as van Goghs thirty paintings, for an average price of more than 10,000 marks, of which it could be established that none had been painted by van Gogh." He was accused of "uttering these paintings as genuine van Goghs, while knowing them to be false, at prices such as are paid only for genuine van Goghs."

The Berlin police stated next day that they had "confiscated from the premises of the Düsseldorf taxidermist Wacker, a brother of Otto Wacker, a forged painting bearing the signature van Gogh of which the original could be found with Otto Wacker."

On April 6, 1932, the trial of Otto Wacker, now a man of thirty-three, opened at the central lay assessors' court in Berlin. Among the experts subpoenaed to attend were Bremmer, Professor Justi, Stopperan, Dr. de la Faille, Vincent Wilhelm van Gogh (a nephew of the artist), the proprietor of Hodebert, the Paris art dealer's, the Dutch collector Scherjon, a director of Wildenstein, the

New York firm of art dealers, the painter von König, the technical expert Wehlte, Dr. Thormaelen, Dr. Ruhemann, a chemist from the State Museums of Berlin, Professor Brittner the art historian, the art critic Julius Meier-Graefe, the art dealers Dr. Feilchenfeld and Dr. Grete Ring from the Galerie Paul Cassirer, the owner of the Thannhauser art salon at Munich, Zatzenstein, proprietor of the Galerie Matthiesen, Professor Eugen Spiro, and others.

Seen in the sober setting of the Moabit courtroom, the controversial van Goghs looked somewhat theatrical, transforming the scene into a fantastic, vaguely surrealistic art gallery.

The only substantial result of Wacher's personal interrogation was, apart from a rough outline of his life story, an assertion that he not only believed the paintings to be genuine van Goghs when he sold them but still regarded them as such. He again refused to disclose the name of the Russian aristocrat.

Vincent Wilhelm van Gogh stated in the witness box that after his uncle's death in 1890 the majority of his estate went to his brother Theo, who followed Vincent to the grave a few months later. The witness's mother then became the sole beneficiary. The sale of paintings began in 1891, but not before they had been catalogued and their exact descriptions recorded. The witness could remember various paintings in detail. Only two of Wacker's paintings, at most, could be identical with the subjects of two pictures in the van Gogh estate. Apart from the Moruschov Gallery, which contained about twenty van Goghs, the witness was unaware of any Russian collection which possessed a substantial number of his uncle's works. He further stated that the artist's own extensive notes had not contained any reference to a Russian collection.

For the defense, Dr. Goldschmidt asked the witness if it were not true that piles of pictures had lain about in the attic of the van Gogh house like so much wastepaper, accessible to countless peo-

ple of varying artistic interests, later to be hawked from carts in
the street like junk dealer's wares.

Vincent Wilhelm van Gogh replied in the affirmative, but added
that this had applied only to pictures from van Gogh's Brabant
period.

Counsel for the defense drew attention to the self-contradictory
nature of this testimony: on the one hand, the pictures had been
catalogued; on the other, they had been peddled like bric-à-brac.

Dr. de la Faille's evidence showed that a credulous art historian
is prepared to believe a lot of the tall stories that are trotted out for
his benefit. When asked by the president of the court whether it
were really true that his suspicions had not been aroused by the tale
of the mysterious Russian, de la Faille answered with disarming
naïveté that "there are large numbers of mysterious people in the
world, and these may well include some Russian noblemen."

Before the witness was released, he handed the president a written
deposition which, coming on top of the more colorful than informative give-and-take of the various other witnesses, caused a
considerable stir in court:

> I became confused by the daily sight of now familiar fakes. After re-
> examination and fresh research, and having regard to evidence in letters
> by van Gogh, I declare that when, in 1928, I believed that I had been
> involved in a fraud, I probably gave way to excessive skepticism and lost
> my absolute objectivity. For this reason I now declare that, in respect to
> five of the thirty paintings, I withdraw my opinion that they are spuri-
> ous.

The witness went on to give a precise description of the five
paintings which he now regarded as genuine. He dropped a hint
that the supplementary volume of the oeuvre catalogue, in which
he had classified the thirty Wacker paintings as forgeries, would

be followed up by a further supplement devoted to final recognition of the five paintings' authenticity.

The art critic Meier-Graefe laid stress on his own good faith. He had made vigorous attempts to get Wacker to accompany him on a visit to the mysterious prior owner of the paintings in Switzerland, as Wacker himself had suggested to the police. The trip never came off, however. When their date of departure had already been fixed, Wacker broke the news that his Russian was no longer in Switzerland but had gone to Egypt. Meier-Graefe went on to make a statement which was as clearly formulated as it was unwelcome and unsatisfactory. Some of the van Goghs formerly in Wacker's possession, he asserted, were of such high quality that, were their falsity proven, any possibility of distinguishing between genuine van Goghs and fakes would in future be precluded.

If Dr. de la Faille had caused a sensation with his statement of the day before, Dr. Goldschmidt, counsel for the defense, now provided another by doffing his robes and entering the witness box.

He testified that his client had actually tried to contact the Russian aristocrat with a view to securing permission to reveal his name. To this end, Wacker had sent a letter to an agent in Paris, who was to forward it to the nobleman. Being ignorant of his exact whereabouts, Wacker had addressed the letter to a club to which the agent belonged. Unfortunately, the letter was never collected . . . One mystery man already loomed large over the proceedings. It now seemed that there was another, a minor mystery man who neglected to pick up his mail!

Dr. Kreutzberg, a psychiatrist from Berlin's Charité Hospital, described the accused to the court as a psychopath who had done all he could to hinder investigations but was definitely not insane.

The Dutch expert Bremmer stated that there were hundreds of fake van Goghs, just as there were thousands of forged pictures by other painters. Some of Wacker's van Goghs were probably genuine, others probably spurious, and others unverifiable.

Professor Spiro doubted the authenticity of most of the pictures but did not regard them as "altogether bad, viewed in the spirit of van Gogh."

The artist von König described some of the pictures as fakes and others as genuine.

The technical expert Wehlte concluded from the results of his X-ray examinations that Wacker's pictures were painted much later than the undisputed van Goghs used in comparative tests. Brushwork and technique differed considerably. The paints in Wacker's pictures had probably been dried by artificial means.

Professor Justi concluded his exhaustive report with the words ". . . all the paintings which the accused put on the market as genuine van Goghs represent fakes of inferior quality."

At his own request, Meier-Graefe, having been examined as a witness, now took the stand in his capacity as an expert. The most significant part of his testimony ran as follows: " 'Anyone who buys pictures and pays enormous prices for them on the strength of expert opinions alone deserves to meet with disaster.' "

Ruhemann, restorer for the Prussian State Museums, described the great majority of Wacker's van Goghs as obvious fakes. His certainty that forgery was involved was attributable to the advanced methods of scientific research employed. Ruhemann submitted to the court X-ray photographs first of the genuine Vincent van Gogh painting *Reaper in a Cornfield* and then of a Wacker picture portraying a similar subject. The expert demonstrated the existence of differences so pronounced as to exclude the possibility that both pictures had been painted by the same man.

Ruhemann illustrated the differences between a genuine and a fake van Gogh by pointing to characteristic gradations clearly revealed by the X-ray picture — whereupon Meier-Graefe declared that this technique was not typical of van Gogh — whereupon Ruhemann observed that genuine pictures by van Gogh displayed cast shadows only where they would naturally appear in bright sunlight — whereupon Professor Spiro stated emphatically that he had never seen cast shadows in a van Gogh.

After this flurry of contradictory statements, Ruhemann demonstrated on the basis of his enlargements that in genuine van Goghs the picture remained recognizable when X-rayed, whereas in the fakes the layers of paint were disguised by the forger's totally different technique.

Dr. Goldschmidt inquired whether the chemical experts had, on the basis of their laboratory tests, arrived at the same conclusions as were allegedly supported by the X-ray photographs. His query elicited an unqualified affirmative from Ruhemann and an equally unqualified negative from the Dutch restorer de Wilt.

From a review of the expert testimony given at the hearing, the following inferences might have been drawn:

(1) All the pictures were genuine.

(2) Some pictures were genuine and some spurious.

(3) All the pictures were spurious.

(4) Some pictures were spurious and some genuine, but the genuine ones were those stated to be spurious and the spurious those stated to be genuine.

On April 19, 1932, the court of lay assessors sentenced Otto Wacker to a year's imprisonment "for persistent fraud, partially coincident with grave and persistent falsification of documents." He was acquitted of the charge alleging breach of contract. The court issued a warrant for his arrest because there was a suspicion that he might try to leave the country, but it was held in abeyance on condition that he reported to the police twice a week.

From the formal aspect, the court's decision censured the reprehensible activities of the accused, but its deeper implications redounded to the discredit not only of experts but of imbecile collectors who buy works of art not because they see something in them and are willing to pay a determinate price but because they judge them by the name signed in the corner and the expert opinions that go with them.

Appeals were lodged both by Wacker and the public prosecutor's office, and a new hearing was held in Berlin's supreme court. On this second occasion, Wacker was sentenced to nineteen months in jail, a fine of 30,000 marks, and forfeiture of civil rights for a period of three years. He was arrested in court.

13

❦❦❦❦❦❦❦❦❦

Twentieth-Century Vermeers

AMONG the numerous Allied special commissions which
swarmed through defeated Germany in early 1945 were
various art commissions. All the paintings, sculptures,
pieces of furniture and carpets, often of great or very
great artistic merit, which had been so eagerly accumulated during the war by German collectors were to be traced and restored to
their rightful owners.

The government of the Netherlands was represented on all these
art commissions by experts. For centuries the home of glorious
works of art, little Holland had to mourn the loss of many of her
former treasures. It was assumed that they had been stored in secret
caches and that many who knew their location were either staying silent or had been silenced for ever. Initially, therefore, the
search for Dutch works of art was concentrated in Germany.

While the Dutch members of the main commission were examining pictures from the Hermann Göring collections, they came

upon a painting of *The Woman Taken in Adultery*. The connoisseurs' animated conversation ceased abruptly as they gazed in silence at the picture before them. There, confronting them in the glow of the powerful lamps, was a Vermeer — a magnificent work, even by that great master's standards. The only question was: how had a hitherto unknown Vermeer of such exceptional quality entered Göring's collection?

The first task was to identify the picture. Where could it have come from if not the Netherlands? This must surely be a case in which some private collector's closely guarded treasure had arrived in Göring's possession by irregular means — by illicit means, furthermore, since all Vermeers were protected by statute and it was a punishable offense to export a work of such importance. Anyone who had handed it over to the enemy was a criminal and, still worse, a collaborator.

The police were alerted, wires began to hum, and a full-scale inquiry was instituted with the object of tracing the Vermeer's origin.

While this investigation (classified as Top Secret) was being pursued, a prematurely aged man sat in a finely carved armchair in the living room of Number 321, his lovely old house on Amsterdam's venerable Keizersgracht, looking out idly at the sluggish waters of the canal. It was Han van Meegeren, the man who had painted the Vermeer known as *The Woman Taken in Adultery*. But he alone knew that.

During their painstaking examination of all the complex accounts and transactions associated with Göring's artistic possessions, the investigators repeatedly met the name of Alois Miedl, a German banker with an interest in Goudstikkers, the Amsterdam firm of art dealers by whose agency the former Reichsmarschall had augmented his various collections. All attempts to trace Alois

Miedl foundered because of that wary individual's successful disappearance. However, the prompt seizure and examination of Goudstikkers' business records produced some valuable disclosures. The unknown Vermeer had passed through three hands. The names that came to light were those of Walter Hofer, Alois Miedl and Reinstra van Strijvesande. The first was one of Göring's intimates, Miedl the financier, and the last an art dealer.

The military police asked van Strijvesande who had been the original seller of the picture. The man's name, apparently, was Han van Meegeren, painter and art dealer of Keizersgracht 321, Amsterdam.

Preliminary confidential inquiries into the identity of van Meegeren yielded some surprising results. The artist-antiquarian owned several houses in Amsterdam and Laren. He was said to be rich, extraordinarily generous and slightly eccentric. His neighbors liked him in spite of his, by their bourgeois standards, extremely easygoing way of life. He lived in rather complex circumstances under the same roof as his ex-wife. There were dark rumors of wild affaires, debauches, abnormal tastes. Eccentric he might be, but no one dreamt of suspecting him of being a collaborator.

Two plainclothes detectives called on him. They were cordially received and gladly accepted their host's invitation to sit down and have a drink. In accordance with time-honored police tactics, they chatted of trivialities before putting their carefully rehearsed questions about the Vermeer. The master of the house had just as carefully been arming himself for many years against questions of this nature. He refrained from evincing any surprise. Certainly, Vermeer's *Woman Taken in Adultery* had been sold by him to a Dutchman of the highest reputation. He had only learned much later that middlemen unknown to him had passed the painting on to Göring. He had tried to prevent the transaction, but was given to understand that it had been made in the national interest, since

the Germans had not paid in German currency but had exchanged the painting for a superb collection of Dutch masters
whose total value exceeded that of the Vermeer several times over.

The detectives were satisfied with this explanation as far as it
went. Van Meegeren's account corresponded with the details
already known to them. However, they needed an answer to one
more important question, this time to do with the origin of the
painting. Where had it come from, and from whom? What Dutchman had owned such a work of art unknown to the state collections?

Han van Meegeren had long been prepared for this question,
too. In an emergency he was covered by the following story, carefully thought out over the years. He had discovered the Vermeer
in Italy while visiting the gallery of a distinguished but impover-
ished patrician family who wanted to dispose of various works of
art under pledge of complete and unconditional secrecy. He could
not, therefore, divulge any names.

The detectives made no comment. They took notes, eying their
host in some perplexity. His last answer was hardly satisfactory,
but time would tell. They took their leave. Han van Meegeren
breathed a sigh of relief. He could not prove his Italian story, but
nobody could disprove it.

The next day his optimism turned out to have been ill founded.
Two members of the political police presented a warrant for his
arrest. On May 30, 1945, the examining magistrate informed him
that he was under definite suspicion of "collaboration with the
enemy," a charge which, once proved, could mean a very heavy
sentence.

When Han van Meegeren returned to his cell after the preliminary hearing he had time for reflection. Two choices lay open
to him: penal servitude, possibly for life, for services rendered to

the enemy; or imprisonment, perhaps of short duration and subject to commutation, for forgery. By May 31st he had made up his mind.

He signed a confession alleging that he had faked "fourteen classical Dutch masterpieces." Of these he had put nine on the market. The proceeds of their sale totaled 7,167,000 gulden. His share, after deducting agents' fees, had been 5,460,000 gulden.

It seemed as clear as daylight to the examining magistrate that van Meegeren was only putting forward these fantastic statements because he preferred jail for forgery to penal servitude for active collaboration with the enemy. Undoubtedly, Han van Meegeren was an accomplished liar.

However, he eventually supplied the court with so many verifiable details that his confession ceased to be a matter for doubt. He was asked a final question: whether he would be prepared to paint a new "old masterpiece" in his cell in the presence of experts. He agreed.

The judicial authorities released details of the van Meegeren case, and the international press had a sensation on its hands. Art critics of international standing, leading authorities from the Dutch national museums, art dealers with hitherto sacrosanct reputations — all read the news and saw their world collapse in ruins. A single man had succeeded in casting the high priests of aesthetics as ludicrous marionettes in a farce costing some $2,200,000 — a sum which he had been able to pocket, less commission, thanks to the expert opinions of those same authorities.

The trial which, after two years of preliminary investigation, followed upon van Meegeren's confession yielded little more — apart from the humiliating appearances of expert witnesses — than the sentence. Han van Meegeren was sent to prison for a year. No very substantial details about the accused man came to light at the proceedings. The court was not, after all, concerned with the investigation of Han van Meegeren as a person, with his motives or character.

Who, then, was this slightly built man whose pictures had been acquired by experienced buyers for a sum of around five million dollars in present purchasing power?

Art historians, chemists and physicists filled volumes with their researches into the paintings of Han van Meegeren, but his life remained a closed book. Apart from painstakingly collected press cuttings, vague hints from his former circle of acquaintances and anecdotes of dubious worth, the only other material consists of fragmentary accounts by his daughter Inez and son Jacques, as pieced together by John Godley.

In Deventer on the Ijssel October 10, 1889 was a rainy autumn day like any other. Henricus van Meegeren conducted his classes at the Kweek School just as he did on any normal weekday, while his wife Augusta was giving birth to a baby boy at home. The child was sickly like its mother. Henricus van Meegeren did not return home until late that afternoon. Duty was higher than man, he held, and God alone stood above duty.

Like the school, the van Meegeren household was ruled with puritanical harshness by its master. The van Meegerens' firstborn, scarcely one year old, was a stranger to laughter, and his new brother was to be reared in an equally joyless atmosphere. Yet the two boys' personalities soon diverged. Herman, the elder, submitted; Henri, the younger, rebelled.

Van Meegeren senior managed to subdue the younger boy's temperament until he reached the age of twelve, when he developed a talent, probably inherited from his mother, which proved stronger than his fear of parental disapproval. He began to draw — fanciful dream-pictures which he studiously concealed from his father's gaze. When he started to fall behind at secondary school, however, Henricus decided to get at the root of the matter. He found the drawings, tore them up and summarily consigned them to the stove.

For Henri, this represented the hostile intrusion of authority into his life. Shortly after this formative experience, Henri was passing the local police station when he noticed, no doubt at first subconsciously, a key protruding from the outside of the gate. Laying his plans with considerable ingenuity, he cautiously crept back, pushed the door to, locked it, and threw the key away. He looked round, but no one had spotted him. Walking slowly to the next corner he secreted himself in a doorway which commanded a view of the police station, and waited.

A few pedestrians hurried on their way. After a while the curtain rose on the little comedy which Henri had devised and produced. Uniformed policemen clambered out of the windows of the locked building. They tried to open the gate from outside and when it refused to budge had to break it down. A group of sniggering onlookers collected.

Henri mingled inconspicuously with the bystanders. Many of them knew the pale, slender, narrow-chested boy by sight, but none would have thought of connecting the schoolmaster's weakling with what had happened.

It was a moment to be savored. Henri had avenged himself on authority. He would much rather have stepped forward and claimed credit for his successful plan. It would have done the police good to know that the one who had managed to make fools of them was little Henri van Meegeren.

Decades later a markedly similar scene was enacted at Rotterdam. Han van Meegeren, formerly the boy Henri, entered the main hall of the Boymans Museum in Rotterdam almost unnoticed amid a throng of eminent guests. "Vermeer's most important work," *The Disciples at Emmaus,* was to be presented to the public by state decree. There was much speechifying in lofty terms as the assemblage gazed enraptured at the painting. Heavy ropes of red silk enclosed the space in front of it, reminiscent of a lying-in-state. The floor was richly carpeted, the atmosphere redolent of reverence and devotion.

In one corner on the left stood Han van Meegeren. He looked ill and older than his forty-nine years, his small, unkempt mustache lending emphasis to the deep lines on his face. He watched the eminent gathering as if through a veil. The only thing he distinguished with complete clarity was his painting as it hung there under its special lights. Perhaps he was seeing an old street in Deventer, a police station and constables climbing through windows to break down a gate.

Han van Meegeren's thoughts returned to reality. Just as he had made fools of the police so long ago, so he had duped these worthy citizens, museum Goliaths, critics and experts — all those who had disparaged Han van Meegeren, denied him true artistry and genuine ability, done him an injustice, refused him consideration.

Spellbound they gazed at the newly discovered Vermeer, a masterpiece among masterpieces, a uniquely perfect work of art which surpassed all that was hitherto known to have come from the hand of the Grand Master of Dutch painting — and which had been painted by him, Han van Meegeren, the insignificant little man who stood on the fringe of this illustrious gathering.

Many years had passed since he had first used a hoax to avenge himself on authority. Now the curtain had risen on the second comedy, the tragicomedy. Once more he was tempted to come forward and take a bow, and once more he refrained.

If it had been fear that induced him to conceal his responsibility for the little episode in Deventer, there were now more material inducements to secrecy: a strong reluctance to gamble wih the fantastic profits he had made, and an equally compulsive desire to go on gambling.

The affair of the incarcerated policemen passed off without any repercussions for Henri, except perhaps in a field of experience which cannot fully be explored. When Henri was thirteen, something happened which was to play an important role in his life. Bertus Korteling, the school's drawing master, took him under his wing. The sickly boy proved an eager pupil, and his undisciplined fantasies soon gave way to organized work. Outside his capacity as a teacher, Korteling used to work as an artist in his own right, and his pictures, all done in an early naturalistic style, found a ready market. Henri saw in his master both an example and the fulfillment of his ambitions. He adopted the whole of Korteling's archaic manner of painting, modeled as it was upon the classics. The only path to success lay in a study of the old masters: such was his teacher's maxim.

Father van Meegeren remained inimical to all ideas of an artistic career. With an iron hand he steered his elder son, Herman, into the priesthood. The younger boy could study to become an architect if he wanted, but that was as far as his father would go.

Han (he was bored with the name Henri) went to Delft University, though not to study. He had no wish to become an architect, but Delft meant freedom and a monthly allowance from Henricus which would take care of his living expenses.

In fact, Delft brought him a freedom other than the one he had longed for, the freedom of the lonely. He was the weakest of all his classmates. He could do whatever he chose, but alone. He had no friends, no romantic attachments. The only alternative was to bury himself in work which had little to offer him. He began to paint more intensively, but without showing anyone the results. He dispensed with recognition or rebuff, commendation or criticism.

This state of affairs continued until he met Anna de Voogt, a girl as lonely as he was himself, the daughter of a Dutchman and a Sumatran. In early 1912 they married. Their new home at Rijswyk was an abode ruled by love, painting and poverty. The future held two problems: what was to happen to the baby which Anna was expecting, and how Han was to combine his studies for the examinations at Delft with work on a picture for the exhibition at the Hague Academy, which awarded five yearly prizes.

Han settled for art and toiled away like a man possessed at his *Interior of the St. Laurens Church in Rotterdam*. This picture gained him the gold medal and a fee of 1700 gulden. He failed his examinations at Delft, but that mattered little as long as he was painting. There was a market for pictures by the holder of the Hague Academy's gold medal, and Han knew why. The buyers were not after a work of art but a work signed by a gold medalist.

His blaze of glory all too soon forgotten by the buying public, Han saw his clientele melt away. Critics left him severely alone. Dealers turned their backs on him. Money ran short. The gold medal found its way across a pawnbroker's counter. Meanwhile, a son had arrived. Anna's grandmother helped the young couple during this difficult period.

Realizing that he must acquire a name, a title or a diploma, Han applied to the Academy of Art at The Hague and was allowed to sit for its examinations. In portraiture he was marked "unsatisfactory." His last chance lay in the practical test to be held before the assembled faculty. For this, candidates had to paint an interior scene in the style of the seventeenth century. They sat in a semicircle, professors in the background.

Han van Meegeren, rejected as a portraitist, decided to demon-

37 *a*.   Rubens, *Adoration of Venus*: National Museum, Stockholm

37 *b*.   Titian, *Adoration of Venus*: Prado, Madrid

38 a. Renoir, *Girls at the Piano,* a variation on the picture of the same name in the Louvre

38 b. Renoir forgery, from a Paris collection

39. One of the innumerable van Gogh forgeries with which art dealers, collectors, and even museums, have been inundated. This 'self-portrait' is nothing but a pastiche of three genuine van Goghs: the head is taken from *Old Provençal Peasant* (in the Chester Beatty Collection, London), the coat from *Self-Portrait with Pipe* (Leigh Block Collection, Chicago), and the features of the face from the *Self-Portrait* in the Wertheim Collection, Fogg Art Museum, Cambridge, Mass.

40. G. Courbet, *Sleeping Girl with Setter:* formerly in the Kunstmuseum, Basle. Forgery executed about 1870. Note the lack of proportion between the dog and the figure of the girl.

41 *a*. Han van Meegeren, *The Last Supper*, painted in the style of Vermeer on a canvas of A. Hondius.

41 *b*. The zinc plates which the artist used as models

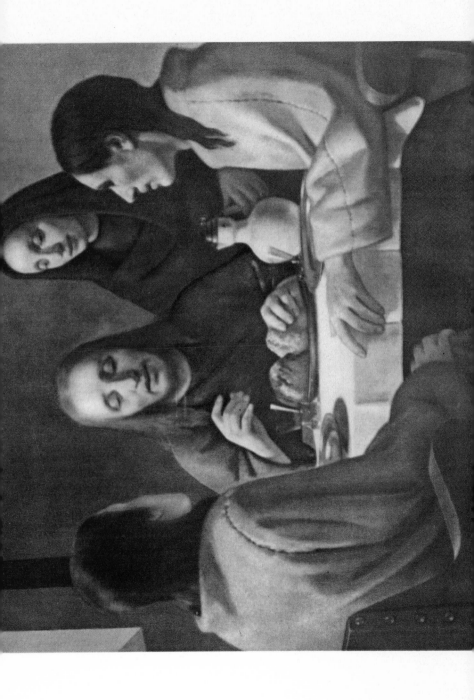

42. Han van Meegeren, *The Disciples in Emmaus*: Boymans Museum, Rotterdam. It was this work which started the scandal of the Vermeer forgeries.

strate the injustice of that verdict. Whereas all the other competitors kept strictly to the subject and essayed a faithful reproduction of the old-fashioned chair, décor, vase and candlesticks, Han van Meegeren not only painted those aspects of the subject but added portraits of the academicians seated in the background.

His painting won the Academy's prize and was duly exhibited. Commissions started to come in shortly after the opening. It was a great day: August 1, 1914.

Han was found unfit for military service. This official confirmation of his physical inferiority came as a shock. He declined a professorial appointment at the Hague Academy and acted, though only briefly, as deputy to a Professor Gips. Artistic activity alone could restore his self-respect and confidence, and he drove himself hard. Then he became restive, staying away from home for nights on end. Anna, his son, and a new daughter who had nearly cost her mother's life now seemed insufferable links with his bourgeois past. Han wanted to be free, devoid of obligations to anyone. His brother, the only person to whom he had ever felt genuinely drawn, had been forced to abandon the priesthood by ill-health and had died from neglect. No one meant anything to him any more.

Han's irregular habits made him ill and adversely affected his work. In spite of the many substantial fees he earned, debts were piling up. All this he laid at the door of a public which had once more forgotten him, of critics whose indifference was strangling his career, and of Anna, the eternal millstone about his neck and reproach to his conscience.

After an encounter with his former master, Korteling, Han once more began to work like a man possessed. A special exhibition of his pictures brought him genuine success. Commissions again rolled in. Dealers competed for his paintings, and the world looked rosy. It was in this mood of elation that Han met Jo van Walraven, an art critic's wife and an actress of mixed Dutch and Spanish extraction.

So the years passed for Han van Meegeren, a husband whose loyalties were divided between two women, a father with two children whom he regarded with a mixture of love and hatred, a man simultaneously rolling in money and deep in debt.

A second exhibition in 1921 was another unqualified success. Only one of the leading papers refused to devote a line to the event. To his intimate circle Han van Meegeren attributed this omission to his having refused the critic a material consideration for his services. There is no evidence to support this allegation, but from then on Han nursed feelings of hatred not only towards that particular critic but toward critics in general.

In 1923 he at last divorced Anna. Thenceforth he lived with Jo in an atmosphere plagued by morbid jealousy. Everything he earned, and it amounted to considerable sums, ran through his fingers like water. He had not only to provide for Anna and the children but also to satisfy his own and Jo's every whim. In 1929 he married Jo.

What money his portraits failed to bring in he earned by painting posters for industry. He also did work for printing houses, publicity campaigns and advertising schemes. Amsterdam became too small for him, Holland too cramped. He traveled to Paris and London. In England he made a considerable amount of money with his portraits, but the critics would only credit him with the merits of an excellent photographer in paint. And money was not his sole ambition.

Vainly he sought a path to universal recognition, but exhibition committees returned his paintings and critics refused to be bothered with him. He ran into a brick wall whichever way he turned. In association with his friend and adviser Theo van Wijngaarden, he undertook the publishing of a magazine which he named *De Kemphaan,* but "The Fighting Cock" was not destined to survive for long.

Then, one night, after hours of discussion over a bottle, Theo van Wijngaarden, who was a man of wide interests, brought the subject round to old paintings, genuine and faked. It seemed that when Dr. Abraham Bredius, Holland's leading connoisseur of old masters, had insisted to him that a genuine Frans Hals was faked, Wijngaarden got some old compatriot to forge a Rembrandt for him. Bredius certified its authenticity. Only when the certificate had been signed did Wijngaarden tear up the painting to prove to the expert that it was not what it appeared to be.

Han van Meegeren smiled thinly. So a man like Bredius had accepted the work of some nobody as a Rembrandt original, had he? It only confirmed his opinion of art critics and experts in general.

The thing to do would be to imitate a Van Dyck or a Frans Hals, a Rubens or a Rembrandt, get the counterfeit authenticated by one or, better, several acknowledged experts, and then come forward and admit the hoax. Engrossed in this line of thought, Han was suddenly reminded of his teacher Korteling, that devotee of the old masters, and of his student days at Delft. Delft, which had once produced one of the greatest of all the old masters — Vermeer.

He would paint a Vermeer, get it accepted by the Rijksmuseum, and then announce triumphantly to an admiring throng: "This Vermeer was painted by me, Han van Meegeren." The die was cast.

This goal altered Han's attitude towards work, his daily life, his environment. Resolutely he cut back unnecessary expenditure, gave preference to commissions of a commercial nature, accumulated money.

Such spare time as his commercial commitments left him he devoted to a study of the old masters. He prepared to acquit himself faultlessly of his self-appointed task by studying the technique of the princes of Dutch painting more exhaustively than ever before.

He was worried by the problem of where to carry out his work. In Holland, people lived in each other's pockets and walls had ears. One unexpected visit to his studio would put an end to all his plans. It became obvious that the elaborate preparations necessary to a fraud on the projected scale could be successful carried out only in complete privacy.

From acquaintances who had returned from the Côte d'Azur Han learned that conditions there had become very favorable for foreigners in the postwar period. A suitable little house could be acquired for a comparatively small sum. For his wife's benefit, Han based the proposed move on artistic and health considerations, telling her that he needed the sun's warmth to help him work and alleviate his physical discomfort.

Traveling to Nice, he and Jo drove along the coast road until they came to Roquebrune, where they eventually found an isolated house which fulfilled all his requirements and would protect him from surprise visitors. Then they returned to Amsterdam to prepare for the move.

Han van Meegeren spent the last few weeks in further intensive study. In a little antiquarian's shop in Amsterdam he found a copy of the book by A. M. de Wild, long out of print, called *Vermeer's Technique.* In Arnhem he ran to earth an even rarer work, *On Fatty Oils,* by Professor Alex Eibner. It was hardly a painter's book, but van Meegeren knew how essential it would be to a man who wanted to make a picture look as though it had originated three hundred years earlier. He had to count on the likelihood that experts would test the authenticity of a newly discovered Vermeer with every scientific method at their command. It would be an additional satisfaction to delude them by exploiting their own teachings and discoveries.

Patiently he explored countless antique shops in the role of someone looking for an old painting to hang in his drawing room, but his eyes tested the pictures for one characteristic alone: genuineness of material. The painting itself meant nothing to him, for it would have to be carefully removed. He was interested only in the old canvas and wood. Eventually he acquired for sixty gulden a *Raising of Lazarus,* a wretched piece but one which had undoubtedly been painted in the seventeenth century. The picture's dimensions were 125 x 127 centimeters — by a curious coincidence the same as those of *The Disciples at Emmaus.*

Jo showed no surprise at the various chemicals which her husband brought home. To her they were just painting materials like all the rest. It did strike her as odd when Han bought a large collection of shaving brushes, but then he did a lot of incomprehensible things. She had no inkling of the connection between the collection of badger-hair shaving brushes and the fact that Vermeer painted exclusively with badger-hair brushes. Han knew full well that a single alien brush hair found during a careful scrutiny of the paint layers in his Vermeer would expose the whole fraud.

Jo wondered a little at Han's habit of bringing home curious old goblets, utensils, candlesticks and cloths. He told her that they would help to make the house on the Mediterranean look more homely, but only he knew that they were to form the décor of the proposed fake. It had to be genuine down to the smallest detail.

In the autumn of 1932 Han and Jo moved into the house at Roquebrune. Pleading financial difficulties, Han refused to allow his wife a maidservant, thus eliminating the unwelcome presence of a witness on the premises.

During the ensuing years Han van Meegeren led a dual exist-

ence. One Han painted portraits; the other lived in a world of
secret attempts, reminiscent of alchemy, to find a sort of touchstone
which would enable him to paint a genuine Vermeer. Increasingly
obsessed with an urge to attain the unattainable, he took refuge in
the mental transformation of Han van Meegeren into a resurrected
Vermeer. In empirical research, in experiment, and in the intellectual exploration of the Biblical theme which he had already
selected for his picture, he ceased to draw a distinction between
reality and appearance. The boundaries between them had dissolved.

After trials with homemade paints and binding agents prepared
according to ancient recipes, after attempts at drying with oils and
varnishes, after the application of the celebrated Vermeer blue
(derived from lapis lazuli which he imported from London and
laboriously ground by hand in a mortar), Han subjected his surfaces to a baking process in the kiln. Those experiments took
weeks. Months were spent in testing the reactions of paint, varnish
and canvas to warmth and heat. The problems raised by the
necessity for rapid and permanent hardening were innumerable.
Moreover, Han was continually forced to tear himself away from
his series of tests and return to the present, where he had to paint
convincing portraits of masculine and, more especially, feminine
members of the *haut monde* in order to keep the wolf from the
door. Beside his prudently covered, banal portraits of society women
stood, even more carefully protected, the paints, materials and hardening experiments for his Vermeer.

What intrigued many visitors and also provoked occasional
questions from Jo was Han's sudden passion for fresh flowers,
especially elder blossoms. Regardless of cost, elder flowers scented
the air in his studio, in the corridor, on the veranda. There were

concrete and quite unsentimental reasons underlying this new craze.

Flower oils occurred frequently in the paint recipes of the old masters. After experimenting with every conceivable kind, Han found that elder oil made a particularly good agent for binding solids. His tests with volatile oils produced a strong odor. If he were to avoid awkward questions, there had to be plenty of fresh elder blossom in evidence.

Having overcome the difficult and at first apparently insoluble problems of paint, varnish and surface texture, he set about removing the paint from his *Lazarus*. Its powers of resistance defied all his efforts. It seemed completely impervious and withstood every attempt at softening.

The *Lazarus* was a genuine picture of the seventeenth century. Its paints, dried to the consistency of stone, could not be dissolved either with alcohol, turpentine or benzine. True, the topmost layer yielded slightly here and there, but the bulk of it appeared to be impenetrable.

Han detached the canvas from its frame, carefully preserving the handmade nails and old leather cornerpieces. He spread the stiff material on the floor and began to remove the paint. The upper layer he rubbed off with sandpaper, substituting a rounded pumice stone as he got nearer the canvas. It was an endless task: too much pressure endangered the precious old canvas, too little would not shift the paint.

After weeks of effort the canvas was at last free of paint except for a few white patches where the threads and white lead had become chemically fused. Since Vermeer had worked with metallic white, even the smallest traces of lead would become treacherously apparent under X-ray. There was only one way to combat this. Han van Meegeren had to construct his picture so that the rem-

nants of white paint on the old picture were once more covered by
white paint. In fact, he disguised the old traces of white lead under
the white lead surface of the tablecloth in *The Disciples at Emmaus*.

The old canvas was now ready to receive new priming for the
Vermeer, but van Meegeren immediately had to remove the first
applications. The canvas was not only hard but brittle, and there
was a danger that paint would penetrate the priming during forced
drying in the oven. Tentative efforts had to be made to render
the old material pliant, homogeneous and malleable, to ensure the
suppleness essential for subsequent *craquelure*. What was more, the
old canvas needed support from a new one at the back.

When it seemed that all his preparatory work had been successfully concluded, Han was obliged to relax for a while. His physical condition left much to be desired. Whereas city dwellers make
for the sea to recuperate, Han and Jo now turned their backs on it
and visited Holland, France and the Olympic Games in Berlin. In
the autumn of 1936 they returned to Roquebrune, and in late
autumn Han started work on *The Disciples at Emmaus*.

He scrupulously followed Vermeer's methods down to the
smallest detail. He had steeped himself so thoroughly in the master's technique that what he had assiduously memorized had now
become an integral part of his own store of knowledge. Priming,
composition, light distribution, perspective, figure work, method,
color heightening and brushwork were no longer those of forty-
seven-year-old Han van Meegeren: he had become the medium of
the man whom he wished to imitate.

The prior hardening of paint had become a difficult and time-
consuming problem. Quite by chance Han was reminded of bake-
lite, and this led him, after studying its method of manufacture, to
blend phenol and formaldehyde with his pigments. There was a
risk that pre-mixed paints would set too quickly. This he obviated

by adding the hardening agents to his paints immediately before use, thus preventing them from setting on the palette. The final, almost adamantine finish was achieved by baking the completed picture in the oven. This, while avoiding an unnaturally glassy surface, endowed his paints with an inner solidity which would otherwise have required centuries of natural drying.

The problem of hardening had been solved, but not without risk. Phenol and formaldehyde did not appear until two hundred years after Vermeer's time. Evidence of these substances in the paint would give the fraud away. Even so, it would be almost impossible to discover any telltale particles remaining in the hardened mass of paint once it had been baked. And who would try to find any at the risk of desecrating a Vermeer?

One more almost insuperable problem was that of models. He would of necessity have to rely upon painted references if he were not to reveal his secret. But, while he had formed a clear idea of how to portray the disciples, his powers of imagination were unequal to a Christ.

Here chance took a hand in the shape of a beggar who one day rang his doorbell. To Han, the alms seeker who stood diffidently on the threshold presented a heaven-sent opportunity. He decided to give his Christ the features of this unknown man.

After six months' work the painting was finished. All that remained was to age it. Overlaid with the varnish which he had himself made according to ancient formula, the canvas went into the oven for a second baking. Personal experiment had shown Han that the ideal temperature was a fraction over 110 degrees centigrade.

After cooling, he rolled the canvas round a thick metal tube, painted side outermost. Into the minute cracks and fissures which resulted from this treatment he rubbed a slightly dampened neutral pigment which, when the canvas was laid flat once more, was extruded from the crevices and could be cleanly wiped off. Any paint dust remaining in the network of minute cracks became fused with the layers of paint in which it was embedded once drying was complete.

Not until some days later did he reattach the canvas to its old frame with the handmade nails and old leather fittings.

Weeks passed in agonies of doubt and indecision. Behind locked doors, Han van Meegeren studied his picture again and again.

Slowly, conviction dawned. On the easel stood a Vermeer — indistinguishable in any respect from a Vermeer painted by the master himself. It was *The Disciples at Emmaus,* a painting by Vermeer, a work dating from his obscure youth, which he had probably spent in Italy. That would also explain the choice of theme.

Han van Meegeren stood at the crossroads in a journey which hatred had impelled him to make. He wanted the completed work to demonstrate that art critics, art historians and the greatest of experts could be wrong.

But would this hoax, which properly belonged in the realm of tragicomedy, be worth the years of effort? Why not try to *sell* the painting as a Vermeer? If the attempt were successful it would undoubtedly bring in a sum worth many hundred of thousands of gulden. Besides, paying these gulden for a van Meegeren instead of a Vermeer would teach his arrogant detractors a lesson. In five years' time, after the statute of limitations had come into effect, he could safely tell them that their precious Vermeer van Delft was a Vermeer van Meegeren.

In order to put the picture on the market he took it to Paris. There he deposited it at the Crédit Lyonnais and offered it to an agent, telling him that it was the heirloom of an aristocratic Italian family of Dutch extraction whose name could under no circumstances be revealed. The agent questioned him no further.

All now depended on the picture's authentication, and the only man for that job was Bredius.

Dr. Abraham Bredius, the eighty-year-old Nestor of Holland's art historians and an authority on the Dutch masters, examined the painting and pronounced it to be a work by Vermeer. The "four tests of authenticity," at that time still regarded as infallible, were carefully applied:

(1) Resistance of the paints to alcohol and other solvents.

(2) Evidence of white lead in the white portions.

(3) X-ray examination of the substratum.

(4) Microscopic and spectroscopic examination of the principal pigments.

These tests produced nothing which cast doubt on the picture's authenticity.

Bredius, convinced of the infallibility of his judgment and unwilling to await the result of the tests, had already published in the November issue of the *Burlington Magazine* an authoritative article entitled "A New Vermeer" in which he pronounced *The Disciples at Emmaus* to be an early work by Vermeer, "a masterpiece, his crowning achievement."

As a result, the Rembrandt Association, a society of moneyed art lovers, decided to "preserve" the picture for a Dutch museum provided that other experts gave their confirmation. Professor Martin and Dr. Schneider of the Mauritshuis, Dr. Schmidt-Degener and Jonkheer Roëll of the Rijksmuseum, Dr. van Gelder and Dr. Hannema all confirmed that *The Disciples at Emmaus* was a masterpiece by Vermeer.

The picture passed into the possession of the Boymans Foundation at Rotterdam as a gift from the Rembrandt Association. The cost was 550,000 gulden, of which van Meegeren received 340,000 and the agents 210,000.

Then came the day when the Deventer story repeated itself. The schoolmaster's son, now a middle-aged man, watched the farce which he had staged unfold before him. This time the gratification of what in Deventer had been unalloyed revenge was overlaid by the stigma attaching to ill-gotten gains. A youthful hoax had matured into a full-scale fraud. The "Vermeer" formed the central attraction at an exhibition of 450 classical Dutch masterpieces held in the Boymans Museum to mark Queen Wilhelmina's jubilee.

The leading monthly *Pantheon* asserted that "few other works of art have ever become so widely known in so short a time," and the *Journal of Art History* proclaimed that "the spiritual focus of the exhibition, despite the distinguished works by Rembrandt, Hals and Grünewald, is Vermeer's Emmaus picture."

Van Meegeren's "Vermeer" had won a place in the history of art.

All the superlatives in the dictionary were lavished upon Vermeer's *Disciples at Emmaus* during the following weeks. The art historian de Vries wrote of "the ideal content, the especial inspiration" of the painting, and went on: "The miracle of the Manifestation has been transformed into a miracle of painting."

However flattered van Meegeren was by the admiration accorded to the Vermeer, what was more important to him than all the art historians' praise was that his picture had withstood the scrutiny of the expert restorers who carefully cleaned his newborn child before its exhibition in the Boymans Museum. It had passed through their hands unchallenged as a genuine old painting — so old, indeed, that it had been found necessary to restore it in order to eliminate the defects and irregularities with which Han van Meegeren had prudently provided it.

He told his wife the tale of the aristocratic Italian family, and she accepted this explanation of their sudden affluence without question. Han bought a palatial villa in Nice. The months passed in a whirl of gaiety and enjoyment, but money flowed through his fingers like water and he was soon in need of more.

A second Vermeer seemed too risky a proposition. But, after all, there were plenty of other names on Holland's artistic roll of fame!

Han settled on Pieter de Hooch. Admittedly, he stood lower than Vermeer in the price scale, but that made him considerably safer to put on the market. The appearance of a hitherto unknown de Hooch might pass virtually unnoticed. He accordingly produced *The Drinking Party* and *The Card Players*.

The former picture was acquired by the leading collector D. G. van Beuningen for 219,000 gulden, the latter by W. van der Vorm for 220,000, of which sums van Meegeren received 175,000 and 170,000 gulden respectively.

While Han was contemplating the production of a new Vermeer, the Second World War broke out. He became extremely worried about the large sums of money which he had made (he accounted for them by telling everyone that he had won the *grand prix* in the Loterie Nationale) and wondered what would happen to the franc and the gulden. Not wishing to spend the war abroad he decided to return to his native land. Jo would rather have stayed in Nice, but he insisted that they should at least keep an eye on their property in Holland. The war would soon be over, he argued, and within a few months they would be back on the Côte d'Azur. Taking only a small quantity of luggage they closed up their little palace and left, little guessing that they would never see it again.

When, years later, the house was next visited, it was by detectives and experts ransacking it in quest of fakes.

In early 1940 Han and Jo moved into a villa in Laren, away from the all too watchful eyes of Amsterdam but not too far from the center of things. The greater part of Han's fortune was salted away in Nice and could not be realized. There were no purchasers about, and the international flow of currency was at a standstill. Once the Germans occupied Holland all communication with the rest of Europe ceased.

Van Meegeren, accustomed to unlimited supplies of money, found his lack of ready cash unendurable. Moreover, it was hardly an appropriate time for people to have their portraits painted. Accordingly, Han began to assemble a new forger's workshop. After his experiences in Roquebrune everything went considerably faster.

Exactly why he confined his activities exclusively to Vermeer from now on remains unknown. Perhaps he wanted to imitate the most valuable — and the most conspicuous — master of all. Perhaps he had lost his taste for any but the hardest of problems. Perhaps he merely wanted to dice with destiny, and no other method of deceiving the foremost connoisseurs, experts and collectors could give him the same thrill. Certainly, no artist was more highly prized than Vermeer, and van Meegeren had never become so deeply absorbed in the style of any other.

He began with sketches. He was so pleased with a head of Christ that he aged it and introduced it into the van Beuningen collection via the art dealers Strijbs and D. A. Hoogendijk as a "study by Vermeer for an unknown work." The 325,000 gulden which were his share of the purchase price of 400,000 covered all his debts, but he spent the balance so recklessly that it lasted him only a few months.

With a certain obsessive logic, he followed up the study by producing the painting itself. Once more it found its way into the same collection via Strijbs and Hoogendijk. Curiously enough, no one found it odd that the same man who had succeeded in unearthing the *Study* should now have managed to lay his hands on a painting incorporating a head of Christ for which it had obviously served as a model.

This *Last Supper* cost van Beuningen 1,600,000 gulden, of which Han received 1,350,000. It was his first million — and this time he had not even bothered to remove the old paint from the canvas on which he had perpetrated his forgery. He left the *Hunting Scene* by Hondius, an unimportant contemporary of Vermeer, just as it was, and painted his Biblical picture on top.

What explanation can there be for this lack of discretion? Was he drunk with success, or impelled by an unconscious wish to be finally unmasked and thus relieved of the necessity for further masquerades?

The following two years saw the appearance of *Isaac Blesses Jacob, The Woman Taken in Adultery,* and *The Washing of Feet.* Their sale netted 1,275,000, 1,650,000 and 1,250,000 gulden, of which van Meegeren received a total of 3,100,000 gulden. The purchasers were van der Vorm, Göring and the Dutch government.

Van Meegeren now oscillated between extravagance and sound business acumen. He bought houses in Laren and Amsterdam, shares and other securities. He always took his share of the proceeds from the Vermeers in cash, never in checks or promissory notes, which meant that he could always make his own purchases for cash.

Since the Dutch government applied extremely rigorous conditions to the purchase of pictures, Han van Meegeren arranged that *The Washing of Feet* should be passed by Jan Kok, a friend of his youthful days in Deventer, to P. de Boer. The latter gave it to Dr. D. Hannema for expert opinion. Hannema accepted the painting as a genuine Vermeer and his example was followed by the members of the Art Commission, at whose suggestion Professor J. van

Dam, Secretary General to the Ministry of Education, instituted negotiations for its purchase.

By this time rumors were already rife that van Meegeren was taking drugs. How much truth, if any, there was in this surmise remains uncertain, but his alternate fits of melancholy and euphoria indicated that he was suffering from acute nervous instability. His marriage started to break up.

His behavior was sometimes odd, sometimes quite normal. He dealt in old paintings, buying weak pictures from small dealers, cleaning them up and reselling them at a considerable profit. He hid large sums in unlikely places, kept hundreds of thousands of gulden in cashboxes. One of these he buried in the garden of his house at Laren, where it was later discovered by Allied troops hunting for unexploded ammunition. The local inhabitants gaped in amazement as the soldiers opened the tin canister and found van Meegeren's cache of thousand-gulden notes.

In 1944 Han and Jo were divorced, but continued to live under the same roof owing to the desperate shortage of accommodation in Holland. After one of their innumerable quarrels he collapsed. On coming to, he murmured some incoherent phrases. "I shall soon be dead," Jo thought she heard. "I must make a full confession . . . write it down . . . I'm tired . . . this is the end . . ." That was as far as it went, however. Van Meegeren did not commit his confession to paper.

But he did make a full confession to the court which, on October 12, 1947, after two years of preliminary investigation, sentenced him to a year in jail. The public prosecutor had demanded two years, half the maximum sentence allowed by law.

After sentence was pronounced van Meegeren asked the president of the court for permission to paint in prison. The granting of this request was the signal for a flood of portrait commissions. From the United States came a contract to illustrate a book. Collectors, artists, dealers and agents from London and Paris, Monte Carlo and Zurich all developed an interest in "the man who could paint like Vermeer."

Actions for damages, governmental demands for arrears of taxes and very high court costs necessitated the opening of bankruptcy proceedings. Despite all his assets, Han's fortune could only cover a proportion of the claims put forward.

However great a fillip the lenient sentence seemed to have given his spirits, Han's strength began to fail. He had to be transferred to the Valerius Clinic, where he died on December 30, 1947, at the age of fifty-eight.

Now that the play's protagonist had made his exit, a mob of extras tumbled onto the stage to fight a bitter rear-guard action. While some regarded van Meegeren's work as a hodgepodge of fakes and inferior originals, others picked out individual works and pronounced them genuine.

What, they asked, if his confession had merely been motivated by fear of a severe penalty for collaboration? Perhaps everything he had told his son and daughter — including those hints about yet another world-renowned painting which was still hanging in a gallery somewhere, faked by him — had sprung from fear or was no more than a sick mind's flight into the comforting twilight of self-delusion?

Could it really be true that the most important of the pictures, *The Disciples at Emmaus,* was not a genuine Vermeer? And what about *The Woman Taken in Adultery?*

Considering how easily solved the whole matter had at first seemed, it was only to be expected that the unusual nature of the general summons issued to experts to settle the question of authenticity should give rise to much speculation. The wealth of scientific knowledge brought to bear on the problem becomes apparent from a mere glance at the list of authorities whose aid was enlisted: Dr. P. B. Coremans, Director of the Central Laboratory of the Belgian Museums, Brussels; Dr. A. van Schendel, Director of the Department of Painting at the Rijksmuseum, Amsterdam; W. C. J. Wooning, Inspector of the Dutch Ministry of Justice; Professor R. J. Gettens, Fogg Museum, Harvard University; H. Gravenstein, Lecturer in Microchemistry, Delft Technical College; Dr. J. C. A. Kappelmeier, Director of Sikkens Varnishes, Sassenheim, Holland; L. Loose, Assistant at the Central Laboratory of the Belgian State Museums, Brussels; Professor P. Terpstra, Crystallographic Institute of Groningen University; D. C. Hodgskin, Crystallographic Institute of Oxford University.

Among others who co-operated with the above in their quest for the truth were the boards of directors and experts of the Rijksmuseum, the Mauritshuis and the Boymans Museum.

Despite the eminence of this band of connoisseurs, it was mooted that the motive underlying such an impressive display of qualifications was a wish to hush up the fact that *The Disciples at Emmaus* and *The Last Supper* (in its second and final version) really were original works by Vermeer.

The question whether all or only some of van Meegeren's pictures are fakes is still debated today. In 1951, while his son was declaring in Paris that still more greatly admired masterpieces in various galleries had really come from van Meegeren's hand, Donker published in Rotterdam an article by Jean Decoen entitled '*Retour à la vérité!*' which set out to prove the authenticity of *The Last Supper* and *The Disciples*. In Leyden, A. W. Sijthoff published M. M. van Dantzig's book *Johannes Vermeer, de 'Emmausgangers' en de Critici* with the opposite end in view.

Many are inclined to favor those who contradict the experts. Their argument, which lacks neither logic nor popular appeal, runs as follows: since the leading authorities who once pronounced the Vermeers of van Meegeren to be well-nigh divine works of art now opined that the same pictures were naïve hackwork, their figures wooden and maladroit, lacking in depth, plasticity and perspective, it was hard to tell why their expert judgment should be any worthier of credence this time than last.

The Scribes, painted in prison, fetched 3000 gulden. Equipped with the signature "Vermeer" it would have found its way into a private gallery or museum for several hundred thousand gulden . . .

An auction of pictures and effects from van Meegeren's estate held at Haarlem in 1958 gave fresh impetus to the controversy over *The Disciples at Emmaus* and *The Last Supper.*

A decisive share of the *proof* that van Meegeren's pictures involved forgery was furnished by Professor Coremans of Brussels. (After all, van Meegeren's confession should not necessarily be taken at face value.)

The scientific evidence of fraud rested to a large extent on Coremans's assertion that the paints in works purporting to date from the seventeenth century contained a synthetic resin not discovered until 1900.

Professor Meurice of the Chemistry Faculty of Brussels University thereupon demonstrated that medieval binding agents gave precisely the same reactions as synthetic resin when subjected to Coremans's method of analysis.

A Basel chemistry professor, Dr. Grob, announced that "the microchemical analyses on which Coremans has based his findings yield no evidence that any synthetic resinous products are present in the layers of paint on the picture under examination."

Similarly, the proof of forgery on microphotographic grounds which Coremans buttressed with numerous shots of brush strokes has, on the strength of more recent photographs, been declared misleading and erroneous.

The scientific rebuttal of at least a considerable part of Coremans's evidence for the faking of *The Disciples* and *The Last Supper* resulted in his being sued for damages by D. G. van Beuningen, the purchaser of the latter picture, on the grounds that he had "given it as his expert opinion that a genuine Vermeer was an imitation by the hand of the painter van Meegeren."

Coremans retorted with a counterclaim alleging derogation of his expert qualifications. He won his case on the following, purely juridical grounds: that since the judges at Amsterdam had accepted Coremans's expert opinion in van Meegeren's trial for forgery, their colleagues at Brussels were also obliged to regard it as conclusive.

Decoen and Dantzig vainly tried in various published utterances to incite Coremans to bring an action against them, but the Brussels professor declined any legal clarification of the charge that his unreliable methods had produced unreliable results.

Thirteen years after the Amsterdam court's decision, the van Meegeren case is still shrouded in the same cloak of obscurity which characterized the life of the man himself.

14

❧❧❧❧❧❧❧❧❧

Malskat and the Turkey

IN the year 1940 there appeared a large art book entitled *Schleswig Cathedral and Its Mural Paintings*. Edited by the art historian Professor Alfred Stange, it devoted twenty-four pages of text and thirty-three plates, some of them full-page, to paintings "which have been restored to us by cleaning and treatment as restrained as it was careful" and which, in the editor's opinion, represented "an excellent demonstration of the ties, permanent because they spring from nationality, which bind Schleswig to the Saxonian-Westphalian area and its art." Of a frieze in the form of animal medallions, Stange had this to say: "Some of them are imaginary animals commonly found in medieval art, but others are taken from real life, and the latter are portrayed so faithfully and with such animation that this frieze appears to be unique in its period. With astonishing powers of discernment, the painter has observed and reproduced the creatures' individuality and smallest idiosyncrasies.

The portrayals are not, as so often, borrowed from reference books, but are based on a high degree of personal observation."

This slightly prolix but enthusiastic description referred to some original murals by an unknown painter of the twelfth to fourteenth centuries, recently restored. Although the pictures and frieze were "not painted, but only drawn in ruddle on the plaster of the wall," the Professor considered it "unnecessary" to entertain any doubts or to assume that they were always in their present condition, i.e. unfinished.

Professor Stange attached particular importance to these "early Gothic ecclesiastical frescoes" in Schleswig Cathedral. The turkeys were the only disturbing feature. All the other creatures depicted — and these included kings, saints, knights and jesters — were at home in early Gothic painting: the turkey was, so to speak, the odd man out. It had not been introduced into Europe by the Spaniards until 1550, and before that time was known only in North America and Mexico. How, then, could a Schleswig painter have depicted a lifelike turkey during the thirteenth or fourteenth centuries?

The turkey had to be supplied with an historical basis, and that, at a time when Germany was infected with a mania for things Nordic, did not present too much difficulty. The theory was that long before the Spaniards ever arrived, America was discovered by bold blond seafaring Vikings, and that they were responsible for importing the first turkeys. The Gothic artist's turkeys in Schleswig Cathedral were thus members of a species of poultry known in Germanic lands during the thirteenth and fourteenth centuries.

Combining art with history, Professor Stange wrote:

"The author of these paintings is one of the 'greats' in the realm of art. The painter's kings help us to determine his historical location. He worked in Schleswig *circa* 1280 and hailed from the time of the Hohenstaufen emperors. We do not know his name."

Thirteen years after the appearance of this authoritative work on

Schleswig Cathedral and its frescoes, the name of the unknown painter was on everyone's lips. It was Lothar Malskat.

Among those who had acted as models for the figures and faces in the murals in Schleswig Cathedral were: his father, his sister Frieda, his friend Kurt Meiser, Jörn Ross, sacristan of the Cathedral, and the film actress Hansi Knoteck. The "early Gothic" artist was born at Königsberg, East Prussia, on May 3, 1913.

On September 2, 1951, the Church of St. Mary at Lübeck celebrated its seven-hundredth anniversary. This long-awaited event, for which elaborate preparations had been made, was signalized by the presence of high ecclesiastical dignitaries from Germany and elsewhere, senior representatives of the federal and provincial governments, envoys and ambassadors, professors and municipal councilors.

The central feature of the occasion was not so much the structural restoration carried out on the venerable old church as an artistic event: the resurrection of some unique mural paintings.

When the Federal Chancellor, Dr. Adenauer, asked to be shown the "unique frescoes," Dietrich Fey, the restorer, described the great difficulties which had attended their restoration. The Chancellor observed that it remained for the art historian to carry out the hardest but perhaps the most pleasant task of all. They were prophetic words.

Sweden's National Curator, Dr. Berthil Berthelsson, pronounced the mural paintings to be "entirely unique; they are to be found nowhere else in the world." No one could quarrel with that statement, either.

In a disquisition published by the Institute of Art History at Kiel University, the works of art at St. Mary's, Lübeck, were described as follows:

There is so little "prettiness" about the splendid Madonna that we can only assume that the author of this masterpiece was a German. The whole group was executed by one brilliant artist. The sacred figures seem to be gazing westwards toward the Last Judgment. Two styles are in evidence at St. Mary's. In the older style, flesh and draperies are uniformly outlined in black, while the younger naturalistically reserves the red sub-contours for flesh and models only the draperies with black lines.

The early medieval artist to whom Lübeck owed this work was unknown, for he was apparently one of those artists of long ago who put work before personality. Neither their names, ciphers nor monograms have survived. The Federal German Post Office used three of the finest and most expressive figures as a subject for two large welfare stamps. They can be found listed in the West German section of Stanley Gibbons's catalogue as Numbers 1065 and 1066: "Charity. 700th Anniversary of St. Mary's Church, Lübeck." The extra five pfennigs payable on each stamp went to the administrators of the Evangelical Lutheran Church of St. Mary, Lübeck.

Lübeck's early Gothic masterpieces provided a favorite theme not only for newspapers at home and abroad but also for several essays by art historians. In Switzerland in 1952 Hans Jürgen Hansen published a treatise, illustrated in color, on "The Mural Paintings in St. Mary's Church, Lübeck." It contained the following passage:

After the fire, the frescoes were very badly exposed to the elements. However, it proved possible to save them by careful restoration which added nothing new but merely preserved what had survived. The Virgin and Child form the central figure in one of the triple groups of murals. . . . The painting dates from *circa* 1300. The brilliance of its colors has survived with unusual freshness because until their discovery after the incendiary-bomb raid in the year 1942 the murals had lain hidden under a layer of white plaster for almost five hundred years. . . .

Most impressive are the triple groups of saints. . . . They stand . . . beneath the windows of the central aisle. Above the high altar is a portrayal of the Virgin together with St. Anne and St. John, the two co-patrons of the church, and in other parts of the choir are triple groups of apostles, patriarchs and monks. These exhibit a severe style, Byzantine-influenced and still almost Romanesque, and undoubtedly originated a few years earlier than the figures in the main aisle. The latter are more animated, softer, entirely Gothic, comparable in character with the celebrated illustrations in the *"Manessische Liederhandschrift,"* to which they also correspond in date.

It turned out later that the only factually correct observation in the long series of enthusiastic treatises on Lübeck's "early Gothic paintings" was H. J. Hansen's closing remark: "Done with a coarse brush, the painting was probably carried out in a very short time."

This supposition hit the nail on the head. Lothar Malskat had, in fact, executed these paintings in a remarkably short space of time.

Lothar Malskat did not spend long as an apprentice painter whitewashing ceilings and kitchen walls in the houses of Königsberg, for he soon abandoned his apprenticeship and was allowed to go to art school. Professors Grün, Marten and Wolff recognized their new student's considerable talents. Professor Marten laid great stress on the young man's "extraordinary, almost uncanny productivity and versatility" and was convinced that he would go places. Professor Wolff thought that "a lot more will be heard of Lothar Malskat." How right both these gentlemen turned out to be!

Even in his student days, Malskat was drawing and painting strongly derivative subjects as well as producing original and imaginative work. In fact, he alternated between original composition and work which was based on references. After a successful local exhibition of his pictures, Malskat, who was a restless young man, left Königsberg and set off for Berlin.

Armed with a letter of recommendation, he called on the well-known church painter and restorer Professor Ernst Fey and showed him some of his work. Fey at once recognized the shy youth's unusual gifts and decided to exploit them for his own ends. To provide Malskat's remarkable versatility with a solid foundation, he gave him rough manual work to do and at the same time encouraged him to study richly illustrated works of stylistic criticism dealing with early ecclesiastical painting.

Having followed theoretical instruction with practical demonstration, Fey went on a tour through Silesia, accompanied not only by his son Dietrich, who was his constant collaborator, but also by his new assistant. Dilapidated church frescoes were retouched and preserved, and, where original frescoes were missing, new paintings were executed in archaic style. Lothar Malskat was modest and amenable: Fey paid him an hourly wage of 1 mark 20 pfennigs, but kept for himself all the credit for the remarkably successful restoration work carried out in the churches at Oppeln and Neisse.

After completing numerous smaller commissions, the Professor was, in the early part of 1937, entrusted with a task which was to make him famous for a long time to come. This was to clean and restore to their original condition the early Gothic paintings in Schleswig Cathedral, which had been repainted by August Olbers in 1888.

When the upper layers of paint had been removed, however, nothing was left on the brick walls save gray, discolored plaster bearing scarcely perceptible traces of paint. The Gothic frescoes had vanished.

The Feys, father and son, and their assistant, Malskat, stood helplessly in front of the bare expanse. They stood a good chance of being held accountable for the destruction of a priceless national art treasure. Only Lothar Malskat could banish his employer's worries, for he alone could successfully counterfeit Gothic master-pieces — if time permitted and there were no interruptions.

Malskat primed the half-bare brick walls with several coats of lime. On this new ground he sketched figures — of his own de-vising — in the severe manner of the early medieval draftsmen. The two Feys provided the requisite materials and screened Mal-skat's work. Within a few months there had come into being the "early Gothic" portrayals of human beings and animals which were later to furnish so much material for profound essays by art scholars. Only in the case of the turkeys did Lothar Malskat's brush run away with him. They were too early by almost three hundred years.

The "resurrection" of the masterpieces in Schleswig Cathedral set the seal on Professor Ernst Fey's career as an ecclesiastical painter and restorer. Not even the smallest ray of reflected glory fell on Lothar Malskat, and his miserable hourly wage could hardly be regarded as adequate compensation. He pondered on ways of improving his position, but a national art treasure of the first rank was involved, and to pick a quarrel with Fey might in-volve greater risks for him as the executant for the work than for Fey as the man who had commissioned it.

On the outbreak of the Second World War, Malskat exchanged his paintbrush for a rifle. He was not destined to die a hero's death fighting for his country, but survived the war as an artist-soldier in Norway, drawing landscapes, fellow soldiers and Nordic beau-ties.

When the war ended, the tide of returning humanity carried him back to Lübeck, where he tried his luck as a window dresser. He acquired new painting utensils, one by one. Then, selecting the best nude studies from his first finished pictures, he took them off to Hamburg, where he found a ready market. His subjects (full-bosomed girls) were in great demand.

Malskat knew that Dietrich Fey lived in Hamburg. He had no idea what he was doing, but Professor Fey's son was the sort of man who always fell on his feet. Then, quite by chance, he bumped into his former colleague, and Fey invited him home.

For some time conversation centered on their common past, but the future was more important. At first tentatively but with growing clarity, plans for future collaboration took shape.

In the weeks that followed, the two men set up a "picture factory." Dietrich Fey handled the business side while Malskat's unerring hand conjured up, on paper or canvas, whatever Fey's customers required: Barlachs, Chagalls, Utrillos, Munchs, Henri Rousseaus or Beckmanns, Pechsteins and other Expressionists — sometimes a genuine Lothar Malskat, too.

The opportunist dealers who sprang out of the ground like mushrooms in the postwar years did not inquire too closely about the authenticity of a picture. They only wanted to know where it had come from, for fear of handling stolen goods. To this ever-recurring question, Malskat could reply with a clear conscience that none of his pictures was stolen and every one belonged to him. He would even give a written guarantee if requested.

The products of the Fey-Malskat picture factory were not intended for the connoisseur but for the superficial observer. When Malskat showed his portfolio of "original prints by French Impressionists" to an experienced art dealer in Stuttgart, they were at once identified as fakes.

After the currency reform, which struck a new note of harsh reality into Malskat's shady existence, vigorous preparations were made to rebuild the Church of St. Mary, Lübeck, which had been gutted by the severe fire of 1942. Church authorities, senate and citizens assembled the materials needed to reconstruct the roof of the nave in order to protect the interior of the medieval building from further damage and enable renovation to commence.

Dietrich Fey was entrusted with the restoration of the celebrated frescoes, a contract which came at a most opportune moment, for the new official mark had swept away a large number of dubious businesses.

What had succeeded so well in Schleswig Cathedral was to be equally successful at St. Mary's. Relying on his fruitful partnership with Lothar Malskat, Fey undertook the restoration of the church's early murals.

Very little of the early Gothic frescoes had survived the conflagration. Fey and Malskat could only resort to the methods which they had already employed at Schleswig. The surface of the walls was ruthlessly cleaned. The crumbling, smoke-blackened old plaster, which bore only faint traces of paint, was removed and the stone reprimed. Then, when the surface had been dried and slightly discolored to simulate age, Lothar Malskat adorned it with his early Gothic figures, faces and animals.

If this form of "restoration" were to be safeguarded from discovery, all visitors had to be kept away from the interior of the church while work was in progress. Any inquisitive intruders were halted at the threshold by a notice warning them against the dangers of falling masonry. When art historians dropped in, as they occasionally did, they found their passage barred by precarious scaffolding. A confederate of Fey and Malskat used to signal the unwelcome approach of visitors by hammering. The areas on which Malskat was working were hastily screened by sliding wooden partitions. Visiting art historians and churchmen were welcome to see what had already been "restored."

Just as at Schleswig, Lothar Malskat performed the whole of the

actual painting work anonymously and for a minimal fee. Dietrich
Fey was the organizer and figurehead, while the man who had
conjured up the early Gothic masterpieces remained in the background. Moral and material recognition were denied him. He did
not even receive cash compensation for the fact that he was not
appreciated as an artist. It is not surprising that Malskat gradually
developed a hate-complex against someone who calmly accepted
not only the growing chorus of approbation but the entire financial
benefits as well.

Malskat, who was fundamentally not an intellectual imitator but
a technically and stylistically competent forger, became firmly convinced that he had been exploited and deprived of his rights.
Suppressing the thought that he himself was responsible for this
situation, he nursed a day laborer's resentment of the successful businessman.

Dietrich Fey's triumph at St. Mary's seven-hundredth anniversary celebrations, which Malskat, unnoticed by the festive crowd,
was forced to witness, sparked off the explosion which had been
pending for so long.

When the celebrations were over, Malskat received his share of
the honors: a good-humored pat on the back from Fey and a few
beer and schnapps tokens which could be exchanged at a hostelry
in the neighborhood.

At that moment, Lothar Malskat remembered the report which
the provincial curator Dr. Hirschfeld had sent to the church
authorities at Lübeck when restoration work began, and had also
forwarded to the Ministry of Culture at Kiel, the municipal board
of works, the West German Association for the Preservation of
Ancient Monuments, and the administrators of Lübeck Museum.
Marked "Secret," this document was an expression of the strongest
reservations, and its phrasing left little to be desired in the way of
clarity:

The restoration of defective medieval mural paintings is, in the last analysis, a question of trust. Dietrich Fey will not guarantee that he has never done any overpainting in an unguarded moment. I therefore declare that I dissociate myself from the working methods of the restorer Dietrich Fey. If Lübeck's monuments are to be properly preserved, work can only continue under a restorer who is absolutely trustworthy at all times and never carries out secret overpainting or amplification. I decline all further responsibility.

This document was filed at the public records office, but Dr. Hirschfeld's violent arguments with Dietrich Fey had no effect on the progress of the so-called restoration work. The provincial curator made repeated demands that Fey should not overpaint old painted surfaces in color, but without success. Watched over by an invisible guardian angel, Fey continued to adorn the church with Lothar Malskat's early Gothic frescoes.

A vote of no confidence by Professors Deckert and Scheper was equally ineffective. On the contrary, despite any misgivings, the West German Association for the Preservation of Ancient Monuments proposed to grant a further 150,000 marks "for the maintenance of the rediscovered mural paintings in St. Mary's Church."

Malskat, having formed the decision on September 2, 1951, to seek refuge in publicity, as it were, did not act on it until more than eight months later. During that time he remained in Dietrich Fey's employ, working on restorations in the Lübeck Rathaus. In a turret room there, Fey found some "Gothic murals" which he graciously "restored to the present and to posterity" on the principle that what was good for St. Mary's could not do the venerable old Rathaus any harm!

On May 10, 1952, Malskat sent Dietrich Fey a registered letter challenging him "to inform all interested parties that new paintings, not discoveries, are involved."

This sudden and belated regard for the truth should be viewed, assessed and analyzed with close reference to his later apologia. Malskat did not invoke a "subordinate capacity" as expressly defined by law. On the contrary, he claimed full responsibility for the work and at the same time tried to save his skin:

My religious pictures in the churches of Schleswig-Holstein are not forgeries. They became so only because of Dietrich Fey's willful and fraudulent misrepresentations. I had nothing at all to do with these fraudulent misrepresentations. The boundless confusion in the press and among art experts is due only to the fact that Dietrich Fey turned my paintings in St. Mary's Church into Gothic masterpieces.

As a painter of no mean ability, Lothar Malskat must have known that pictorial works which had survived in vestigial form could not be restored but only painted anew in the style of the erstwhile originals. This task he performed for money. Just as a starving man may be excused for stealing a loaf of bread, so artistic frauds committed *in extremis* need not be too harshly judged. These special circumstances may possibly have applied to the imitations in Schleswig Cathedral, but the fabrication of "French Impressionists" and other pictures provides clear evidence of forgery. Malskat, who could have entertained no doubts about the end product of his imitations, did not admit to forgery as such. He admitted it with qualifications. He was not prompted by an urge to confess the truth — only to hit back at the hated Fey.

And that remained his objective throughout the ensuing course of events. In a circumstantial letter to the church authorities at Lübeck he revealed the whole fundamentally pitiful fraud. When this failed to produce any immediate reaction, he released the details to other quarters at home and abroad.

Little by little, his allegations began to worry the parties concerned. A commission interrogated him. Sworn statements by

AMOSO·DOCTOR·PARESELSVS·

43 a.   Jan Scorel, *Paracelsus:* Louvre, Paris

43 b.   Rubens, *Paracelsus*: Musée des Beaux-Arts, Brussels

44 a.   Van Gogh, *Reapers in a Cornfield,* now at the Pinakothek in Berlin, and an X-ray photograph of the painting (top and bottom left)

44 b.   Otto Wacker, forgery of the preceding picture, and X-ray photograph (top and bottom right). The X-ray of the original shows van Gogh's normal method of painting, while the X-ray of the forgery reveals unsure and fragmentary brush-strokes. All Wacker's paintings have the same characteristics, and are therefore easily recognizable.

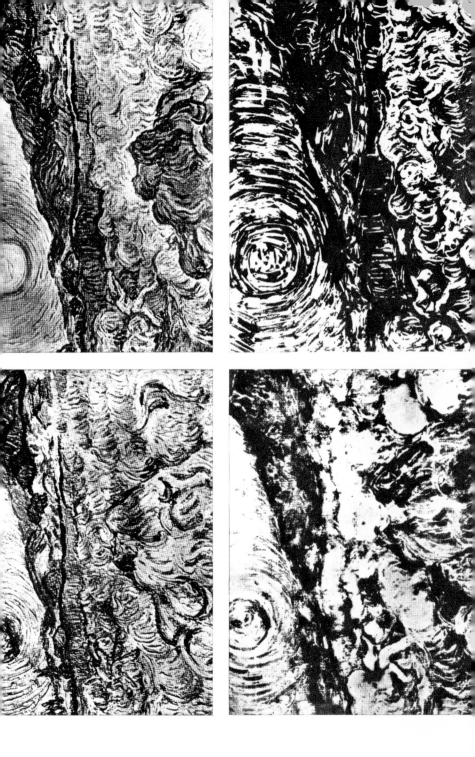

45. Two examples of the Malskat frescoes in the cathedrals of Schleswig and Lübeck; above, the turkey-cock which revealed the glaring forgery

46. Hans Blum, *Portrait of a Commissariat Official*. In the course of barely three years the work was 'transformed' into a *Portrait of a Bavarian Officer* by W. Leibl, and its value rose from 6,000 to 125,000 marks.

47. Joseph Rifesser, *Bishop with Bunch of Grapes*. 'Gothic' sculpture

48. Joseph Rifesser, *Madonna and Child*

bricklayers' foremen and their mates were produced to refute his allegations. This last-minute attempt, as understandable as it was inexcusable, to divert the threat of imminent disaster from the heads of art scholars was frustrated by Malskat's determination to destroy Dietrich Fey.

The strongest piece of material evidence was a roll of Leica film containing shots of the naked walls on which Malskat had later painted his medieval pictures. This knocked the bottom out of all the sworn affidavits that he had only restored what was already there. Malskat had done no restoration at all, merely painted new frescoes which looked old.

Improbable as it may sound, the art experts involved in this painful situation tried to turn their backs on reality. On August 20, 1952, the following statement was issued:

"Any charges at present being leveled at the restorer Dietrich Fey are as yet insufficient to arouse our misgivings. The work of preservation will therefore continue under the restorer Dietrich Fey." This declaration bore the following signatures: Dr. Bruno Fendrich, church architect; Dr. Münter, director of municipal building, retired; Herr Blunck, senior public surveyor and curator of public monuments; Dr. H. A. Gräbke, museum director; and Presbyter Göbel.

Nobody wanted to believe Malskat. Accordingly, he took a decisive step: on October 7, 1952, he instructed his attorney, Dr. Flottrong, to file charges against himself and Dietrich Fey.

The machinery of the law went into action. The first to be caught up in its wheels was Fey. On the strength of a warrant issued by Lübeck police court, he was arrested at Travemünde. The *Hamburger Abendblatt* informed its readers:

The arrest was carried out on the grounds that the course of justice might otherwise be prejudiced. We are informed that the six-hundred-

odd pictures and drawings in the style of many artists, ancient and
modern, which the painter Lothar Malskat faked on the instructions of
Fey have been disposed of to art dealers in Hamburg, Cologne, Munich
and Stuttgart. During a search of Dietrich Fey's house, seven paintings
and twenty-one drawings were seized. The chairman of the committee
investigating the restoration work at St. Mary's, Professor Dr. Grundmann, stated: "We shall not allow ourselves to be influenced in our work
by the human factors and considerations which hover over this affair."

The subject of the "Lübeck art forgeries" was eagerly seized on
by the German press and radio, and the case aroused interest abroad.
Although it had many predecessors, it was generally described as
"unique."

A committee of inquiry was now set up to investigate the affair
from the art historian's angle. On October 20, 1952, the report was
ready. It bore the signatures of Professor Dr. Grundmann of Hamburg, Chairman of the Association for the Preservation of Provincial Monuments, Dr. Sedlmaier, Professor of Art History at Kiel
University, and the Berlin curator Professor Dr. Scheper. Dr.
Scheefe, senior county court judge of Hamburg, acted as legal
adviser, and Professor Dr. Stois of the Institute of Chemistry and
Physics at Munich, one of the leading experts on pigments, was also
invited to give an opinion. On the same day, Dr. Schattenberg,
press officer to the public prosecutor's department at Lübeck, released the following statement to the press:

The twenty-one figures in the choir are not Gothic, but painted free-
hand by Malskat. The results of investigation compel one to distinguish
between the condition of the upper and lower portions of the painted
areas in the Obergaden choir. In the upper portions, the restorers have
at no point penetrated to the medieval layers of mortar. The painting described as old by the restorer, Fey, does not lie on the medieval layer
but on a post-medieval layer, and cannot, if for this reason alone, be
original.

Within the hour, the following statement was released to the press by Bishop D. Johannes Pautke:

The conclusions reached by the committee of inquiry divest the paintings in the choir of their medieval character. If the restorer Dietrich Fey has fraudulently succeeded in getting his work recognized as faithful restoration, this was possible only because of an extremely cunning deception which misled not only the church administration, as proprietor, but also curators and art experts.

On January 23, 1953, Lothar Malskat was arrested at his home and taken to Lübeck jail. A writ of habeas corpus was refused because it was surmised that Malskat might disappear or pervert the course of justice.

Malskat saw things differently. He had been enjoined not to give the press any information about the "early Gothic paintings," but the newspapers continued to come out with new details, and he was suspected of being the source. Despite all protestations to the contrary, his remand for questioning was upheld. No one believed him. The case had raised up so much dust that many people thought it advisable to remove the protagonist from contact with the outside world.

A preliminary hearing was held on October 27, 1953, and the main proceedings began on August 9, 1954. The ecclesiastical paintings were proved beyond any doubt to be fakes. Variously estimated at one time to be six, seven or eight hundred years old, the frescoes were in fact brand-new.

Even though it proved impossible entirely to dispel the fog of obscurity which hung over the whole affair, one or two noteworthy facts came to light. The Frankfurt art dealer Wilhelm Henrich stated that he had, through a colleague, bought a "Chagall" and sent it to the artist, who was at that time resident in the United States, with the request that he should certify it as genuine. Chagall apparently tore the picture up because it was a "miserable fake." This painting was the work of Lothar Malskat. It is uncertain how many drawings and paintings he actually faked, but they reached the market under the names of at least seventy different artists.

The sentence of the court was not announced until January 25, 1955. Fey got twenty months' imprisonment, Malskat eighteen. Malskat fled to Sweden. He found no lack of work there, for he displayed at least an average talent in his own right. It is only fair to mention that he took no advantage of the many questionable propositions he received. After his appeal had been dismissed, he returned to West Germany.

Malskat's early Gothic paintings vanished from church walls. Greatly though they had once excited the admiration of so-called authorities on art history and found favor with ecclesiastical, federal and local bodies when they were still medieval masterpieces, now, after Malskat's admission that he was their author, they were just as vehemently condemned. Why, in fact?

There are two schools of thought about the destruction of Malskat's paintings. It is impossible to refute the argument that his work, per se, remained what it had been before. His frescoes had rejoiced the eye of the beholder. They remained identical before, during and after the denouement. The admission that people of our own time had served as models for twelfth-century figures did not alter them in the slightest.

The pictures were washed off. There seems little doubt that this radical measure was intended to do more than merely clean the walls, but it is a curse — and sometimes a blessing, too — that what has once been done cannot be undone.

Anyone examining the Picassos, Chagalls, Barlachs and Utrillos forged by Malskat will be astonished, at first glance, by his fluent draftsmanship, his water-color technique and the facile manner in which he played with the shapes and colors of creative artists. His works will not, however, stand up to serious stylistic analysis. They are no more than competently painted fakes.

15

❦❦❦❦❦❦❦❦❦

Through a Glass Darkly

THE forgery of works of art knows no set rules, in either the technical or the intellectual sphere. Boundaries are always fluid and difficult to determine except in the case of straightforward, uninteresting imitations on a professional or industrial scale.

Nevertheless, there is one instance which illustrates something of universal application, throws the factors of uncertainty into sharp relief and allows us an insight into subsidiary motives which, in a deeper, commercial sense, assume primary significance and are of great value to the collector. The particular phenomenon who affords us this general information is Corot.

COROT

Corot's oeuvre catalogue was compiled by Alfred Robaut. It is regarded as the authoritative work to consult when verifying a picture which has been offered for sale as a Corot. Because the volumes published by Moreau-Nélaton were unfortunately incomplete, Robaut separately identified hundreds of works bearing Corot's signature which are either dubious or definite fakes. These lists have never appeared as a printed supplement to the oeuvre catalogue and can only be seen at the Cabinet des Estampes in Paris.

In them, detailed arguments and numerous reproductions are adduced to prove the unquestionable falsity of many important paintings and drawings signed by Corot in famous museums and collections.

Corot worked under conditions very reminiscent of the workshops of the old masters, a fact from which important conclusions can be drawn. He did not do any actual teaching, it is true, but his gregarious disposition often led him to paint in the company of other artists. This meant that he and his companions sometimes chose a common subject and produced pictures with similar themes. According to the individuality of the artists who worked with Corot, their work showed varying degrees of intentional or unintentional dependence on his style, interpretation, technique and mode of expression. Corot occasionally retouched the work of those who painted with him. It has also been proved that he often signed pictures which other painters produced in his style. The fact that he certified his authorship of such works automatically gave rise to the circulation of would-be Corots which were accepted as originals, for they were so close to his own work in time, spirit, technique and subject that positive differentiation was scarcely possible then — let alone now, after an elapse of decades.

Considering Corot's idiosyncrasies, of which one was to sign work which he had not himself produced, it is not surprising that he sometimes satisfied requests for pictures by handing out pieces which had been corrected and, as it were, authenticated by him. Even members of his own family possessed many undoubted imitations which they had been given by Corot himself. One such example has been positively identified. Corot left his sister, Mme. Sennegon, a study of the north door of Chartres Cathedral. Armed with this absolutely bona fide pedigree, the drawing came into the possession of a collector — only to be identified by Robaut as the work of the architect Poirot. This close friend of Corot's was hard of hearing, and the two men communicated with each other on paper. On one of these message sheets was Poirot's cathedral, which received Corot's signature on its way via the artist to his sister.

Robaut lists a long series of painters who imitated Corot. In the course of time, unsigned drawings and paintings became "Corotized," and, since the artist's effects included many rough sketches and a number of uncompleted works, alert dealers took advantage of this fact by getting works which had been authenticated by the sale-of-effects stamp "completed" by competent specialists and "signed" by others. Because it is now almost impossible to identify the exact proportions of genuine Corot and perfectly imitated Corot in these residuary works, they must in some degree be defined as lying between genuine and spurious. The analogy with medieval studio and pupils' work is clearly recognizable. It is no longer possible to tell what proportion of the whole came from the master's hand.

In his excellent work on Corot, Germain Bazin quotes marginal notes by Robaut referring to an action brought against Vernon, a forger who specialized in Corots. In 1887 the author of the oeuvre catalogue and its vitally important supplement expressed his indignation against imitators and experts in the following terms:

Détrimont, whose father received a sentence for faking the works of Delacroix, is conducting his own business with fake Corots. Tripp, one of Arnold's associates, is in urgent need of Corots and pays good money for these fakes at the Hôtel Drouot. Bernheim [who] gives many people an impression of great acumen, for he supplies the whole of America with fakes of modern French painters . . . George Petit, one of the most imbecile experts imaginable . . . M. Haro, a pseudo-art expert, who one day at the Hôtel Drouot sold a painting by a man called Philippon as a genuine Corot to his fellow expert M. Brame, who passed it on to a M. Clapisson for 5000 francs . . . M. Bague . . . an arrant dunderhead . . . one could scratch this idiot of an expert's eyes out . . . Jackasses, who cannot recognize the authenticity of an original work.

The insatiable demand for Corots had some peculiar results. For example, the Lille Museum acquired *The Castel Sant' Angelo at Rome,* of which it was inordinately proud. Close examination revealed, on the lower left-hand margin, the signature of d'Aligny, one of the artist's oldest friends and painting companions. It is quite impossible to estimate how many paintings, drawings and sketches by Corot's many other cronies later came onto the market bearing his name. His intimate circle included highly gifted artists such as d'Aligny, Bertin, Français, Daubigny, Ravier, Fleury, Jules Boilly, Lessieux, Harduin, Chevalier and Lapitot.

A painter by the name of Prévost worked as Corot's restorer. The artist was always sending him works, some to be mounted and others to be made more marketable. He also employed him as a copyist.

When Corot died, a number of his works were at Prévost's studio. It is unknown how many he copied on instructions and how many on his own initiative, but Corot's signature was not hard to imitate, especially as the artist was so inconsistent that even good graphologists find it impossible to identify his signature with certainty.

It can scarcely be an exaggeration to say that Corot was the most faked painter of all time. His carelessness and his encouragement of emulators and imitators substantially contributed to the fact that, exploiting the existence of these hybrid works, unscrupulous forgers were able to go into production on a large scale.

The universal factor which emerges from this particular case is the extraordinary difficulty confronting any absolutely reliable classification in terms of "genuine" or "spurious." Stylistic criticism and physical examination are both ineffective save in the case of crude and obvious fakes, and the lines of demarcation, even for a true scholar, can be clearly established only in exceptional cases.

Of course, many of Corot's works proclaim his genius so splendidly and unmistakably that all possibility of error is precluded, but it should never be forgotten that many excellent Corot forgeries have been enthusiastically hailed as originals — and how many still enjoy the esteem accorded to works by the artist's own hand will probably never be established beyond all doubt.

MENZEL OR MOCK-MENZEL

If controversies could be clinched by measuring the volume of sound emitted by the participants or weighing the deposits of sulphuric acid left by their ball-point pens, the argument about the Menzel which may or may not be a Menzel would by now have been settled to the satisfaction of at least one of the warring parties. Although attack is supposed to be the best form of defense — an allegedly infallible strategic rule which is often refuted by experience — the problem of the Menzel (with or without quote marks) can be elucidated only in an atmosphere of objectivity, not of polemics.

It all began when the periodical *Das Schönste* published an article by Dr. Wilhelm F. Arntz, art historian, amateur dealer and art archivist. In it, he adduced some thoroughly credible evidence to prove that *The Walk in the Garden*, a Menzel acquired in 1956 by Dr. Günter Busch, director of the Bremen Kunsthalle, for the not inconsiderable sum of 60,000 marks (over $14,000), was a fake. Dr. Arntz's arguments were of three kinds: stylistic, linguistic, and commercial. He denied Menzel's authorship of the picture on the ground of weaknesses discernible to the informed layman as well as the expert; he considered that the picture's title did not fit its subject; and he held that it could scarcely be an undisputed Menzel since it had previously been offered for sale, at a fraction of the price paid by Bremen, without finding a purchaser.

The Arntz-Busch controversy began in 1956 but was not aired in public until 1959, when Dr. Busch published a form of apologia in which he attempted to refute Dr. Arntz's arguments.

Dr. Arntz claimed that the Menzel had been acquired against the advice of Dr. Kaiser, the Menzel expert. Dr. Busch retorted that the latter had called an undisputed Menzel a fake, thereby displaying a lack of expert knowledge; moreover, he had not seen the Menzel until after its purchase.

Against the Menzel, Dr. Arntz cited the fact that it was included neither in the oeuvre catalogue nor in the sale catalogue, whereupon Dr. Busch declared that neither list represented a complete enumeration of Menzel's works.

Dr. Arntz then brought some heavy guns to bear on the Bremen Menzel. The picture's pedigree had been traced back to a sale of effects held by Liebig and Freym at Paris on April 8, 1875. While the Menzel in Bremen's Kunsthalle portrays an angled rear view of a lady in contemporary costume, the sale catalogue of the Paris auction — which Dr. Arntz, but not Dr. Busch, managed to lay his hands on within a matter of hours — gives the following description of the picture:

"Beneath the large trees in a public park, women and children sit or stroll. A gentleman is attentively reading his newspaper, and a servant is carefully pushing an invalid lady along in a wheeled chair."

None of this is visible in the Bremen picture. It merely shows a lone woman out for a stroll.

The Menzel painting acquired by the Bremen Kunsthalle was

supposed to be the one sold at the above-mentioned Paris auction. However, this original is not in Bremen but in the Tretiakov Gallery at Moscow.

To support his contention that the Menzel at Bremen was an original work by that artist, Dr. Busch brought forward some empirical arguments. The painting bore Menzel's signature and the date 1867. Furthermore, an expert had established that the *craquelure* ran right through the signature, which would prove that it had originated at the same time as the picture itself. Finally, the signature had withstood attempts to remove it with alcohol.

The "Notes" by Dr. Busch which the Kunsthalle published as a supplement to its brochure on the disputed Menzel, did, however, contain the following words: "It can be said with certainty that the signatures and date are contemporary with the layers of paint on the actual picture. They are probably by the same hand."

Note the comfortable juxtaposition of the words "certainty" and "probably." Since the director of the Bremen Kunsthalle is here invoking a purely empirical argument he can only be answered with facts ascertainable by laboratory tests, and if Dr. Arntz neglected to undertake this course, there is no reason why we should not adopt it here.

The fact that *craquelure* runs through a signature and that picture and signature are apparently contemporaneous does not in itself prove that a painting is genuine. If a contemporary has simultaneously faked picture and signature the latter becomes an organic part of the paint, and *craquelure* will run through it uninterruptedly. However, this proves merely that picture and signature were painted at the same time. It does not indicate who painted them.

Quite apart from this, there are countless instances where experienced forgers have succeeded in faking signatures after a considerable lapse of time. They remove a strip of paint and embed the signature in the recess in such a way that the *craquelure* — genuine or artificial — runs through the surrounding surface and the signature itself.

The resistance of paint to alcohol or other much more powerful solvents signifies nothing. There are additives which can render a surface so hard that no solvents will affect it — excepting acids which will not only dissolve paints but damage a picture beyond repair.

Newspaper speculation about the authenticity of Bremen's Menzel grew more and more intense. The result was one more usually associated with criminal cases: a member of the public came forward. Kurt Pfoh, a hotelkeeper and enthusiastic art collector, produced a "water-color study for the Menzel in the Bremen Kunsthalle." This work caused a considerable stir. It was executed in a hybrid technique, water color and gouache, and its structural and figurative similarity made it a first cousin of Menzel's *Walker*.

The only trouble was that this study for Menzel's picture was not by Menzel but by one of his contemporaries, the painter Ferdinand Heilbuth, who was born in 1826, worked in Paris for many years, and eventually died there in 1889.

Allowing a variation of only three years for changes in fashion (1867 for Menzel's lady, 1870 for Heilbuth's), even the slight discrepancy in costume between the study and the completed painting disappears. We must remember, too, that fashions did not change as abruptly in the latter half of the last century as they do in our own, nor is it implausible to assume that the lone walker was not dressed in the latest fashion but was a little *démodé*.

The case of the controversial Menzel remains an unsolved mystery. Polemical attacks will do little to establish the truth, and there is absolutely no prospect of authenticating a disputed picture by — as happened in the Busch-Arntz controversy — launching unobjective attacks on a critic who honestly believes it to be spurious.

The Menzel in the Kunsthalle at Bremen *may* be a genuine Menzel provided that the artist ever produced bungling work — for which assumption no other evidence exists. One odd feature is that scientific methods of research have never been employed to establish the empirical facts of the case. This sin of omission, now several years old, would seem to suggest that the parties concerned are not without a suspicion that practical tests could lead to some unwelcome revelations.

In view of the wealth of undisputed Menzels in existence, it would naturally be profitable to submit the picture to comparative examinations on a broad scale. Despite the uncertainty of opinions based on stylistic criticism alone, the variation in quality is so pronounced that negative reports would have carried the day by force of numbers. It is not a question of personalities, but of a painting which has been bought at a price which is only justified if the work passes every test. As long as any facilities for practical and stylistic examination are withheld, the question of the picture's authenticity must unfortunately remain in abeyance.

A "LEIBL" BY HANS BLUM

In March, 1929, the Wallraf-Richartz Museum at Cologne held a memorial exhibition of the sort which is known to the art world at large as "representative" and which possesses more than temporary or local significance. The museum was showing some major works by Wilhelm Leibl. Their quality and pedigree had been scrutinized with the utmost care.

Emil Waldmann, erstwhile director of the Bremen Kunsthalle and foremost expert on Leibl, who had compiled an oeuvre catalogue which is still regarded as a standard work today, shared responsibility for the exhibition with Ernst Buchner, director of the museum which sponsored it. Waldmann later published the book *Wilhelm Leibl als Zeichner.*

Among the works exhibited was a *Portrait of a Bavarian Officer*. This painting, loaned by a private source, attracted special attention. The catalogue described it as follows:

70	PORTRAIT OF A BAVARIAN OFFICER	Oils on canvas.
	circa 1875	100 × 66.5 cm.
	Berlin, private.	Signed bottom right
	Illustration: Plate XLVIII	"W. Leibl"

After the close of the Cologne exhibition, the painting was shown in an equally representative exhibition held by the Academy of Formative Arts in Berlin.

This important work aroused as much enthusiasm among the expert advisers who had been responsible for its inclusion in the two exhibitions as it did among authoritative reviewers for daily papers and art journals and members of the art-loving public.

At Berlin, the painting's value and status were given visible expression. It was accorded "a place of honor among Leibl's chief works," reported the eminent art historian Hubert Wilm in the *Süddeutsche Monatshefte*.

The name of Wilhelm Leibl and the title of the picture, *Portrait of a Bavarian Officer,* prompted the Bavarian paper *Münchener Neueste Nachrichten* to ask the Berlin exhibition for a photograph of the work, once again described as "on loan from a private Berlin source." This incident, though trivial in itself, had undreamt-of consequences.

The elderly Munich painter Hans Blum, a former professor in the School of Arts and Crafts, saw the photograph of Leibl's work and at once called on the editor of the *Münchener Neueste Nachrichten* armed with a catalogue printed by the Munich auction house of Helbing for a sale in July, 1924. Number 48 in the catalogue was the *Portrait of a Bavarian Officer* which had been exhibited as a work by Leibl in Cologne and Berlin, together with the following text:

Hans Blum
Munich

48 Portrait of a commissariat official in dark blue uniform, his right hand resting on a table, his left holding white gloves. This picture undoubtedly originated in the Leibl-Trübner circle.

Oils on canvas.   100 × 66 cm.   Sgd. H. Blum
1880.   G.R.

The editor greeted the seventy-one-year-old painter's allegations with the utmost skepticism. It seemed impossible that a fake Leibl could have been exhibited under the aegis of Emil Waldmann, director of the Bremen Kunsthalle and leading expert on Leibl, and with the concurrence of other authorities. Yet Hans Blum demonstrated his authorship not only with the Helbing catalogue but with a photograph of the picture when it still bore the signature "H. Blum, 1880." On the instructions of the public prosecutor's office, measures were taken which shed a drastic and unambiguous light on the matter.

When dabbed with a pad of absorbent cotton soaked in alcohol, the signature "W. Leibl" vanished, and with it the thin layer of paint on which it had reposed. Traces of the signature "H. Blum, 1880" came to view.

Proceedings against a person or persons unknown had to be shelved because neither the place nor the date of the forgery could be ascertained.

According to research undertaken by the Stuttgart art archivist Dr. W. Arntz, whom we have met in another connection, Hans Blum had been commissioned to paint the portrait by an arms manufacturer from Ingolstadt named Stadelmann. That was in 1880, when he was only twenty-two and studying at Munich Academy under Löfftz and Lindenschmit.

After Stadelmann's death, the painting went to his daughter-in-law, who lived in Munich, and it was she who put it up for auction at Helbing's in 1924. Her reserve price of 800 marks was not reached, and in August, 1924, a Munich painter acquired it by private agreement.

Four years later the picture, now signed "W. Leibl," turned up at an art dealer's establishment in Rome. From there it passed into the possession of the Berlin collector and former Secretary of State for Foreign Affairs Richard von Kühlmann. The price was 110,000 marks. Finally, it was loaned by the von Kühlmann collection to the Leibl exhibitions at Cologne and Berlin.

In 1929, after the fraud had been discovered, the Roman art dealer was obliged to take it back, but not before Hans Blum had signed it for the second time. More recently, the picture was seen in New York, where it was acquired in 1950 by a former Berlin art dealer. In 1957 it was bought by a Munich collector.

Emil Waldmann commented on the case in 1929 in the Berlin periodical *Kunst und Künstler:*

> At the Academy's Leibl Exhibition, the life-sized *Portrait of a Bavarian Officer* was listed in the catalogue as No. 70 and illustrated in Plate No. 48. It was signed "W. Leibl" in the bottom right corner. The picture had not been known as a Leibl until 1928, when it was acquired by a German collector from an art dealer in Rome. A photograph gave no cause for misgivings, even though the pose and expression of the subject appeared unusual, and the picture was provisionally included in the exhibition. Doubts about Leibl's authorship soon arose, however, and the author and editor of a new edition of the Leibl oeuvre catalogue which happened to be in preparation at the time decided not to include the picture.

To read these remarks without prior knowledge of the true circumstances is to gain the impression that Waldmann had guessed in advance that the picture would turn out to be a forgery. He neglected to mention that the fake Leibl was shown at the Cologne exhibition on his personal responsibility, and his admission that doubts soon arose as to its authorship makes it all the harder to comprehend how the dubious picture also came to occupy a place of honor, in its role as a Leibl, at the Berlin exhibition.

Waldmann's allusion to the fact that the work had been excluded from a new edition of the catalogue which he was himself editing seems to imply that this was the outcome of his own detection of the fraud. It need only be pointed out that the new edition appeared at a time (1930) when the fake was already the subject of criminal investigation.

The painting having been acquired for 110,000 Reichsmarks, neither the Roman art dealer nor the purchaser nor any of the exhibition organizers at Cologne and Berlin felt obliged to take a bottle of alcohol and a pad of cotton and carry out the rudimentary test which any genuine signature will pass with complete impunity.

Portrait of a Bavarian Officer had not appeared in the first edition of Waldmann's oeuvre catalogue on Leibl — naturally, since at that time it was still the *Portrait of a Commissariat Official* by Hans Blum.

The transformation of a uniformed official into an army officer should in itself have aroused the experts' misgivings, but they obviously knew as much about uniforms as they did about art.

BALLY VERSUS COURBET

In July, 1957, a Stuttgart antiquarian appeared at the Staatsgalerie of Württemberg with a painting which seemed at first sight to merit attention. It bore the signature of Courbet and depicted a sleeping girl and a setter dog.

Closer examination of the picture revealed a lack of proportion between the figure of the reclining girl and that of the dog on her right. It seemed unlikely that Courbet, who was a first-rate draftsman, would ever have been guilty of such faulty composition or perspective. Quite apart from the disharmony of the portrayal, other features in the picture's execution gave the gallery's experts food for thought.

Scrutiny of the signature with a magnifying glass was enough to arouse further misgivings, for it was in a color which Courbet had never yet been known to use for signatures and "sat" on a foundation which was definitely a later addition. Any discrepancy between the base of a signature and the organic structure of the surrounding paint is always a suspicious feature.

Caution was counseled by yet another circumstance. The Louvre owns an undisputed Courbet dealing with a very similar theme. It seemed improbable that Courbet had produced so inferior a second version of such an excellent work. The Staatsgalerie of Württemberg declined to purchase the picture.

A few weeks later the *Sleeping Girl with Setter* turned up in the Basel Art Collection as a newly discovered Courbet. The administrators of the museum had bought it from a Swiss art dealer for 55,000 Swiss francs.

The pleasure of the museum administrators and their friends was soon marred by a public statement from a Basel art dealer who had formerly been employed as a museum curator. He disputed the picture's authenticity.

The administrators insisted that their picture was genuine. In an acrimonious exchange of letters they expressed the view that one art dealer was not competent to pronounce upon a work of art acquired from another. (Were the same logic applied to museum administrators, none of them would possess the requisite authority to judge pictures in other art collections!)

The archivist Dr. Arntz, making his third appearance in our pages, entered the lists with yet another example of a reclining woman, allegedly by Courbet but actually painted around 1875 by the Hungarian artist Gyula Benczur.

However, quite apart from any arguments based on art history or comparative analysis, there was a far more impressive way of proving that the *Sleeping Girl with Setter* was a fake. Since styles of costume can be accurately dated to within a few years, fashion experts were able to prove that the clothing worn by the *Sleeping Girl with Setter* was of post-1875 vintage.

Experts from the Bally Footwear Museum investigated the development of styles in women's shoes during the nineteenth century and established that Courbet's girl was wearing shoes which were classifiable as a post-1870 style.

Born in 1819, Gustave Courbet had by 1844 already abandoned the technique displayed by the Basel picture. Thus, disregarding the fact that the composition and general arrangement of the picture virtually ruled him out as the painter, he could not have guessed, in the middle of the century, what fashions in dress and footwear were going to look like in twenty years' time.

By 1855, the year when the organizers of the World Exhibition at Paris rejected all the pictures which he submitted to them, forcing him to exhibit his works in a hall of his own boldly entitled the "Pavillon du Réalisme," Courbet was using modes of expression totally unlike those of the *Sleeping Girl with Setter*.

The Swiss dealer who had acquired the Courbet which was not a Courbet from a German colleague was compelled to take the picture back. This he did at the request of the museum administrators at Basel, who were eventually obliged to concede that their undisputed Courbet was only an undisputed fake.

DUVEEN REBUTS DUVEEN

The name Duveen — later Sir Joseph Duveen and ultimately Lord Duveen of Millbank — has won an abiding place in the world of art. His memory survives if only because of the unique collection of ancient sculptures from the school of Phidias and the Parthenon at Athens which he presented to the British Museum, where they are concentrated in three rooms of their own.

That renown was not the only thing which Lord Duveen either merited or acquired is demonstrated by the fact that, though he was the leading art dealer in England and perhaps the world, he found himself constantly embroiled in litigation of the most distasteful sort.

The International Law of Art, an authoritative and comprehensive legal work by Barnett Hollander, cites eight cases in which Duveen was the defendant: once for slander; four times for defamation of goods (Duveen had *disparaged* works of art to the detriment of their owners, and it was indirectly implied that he had done so for mercenary reasons); twice in connection with nonpayment of commission; and once on charges of having sold a "dubious" painting. On the latter count he was acquitted. In the slander case he was ordered to pay nominal damages of one farthing, the court's decision being more significant than the sum involved. In the two disputes about commission a settlement was reached. Two cases were dropped because of the death of the plaintiffs, and four further cases were settled out of court on payment of vast sums by Duveen.

One accusation which aroused particular misgivings was that lodged against Lord Duveen by the collector Carl W. Hamilton, who charged him with having, in the hearing of several potential buyers, described a *Crucifixion* by Piero della Francesca and a *Madonna and Child* by Fra Filippo Lippi as "worthless, retouched, ruined" before their auction at the Anderson Gallery in New York on May 8, 1929. As a consequence of his disparaging remarks, the paintings remained unsold. Lord Duveen had voiced his doubts to such world-renowned collectors as Andrew W. Mellon, Mrs. John D. Rockefeller, William Randolph Hearst and Mrs. Henry F. Du Pont.

The plaintiff Carl W. Hamilton further alleged that Lord Duveen had agreed beforehand to encourage the above-named and other potential buyers to acquire the paintings.

By his statement that the two paintings were relatively valueless, Duveen had, in stark dereliction of his prior agreement, dissuaded potential buyers from making a single bid. Then, through the agency of a middleman, he succeeded in acquiring the pictures himself, the Piero della Francesca for $65,000 and the Fra Filippo Lippi for $50,000 — sums which were only a fraction of what they would probably have brought at auction. Wealthy collectors had failed to bid for either painting on the strength of Duveen's criticism, leaving the coast clear for him to acquire them at the lowest possible price.

Judgment was never given in this case, which involved millions. Duveen paid the plaintiff such an enormous indemnity that he withdrew the charge.

An even greater stir was caused when a Mrs. André Hahn, the French-born wife of an American officer, sued Duveen (then Sir Joseph) for giving an erroneous expert opinion. On June 8, 1920, Sir Joseph had stated in the most explicit terms that a picture belonging to the plaintiff, attributed under the title *La Belle Ferronière* to Leonardo da Vinci, was "a fake, a copy like hundreds of others." He added that "the original *La Belle Ferronière* is hanging in the Louvre in Paris."

The case opened before the New York Supreme Court on February 5, 1929, almost eight years after the suit had first been filed. The defense had delayed proceedings by summoning a string of witnesses from Europe.

In the course of the hearing, which was conducted in an exemplary fashion by Judge William Harman Black, it was established that Mrs. Hahn, the owner of the painting, had in early 1920 entered into negotiations with the curator of the Kansas City Art Museum. The museum's board of administrators had, on the strength of expert examination, come to the conclusion that the painting was an original work by Leonardo da Vinci and decided to purchase it. However, when it became known that Sir Joseph had given it as his considered opinion that the picture was a copy, the museum's offer was withdrawn.

In Sir Joseph's favor, his counsel quoted a report by the internationally celebrated art historian Bernard Berenson which described the *La Belle Ferronière* in the Louvre as an undisputed original and the picture in Mrs. Hahn's possession as a copy.

To support her contention that the *La Belle Ferronière* in the Louvre was not a da Vinci original, Mrs. Hahn likewise quoted Berenson, whose book on the North Italian painters of the Renaissance contained the assertion that although, having studied the *La Belle Ferronière* in the Louvre for forty years and examined a similar painting by da Vinci, he had changed his mind about the picture from time to time over a period of fifteen years, he had "now" reached the conclusion that the Louvre's *La Belle Ferronière* showed absolutely no traces of Leonardo da Vinci's authorship.

Sir Joseph found it hard to refute these arguments in court, having been forced into an admission that he always paid Bernard Berenson ten per cent of the price fetched by any painting sold on the strength of his expert opinion. In his biography of Duveen, Behrmann reports that Berenson served Duveen for thirty years in return for this commission and a fixed annual retainer.

The London art historian Maurice Brockwell was obliged to concede during the hearing that he had based his report on the

La Belle Ferronière on a monochrome photograph. When questioned by the judge, he stated that "in the great majority of cases, experts give their reports on old paintings on the strength of monochrome photographs."

One astonishing feature of the hearing was Sir Joseph's admission that he also had never even seen the painting which he had certified to be a fake. His opinion lacked any solid foundation. In view of his extremely gloomy prospects, Duveen decided to come to terms.

In his biography of Duveen, Behrmann says that Mrs. Hahn withdrew her charges in return for an indemnity of $60,000, all costs and legal expenses being borne by the defendant. It was alleged on the plaintiff's side that the damages were far higher, but there is no evidence of this.

Any attempt to establish the origin of the two pictures comes to a dead stop shortly after Leonardo's death. One trail leads to the royal house of France, but it is impossible to confirm whether the picture which found its way into the collection of Francis I was an original, a repeat performance by Leonardo, or a contemporary copy.

It is superfluous to add that the Louvre very naturally persists in asserting the authenticity of its *Belle Ferronière* and that Mrs. Hahn does the same for hers.

The Berenson-Duveen collaboration is particularly well illustrated by the case of a *Madonna* for which art historian Berenson had supplied a written report attributing it to Masaccio, the highly prized *quattrocento* painter. Furthermore, he accorded the "newly discovered Masaccio" a rapturous article in the art journal *Dedalo*. This "masterpiece" found its way, via Duveen, into the Mellon collection at a price of $395,000. It later returned to Europe after doubts had been raised about its authenticity.

In a book of memoirs entitled *On the Merry-go-round of Art,* the art dealer Martin Porkay claims that the would-be Masaccio originated in a Viennese restorer's studio. The fifteenth-century wooden panel originally displayed a much-repainted Madonna and Child. When the layers of paint, which dated from various periods, had been removed, only vestiges of the picture remained. Since a prominent art dealer was interested in the work provided that it could be turned into a masterpiece, the owner of the restorer's studio dispatched a specialist in "old Italian" to Florence to study some genuine Masaccios. Another two collaborators journeyed to Montemarciano and London on a similar errand.

Then, we are told, the trio of specialists calmly painted a brand-new Masaccio on the old panel, improving the deception by painting over the completed forgery once more so that the "genuine" Masaccio would not come to light until the topmost layer of paint, carefully aged, had been removed.

It would be hard to think of a portable object of great value which has not challenged the forger, whose lure, we must imagine, is as much the prospect of adventure as it is the hope of financial gain. Indeed, as in the conception and commission of less artistic crimes, the possible monetary reward seldom has any logical relationship to the risks involved for even the most intrepid forger. His many miscalculations in the past have, after all, made this book possible.

Index